*You ____________________________ were "Born to Win."*
*But to win please remember that "The Will to Win Is Nothing Without the Will to Prepare."*

# Ziglar On Selling

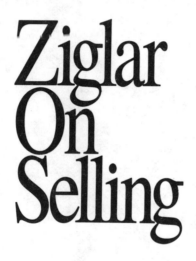

# Ziglar On Selling

Zig Ziglar

OLIVER NELSON
A Division of Thomas Nelson Publishers
*Nashville*

Published in Nashville, Tennessee, by Oliver-Nelson Books, a division of Thomas Nelson, Inc., Publishers, and distributed in Canada by Lawson Falle, Ltd., Cambridge, Ontario.



Printed in the United States of America.

**Library of Congress Cataloging-in-Publication Data**

Ziglar, Zig.
Ziglar on selling : the ultimate handbook for the complete sales professional / Zig Ziglar.
p. cm.
Includes bibliographical references.
ISBN 0-8407-9131-3 (hardcover)
1. Selling. 2. Sales management. I. Title.
HF5438.25.Z545 1991
658.8'5—dc20 91-19535
CIP

3 4 5 6 — 96 95 94 93 92 91

*Dedicated*
*to*
*all enthusiastic and honorable sales professionals*
*who sell goods, products, or services*
*that benefit others*

# TABLE OF CONTENTS

# CONTRIBUTING EXPERTS

The people listed on this page are my "friends in the field," the brave men and women who are applying the principles and concepts talked about in *Ziglar on Selling*. By sharing stories and true-life experiences, each has made a significant contribution to this book!

Bob Alexander
Leonard Allen
Lonnie Amirault
Marvin D. Anthony
Jerry Aull
Bruce Barbour
Donald Bonenson
Bill Callaway
Fred Cardinal
Walt Clayton
Gerry Clonaris
Connie Cox
John Cummings
Jay P. Curry
Nick Dalley
Robert Davis
Howard Donnelly
Andrew Downie
Dr. Ken Dychtwald
Tony Ferguson
Bryan Flanagan
Joe Flower
Gertrude Fogler
Robert Forrest
Robert Gibson
Gerhard Gschwandtner
Walter Hailey
David Halford
Phil Harriman
Jobie Harris
K. J. Hartley
Leonard Harvison
Donald Henry
Rex Hensley
Julie Huntington
Don Jarrell
J. Kevin Jenkins
Tim Jones
Art Lamstein
Dennis Landrum
Dr. John M. Leddo
Joe Lingle
Dave Liniger
Angie Logan
Danielle Logan
Peter Lowe
Randy Manning
P. C. Merrell
David A. Mezey
Jim Norman
Julie Ziglar Norman
Cindy Ziglar Oates
Louise Padgett
Terrence Patton
Roger Peet
David Ray
Cavett Robert
Vince Robert
Rick Robinson
Charles Rondeau
Janet Rush
Ed Sheftel
Fred Smith
Larry Spevak
Deborah Tannen
Dr. Forest S. Tennant, Jr.
Jill Tibbels
Tom Walsh
Greg Watt
Sheila West
Susan Ziglar Witmeyer
W. Phil Wynn
Bob Zaloba
Tom Ziglar
Jean Ziglar

# THANK YOU

Any time a work such as this one is published, you can rest assured that more people than the author were seriously involved. This particular book involved more people—by far—than any of my previous efforts.

To begin, as you will see by reading, a number of sales professionals supplied beautiful, practical, and imaginative examples directly from the "firing line." Each has greatly enhanced the value of this book, and I am indebted to all of them. Their names are listed on the Contributing Experts page.

Since the book is a holistic approach to selling, my family played a prominent role. Daughters Susan Witmeyer, Cindy Oates, and Julie Norman combined their efforts to help "shape" the entire book, specifically to look at the family perspective. Each one gave valuable insights concerning her feelings, and yes, fears, as she was growing up in the home of a professional salesperson. Each one is tremendously important to me on a personal and professional basis. Son Tom shared his insights and wrote a significant portion of the telephone information while making other suggestions. Obviously, he also is vital on a personal and professional basis. Needless to say, The Redhead was very much involved, serving as grammarian, editor, and general consultant for the project. Everything I do in life is influenced positively by her, and I will be eternally grateful for her love and support.

In this particular book, Victor Oliver, our publisher, collaborated and worked with the Thomas Nelson sales staff who, in turn, gave us insights and comments from their personal experiences as well as from numerous bookstore owners concerning the needs and desires of the general public. What they had to say was revealing and enormously encouraging. Their efforts combined with the questionnaires and conversations we had with countless salespeople—both experienced and just beginning—helped us identify needs and desires sales professionals must deal with regularly. In short, we spent many hours doing a considerable amount of research to find out what you wanted, then we made every effort to provide that information.

My friend and coworker Bryan Flanagan has not only tested the principles of this book with his life experiences, he has done an extraordinary amount of research using old-fashioned "elbow grease" ("hard work," for the uninitiated) to prove the principles. Thank you, Bryan, for your unselfish team spirit and for all your contributions to this book.

As always, there are hundreds of hours of typing and word processing that go into each writing project. Laurie Magers, my administrative assistant of fourteen years, again did yeoman work. Laurie stayed late and worked on Saturdays to keep up with her other many duties while helping with this manuscript. Additionally, Debbie Shankle did a tremendous job in keeping the ball rolling and on schedule.

The individual, however, who truly "made it happen" is our senior vice president, Jim Savage. Jim spent countless hours in research, contributing invaluable thoughts and ideas. His insight and tenacity have literally been responsible for bringing this book to the marketplace at least one year earlier than I could possibly have done it. Since he and I are virtually always on the "same page" in our philosophy and thoughts, I had a double advantage of having a dedicated, experienced, bright collaborator who made a magnificent contribution.

I would also like to give my sincere thanks and appreciation to the other authors and speakers who permitted me to use some of their creative efforts. A special thank-you goes to Gerhard Gschwandtner, publisher of *Personal Selling Power* magazine. Gerhard is a good friend and a true selling professional, and his contributions were notable.

To those people whom I unknowingly quoted or whose examples I used without giving credit, I want you to know that we made every effort to find the original source. Though you're not mentioned by name, you are appreciated, and I want you to know that as a fellow professional, I deeply appreciate your contributions—not only to the book but also to the profession.

# Ziglar On Selling

# INTRODUCTION

A crowd of people spent most of a night trying to rescue a black bear caught fifty to sixty feet up a pine tree in Keithville, Louisiana, so they could move it to a wildlife area. Sheriff's deputies, game wardens, and wildlife biologists were in a crowd that gathered for nearly eight hours. A veterinarian fired tranquilizer darts at the critter to get it down. A net was strung to catch the bear when the drugs took hold and it fell from the treetop. It wasn't until the volunteers chopped the tree down Thursday that they discovered they were rescuing a dart-riddled garbage bag.

Far too many salespeople have what they think is a "bear" up the tree when in reality it is nothing but a bunch of "garbage." You can hear them say things like:

> Competition is just too tough in this part of the country for this product. . . . We're in the middle of a recession. . . . Everybody is only interested in price—nothing else—just "who's got the best deal?" . . . People are just not buying domestic (foreign) products anymore. . . . It wouldn't do any good to make the sale; credit's so tight the finance company would turn us down. . . . The economy is just dead in this town. . . . With the rate of unemployment what it is, I don't know how they expect me to make quota . . . !

The question is, How do you deal with all of these situations, succeed in your chosen profession, maintain your sanity, avoid ulcers and heart attacks, continue in a good relationship with your mate and children, meet your financial obligations, prepare for those "golden years," and still have a moment you can call your own? Fortunately, the book you hold in your hands endeavors to answer each of these questions by sharing information, inspiration, laughter, tears, and direction that will allow you to make the choices necessary to have a "balanced" life that leads to personal and professional success.

## CHAMPIONSHIP FUNDAMENTALS AND TIMELESS TRUTHS

The Green Bay Packers won the first two world championships of professional football by outscoring their opponents in Super Bowls I and II. The Packers were coached by the great fundamentalist, Vince Lombardi. When Lombardi's team would fail to play well (which wasn't often), he would begin practice the following week with the same basic comments: "Gentlemen, we performed below the standards we have set for ourselves as a championship football team. This week we are going to return to the fundamentals." Lifting the football he had been holding in his hands to a position above his head so that everyone in the room could see it clearly, Lombardi would intone in that deep, raspy voice he kept hoarse from shouting, "Fellows, this is a football." And without fail, team prankster Max McGee would call from the back of the room, "Not so fast, Coach, not so fast."

Fundamental truths remain constant. Lombardi taught some of the same fundamentals to his Green Bay Packers that Bill Walsh taught to the San Francisco 49ers in helping them become the "team of the decade" in the 1980s. The most successful football team for the 1990s *AND* the most successful sales professionals of the decade are spending time TODAY learning and relearning basic fundamentals.

## THE SELLING BASICS

Selling is more than a profession; it is a way of life. And the sales professional of the nineties is concerned about being fundamentally sound. In addition to fundamentals, any resource tool claiming to be "The Ultimate Handbook for the Complete Sales Professional" must be prepared to address those areas outside the actual time spent in face-to-face (or voice-to-voice) selling. This book is designed to do just that.

We have included not only selling techniques and procedures that will add to your income but also ideas and principles that will add to your "intangible " income (quality of life). How can we move into the "computer age" of selling; how do we deal with the rigors and temptations of the road—from leaving our families (withdrawal) and returning to them after extended absences (decompression) to spending our "nonselling" time in a productive manner; how do we deal with the physical demands of this great profession: fast-food restaurants and lack of time for workouts lead to stress and waist (pun intended); how do we work with the financial arm of the company in such a way that we complement and yet do not duplicate our efforts? These areas, as well as many other concerns, are included.

## GREEN AND GROWING VS. RIPE AND ROTTING

Looking back over my career as a salesman, sales manager, and sales trainer, I have no doubt in my mind that the most successful sales professionals continue to have the attitude of the beginner. The selling pro who gets to and stays at the top of the profession is an "experienced rookie." By that I mean when we approach sales as an ongoing learning experience, we are continually learning the "little things" that make the "big difference" in our careers as sales professionals. (There's no profit on the sale we ALMOST make!)

**Selling is more than a profession; it is a way of life.**

In *Ziglar on Selling,* I have made the effort to take my fundamental selling experiences that began in the 1940s and show how the fundamentals may remain constant, but you and I may not! The two of us (you and I) must continue on our pilgrimage by LEARNING,

LIVING, AND LOOKING: learning from the past without living there; living in the present by seizing each vital moment of every single day; and looking to the future with hope, optimism, *and* education.

The great performers in all professions spend countless hours working on the fundamentals. From Andrés Segovia to Eric Clapton, Enrico Caruso to Luciano Pavarotti, Mary Pickford to Meryl Streep, Jack Dempsey to Mike Tyson, Sammy Baugh to Joe Montana, the daily regimes of four to six hours of practice prior to performance seem incredible and in some ways excessive to most of us. Yet, they have been and are world champions in their professions!

## SOMETHING NEW

When *Secrets of Closing the Sale* was published in 1984, many people were nice enough to call it the definitive sales book of the decade. Over 220,000 trade paper and 250,000 hardcover copies are in print, and on a steady basis we hear from people who testify to the powerful techniques, concepts, and principles it contains. So why a new sales book from Zig Ziglar? There are three basic reasons. In the first place, the sales profession and sales procedures are changing at an ever-increasing pace. This is one of the aspects that makes our profession so exciting! Much has changed since 1984. Those of you who have been on an airplane in the last six months will have noticed at least a half dozen laptop computers and twice that many cellular phones.

On a recent trip, our flight was delayed, and when the pilot made the announcement, there was a mad dash for briefcases. I was the only one in the first-class cabin who didn't have a phone to call and let the client know we were delayed. For "underprivileged" people like me, the GTE Public Phone is now found in most airplanes. In the fast-information, customer-service-oriented society in which we sell, we must deal with changes, or our clients will be dealing with our competitors.

## THE BALANCED LIFE

The second reason I wrote this book is that I have not found one book that addresses ALL aspects of a professional's sales career.

There are so many challenges to the sales staff of the nineties that without some vital information, staying in the sales profession will be very difficult. The sales pro faces questions about travel, family relationships, and personal health concerns that have intensified tremendously in my lifetime. In addition to basic selling skills, I want to share some ideas with you regarding the "balanced life" that means real success for you.

## THE TEACHER AS LEARNER

The third reason for writing this book is that we learn most when we are teaching. The information I have learned in the years since 1984 through reading and research as well as from successful men and women from all walks of life has been enriching and rewarding in my own personal, family, and business life. In turn I have taught the lessons to others, empowering them to become even more successful. I am firmly convinced, based on results we've already gotten, that these tried and proven ideas and techniques will be extremely valuable to you as well.

## WHAT ABOUT YOU?

Countless careers in the proud profession of selling have been aborted with little, if any, chance for success because sales recruits were brought into the profession by callous individuals who played the "numbers" game with lives. Sales managers were told to "hire them in masses and train them in classes," and if they can't "cut the mustard," recruit another class. No wonder so many of our best and brightest young people shunned a sales career or grew discouraged and quit before they gave themselves—or this great profession—a chance.

Today, sales organizations everywhere recognize the necessity of a more comprehensive training approach to maximize our dwindling labor supply. Even companies with sophisticated training programs are becoming more aware of the need for experiential training and the "total person" approach to growth as it relates to our specific profession.

This book is designed to allow you to "feel" real life experiences in the safety of a controlled environment and become better prepared to handle the subtle changes you face daily in the world of selling.

## SALESMANSHIP FOR *YOU*!

Some of the things I am talking about involve the necessity of a change in thinking for many people, and this might include YOU! So let me point out that this book was written primarily for four groups of people. In the first group are the people just getting into the world of selling who understand that a correct start can make the rest of the journey much easier. It's somewhat like the game for which I have such a great passion—golf. When people tell me they're planning to take up the game, I always encourage them to take lessons from a good pro before they go to the driving range or the golf course. If they start properly and learn the basic fundamentals, they will progress infinitely faster and ultimately play much better golf. Reason: They will not have acquired those bad habits that keep many golfers from ever shooting respectable scores. The same is true of selling, so if you are new, I really commend you for reading this book.

Please remember, as you start your journey, that a "green" salesman will sell more than a "blue" one.

## FUNDAMENTALLY SPEAKING

The book is also written for those pros who clearly understand that "you may not need to be told, but the true professional doesn't mind being reminded." Jack Nicklaus, who was voted the outstanding golfer of the century, periodically went back to the man who first taught him the game—his teaching pro, who worked with Jack on some of the fundamental and minute subtleties of the game, changes Jack had made in his game without even being aware. Selling is the same. Even accomplished professionals can drift ever so slowly into destructive patterns and poor sales habits. The fundamentals taught here are reminders, which are combined with the latest data and procedures and will help the "old pro" move to a new plateau of selling.

## WANDERING AND WONDERING

The third group is made up of people who have had one year of sales experience repeated many times. Most of these salespeople are wandering generalities who are wondering why they have not made more progress. Not many of you will fit that pattern because few of these people will be reading these words. If you recognize yourself as a member (actually "former" member) of this group, I'm especially glad to welcome you. The numbers are legion, and when your fire is ignited with new procedures and techniques, a new zest and confidence will open so many doors for you that your whole world—personal, family, and business—will dramatically improve.

**A "green" salesman will sell more than a "blue" one.**

## EVERYONE IS IN SALES

Unfortunately, not everyone realizes that WE ARE ALL IN THE FIELD OF SELLING. The fourth group of people for whom this book is written is the group that realizes that every person in every profession (lawyer, doctor, accountant, engineer, teacher, bus or cab driver, shipping clerk, counselor, receptionist, corporate executive, entertainer, administrator, coach, cook, etc.) is a salesperson. If you are just beginning to understand this concept, then regardless of how long you have been in your business, you are new to the field of selling. In many ways this book will help you even more than those who identify themselves as salespeople because most of your associates haven't recognized the fact that they are members of the selling profession and even fewer have "officially" started their sales training. Competitively speaking, this book will give you enormous advantages.

## THE BEGINNING OF THE END

You are with me right now for one of several reasons. You may be reading this book because you are just beginning a career in the world's oldest (everything begins with marketing), most exciting (how fast does your heart beat at the beginning of a sales call?), and most profitable (but only if you're good) business ever conceived by man; you may be reading this book because you understand the importance of returning to the fundamentals; or you may be reading this book because you clearly know as a sales professional that if you are going to derive maximum benefit from your career, you must take the "holistic" approach and "work" at succeeding in your personal, family, AND business life. The deeper you dig and the further you get into this book, the more you will understand the concept that YOU'VE GOT TO *BE* BEFORE YOU CAN *DO* AND *DO* BEFORE YOU CAN *HAVE*!

At this point let me say, "Congratulations!" With this commitment to yourself, you have taken the most important step in the success formula: You have started! You are miles ahead of the majority of the people entering our profession today. This is truly the beginning of the end of mediocrity—or the sales slump that has been holding you back.

## A FACT OF LIFE

One of the basic truisms of selling is that "slumps" will occur. You are going to hit those plateaus where nothing seems to work very well personally or professionally. Now that may seem negative, but I'm going to be like the little boy who told his dad he was afraid he had flunked an arithmetic test. He was told to be positive, not negative, and so he replied, "O.K., Dad, I'm POSITIVE I flunked that arithmetic test." I'm positive that even the best salespeople get in slumps.

Inevitably, those that slump get away from the basics. In over forty years of selling everything from tangibles like cookware and table appointments to intangibles like securities, insurance, and training, as well as teaching people who have sold literally every item you can imagine (and some you don't want to imagine), I have discovered the surefire way to end the slump: RETURN TO FUNDAMENTALS WITH THE PROPER ATTITUDE.

The primary reason we stay in a slump is a failure to be willing to return to the fundamentals. Basically speaking, we get caught in a rut, and as many of you know, a rut is nothing but a grave with the ends kicked out! It is one thing to get in a rut, but it is an entirely different thing to STAY in a rut. How do we get out? By returning to fundamentals. "The Ultimate Handbook" will be helpful to you in this area.

## THE ULTIMATE HANDBOOK—AND HOW TO USE IT

To make sure you are able to capture and use the ideas woven throughout this book, let me encourage you to keep your pen handy and mark your thoughts right on the pages. I like to make note of the page numbers on the front inside cover of the book for easy review. Some people prefer to get a steno pad and put their ideas in it. Since this is designed to be a handbook and a reference book and is written in a conversational style, I promise you that what the book gets out of you will be much more valuable than what you get out of the book.

**YOU'VE GOT TO *BE* BEFORE YOU CAN *DO* AND *DO* BEFORE YOU CAN *HAVE*!**

I encourage you to keep this book within arm's reach for at least the first month after you've read it. Pick it up and just thumb through the pages to look at your highlighted parts, and you will be astonished at how they will bring additional ideas to you. I also challenge you to wait about two months after finishing the book and then read it again, slowly and more carefully, and this time with a different colored marking pen. I can assure you that you will make more marks and notes and generate even more ideas with the second reading than you did the first time through. Let me say it again. Your purpose should not be to get out of the book as quickly as possible but to get out of the book what is there and let the book get the successful sales professional out of you!

## BRINGING IN YOUR VERDICT

You are the judge and jury in making the decision concerning this book's effectiveness in your life, so as you begin to formulate your decision, let me make a few comments for the defense. For years, the admonition in sales has been to ask the successful person to share "secrets." For that reason, you will notice throughout this book that actual examples are interspersed—illustrations and success stories of outstanding salespeople all the way from New England to New Zealand. Their stories are taken from blue collar, white collar, and "no" collar professions. Those successful sales professionals who are on the firing line, doing the job on a daily basis, can give us valid, up-to-date information that works!

BEWARE: There is a real danger in judging the principles before you have studied them carefully. Just because an example is given from the high-tech world of computers or international finance does NOT mean it will not apply to those of you in direct sales—and vice versa. The stocks and commodities trader uses the same principles of persuasion that the loving parent will want to use. As already stated, each and every one of us is in the business of persuading others. The primary purpose of *Ziglar on Selling* is to help you persuade more people, more effectively, more ethically, more often! And that means, I WILL SEE YOU AT THE TOP—IN THE WORLD OF SELLING!

P.S. In the back of this book, I have included a SUCCESSFUL SELLING SKILLS SUMMARY that will allow you to evaluate where you are today (see page 365). Let me encourage you to give yourself a pretest before reading *Ziglar on Selling.* This analysis will allow you to focus on specific areas you would like to strengthen. If you will check your responses after reading chapters 5 and 11, you will see significant progress, and by taking a posttest after chapter 16, I believe you will see that you have gotten a great deal out of this book. However, and much more importantly, you will KNOW that YOU have gotten a great deal out of YOU!

CHAPTER ONE

# YOU MADE THE RIGHT CHOICE

## *A Career in the World's Oldest Profession*

When the prospect reacted to the door-to-door Bible salesman's request to buy with "I'm broke," the salesman had a pretty fair response. Extending the Bible, he responded, "Would you put your hand right here and repeat that?"

Selling can be and should be fun, so let's make it clear from the beginning that a sense of humor combined with self-esteem that allows you to laugh at yourself will play a significant part in your success in your chosen profession. How I wish someone had made that fact clear to me when I got my start. Laughing more often and feeling better about myself would have prevented many of the bruises to my fragile ego during those difficult days early in my career when I was trying so desperately hard to survive.

## IN THE BEGINNING

I made my first sales call in 1947. After borrowing $50 (a considerable sum of money in those days) to buy a new $22 suit, a new dress shirt, a briefcase, and a hat (all professional salespeople wore hats in the late forties), I was prepared to enter the wonderful world of selling!

My mission was to seek out users of my product line to act as "centers of influence" for "referrals." I didn't really know what that meant except to say that if people were currently using my product, they might be able to direct me to someone else who would want to use it. Much to my great pleasure and eternal gratitude, The Redhead (my wife, Jean) agreed to come along.

After driving for a considerable length of time to find the "right" neighborhood, with fear and trembling I knocked on my first door. The weather was brutally hot that July day in Columbia, South Carolina, but I would have been sweating profusely even without nature's help. A grandmotherly looking lady who would have to rate among the top two or three least frightening or intimidating figures on earth came to the door. She smiled sweetly and acknowledged my presence. I started my "canned" (not planned) presentation and got out almost an entire sentence before I froze. Nothing would come out of my mouth. After about three hours (three seconds can seem like three hours in this situation) this dear, kind lady gently asked me if I would like a drink of water. I managed to nod my head in gratitude, and she invited me in.

I did eventually find out that she was not a current owner of our product, so rather than encourage her to become one or ask if she knew anyone who might be interested, I did the only sensible thing. I rushed back to the car and my waiting wife. Obviously, this was the wrong neighborhood!

Over the next ten days, poor self-esteem, fear of rejection, lack of confidence, and mediocre work habits led to experiences that were not a great deal more successful.

## I QUIT

It didn't take long to reach the end of my financial rope, and my courage bucket soon went "bone dry." I was knocking on doors one hot August day on Adelia Drive, and as I looked down a particularly long block that ended the street, I said to myself, "Self, if we don't get into a house before the end of this block to at least MAKE a presentation, I quit!"

I had been through too many days of *not even* being able to tell my story to get turned down for the sale.

## MY FUTURE—OTHERS' HANDS

In 1947 the overwhelming majority of wives were at home, so my chances for making a presentation seemed pretty good on a long block like this one. Logically, I knew that putting my destiny in other people's hands by determining to continue or quit in this way was not an overly bright decision. But emotionally, I knew that continuing to have doors closed in my face was unbearable. Regardless of who we are or what we do, EVERYONE needs what psychologists call "accomplishment feedback"—*some* success, no matter how small—and I was yet to experience even the slightest hint of getting close to any form of success. The trend continued until only two houses were left.

The next to last home, I learned, belonged to a widow, Mrs. B. C. Dickert. I gave her my presentation at the door, and she told me to go next door to see her brother and his wife, Mr. and Mrs. J. O. Freeman. Those were the first words of hope I had heard in several days. I literally ran next door and enthusiastically told Mrs. Freeman what her sister-in-law had said and that Mrs. Dickert would like to be included if I could come back for a presentation. I got the appointment to come back for a presentation after dinner when Mr. Freeman would be home.

## ACCOMPLISHMENT FEEDBACK

Later that evening, with cotton in my mouth and fear in my heart I made my first sale: product #541 priced at $61.45! I finished writing the order and completely forgot Mrs. Dickert was sitting there. Finally, Mr. Freeman said, "Mr. Ziglar, I believe Mrs. Dickert is interested, too." With all the aplomb of a true professional, I blurted out, "What about it, Mrs. Dickert?" (Smooth, huh?) She said, "Well, I don't have my money with me." Again with considerable tact and diplomacy I said, "Well, shoot, you just live next door. Run get it!" Mrs. Dickert smiled and said, "Well, I think I will." Two sales—I couldn't believe my good fortune!

The Redhead and I bought a quart of ice cream to celebrate, and to the best of my recollection, there was none left the next day.

I decided to stay in the business of selling.

## WHAT ABOUT YOU?

As we get under way in our journey through *Ziglar on Selling*, I would like to begin in a somewhat unusual manner. Let me encourage you to leave the sales profession if you can. Yes, you read it properly. Zig Ziglar is encouraging you to quit selling—if you can. Those last three words are the most important words you can face at this point in your sales career: IF YOU CAN. Those who get into sales because they might make a little more money or might even help other people are "short-termers." You need to get into selling because your heart and your head won't allow you to do anything else!

**YOU CANNOT GET OUT OF SOMETHING YOU HAVE NEVER BEEN IN.**

In sales, you will be treated rudely. People will, on occasion, even slam doors in your face. They will hang up on you for no obvious reason. Some will avoid you at social gatherings. Your family (and even *you*) will question your sanity. You will see people whispering and KNOW they are talking about you and your new profession. People in restaurants will laugh, and you will be sure they are discussing your last presentation.

As humorist and speaker Dr. Charles Jarvis says, "Just because you're paranoid doesn't mean they're not out to get you!" Yes, paranoia can be a side effect of the sales profession.

## GET OUT OR GET IN

My good friend Walter Hailey is one of the most successful men in the world. I talked about his ability to find the good in people and situations in my book *See You at the Top*. In addition to being a "good-finder," Walter is a salesman par excellence (that means he's gooood!) and a winner who has spent his life helping others win.

Despite Walter's success, he had a rocky start in the world of selling. He faced frustration, anxiety, closed doors, low sales, nervous stomach, and virtually every other symptom associated with an individual who is uncertain of his future and how he is going to survive in the sales world. As a matter of fact, his discouragement was so bad, Walter went to his manager and told him he was quitting, getting out of the business. To this his manager responded, "You can't."

Walter dogmatically stated that he was quitting. The manager again told him, "You can't quit." By now Walter was getting a little hot under the collar, and he stated very firmly, "Well, I AM going to quit!" To this his manager replied, "Walter, you can't get out of the insurance business because you have never really gotten into the insurance business."

Walter said the words hit him like the proverbial "ton of bricks." As he reflected on the truth of what his manager said, he realized for possibly the first time in his life that YOU CANNOT GET OUT OF SOMETHING YOU HAVE NEVER BEEN IN. There are many people who "join" a sales organization but never get in the business of selling.

## WHY NOT GET IN THE BUSINESS?

One reason new salespeople never get "in the business" has to do with the information they receive. Are new salespeople told the truth about the job? A resounding "No!" was the answer, according to an article entitled "Shell-Shocked on the Battle Field of Selling" in the July 1990 edition of *Sales and Marketing Management* magazine in which senior editor Arthur Brigg interviewed a large number of salespeople in their first year of selling.

The respondents reported their early days in the field were more rigorous than they ever imagined and were filled with surprises they weren't prepared to handle. If you will permit an observation from someone who has been in their position as a new salesperson and who has hired and trained countless salespeople, ill-informed and ill-prepared salespeople are the rule rather than the exception.

Poor information and poor preparation may have always been the case, and that may never change. But YOU can do a few things to minimize the shock.

## NO FREE LUNCH

*First:* Realize that the majority of highly paid veterans in sales (or in any field) are hard workers. Look around and interview the top performers; ask them specifically about their work ethic. I have been present where the more the hiring managers reinforced the rigorous requirements, the more the candidates ignored the facts and assured the managers they could handle the job. They selectively listened and "heard" what they wanted to hear. Later, when their prospects did the same thing and complained that the salespeople hadn't "told them," the salespeople were amazed and even angered. Solution: Listen well to the entire message, not just the "benefits" portion.

The best-paying hard work in the world is selling, and the poorest-paying easy work in the world is selling!

*Second:* Remember if you apply yourself to the job and absorb the training offered, your productivity will go up, and your stress and fatigue level will go down. In your early days you may be overwhelmed by the amount of time required for the job and the number of details you must manage. I recommend that you adopt a time management and productivity system along with the training required to understand and use the system (discussed in chapter 15 "Organization and Discipline").

*Third:* Work to stay current with the all-important, ever-changing areas of product knowledge and communication skills. Understanding your product and knowing how to communicate that knowledge give a great sense of security in any selling situation. You will want to constantly study the product and any improvements made to it. Some product lines are so large and complex you will need to study daily to keep "up to speed." This is the information age, so take full advantage of your communication technology to stay ahead of the competition.

Important: When your technical knowledge is exhausted, feel free to say, "I don't know." Your company can provide the technical support you need, and you can become an authority on the subject for next time.

## REAL COMMITMENT

Please understand that you may have been presenting your product or service for years and still not have been "in the profession" of selling. "How can you tell when you are *in* the business?" you ask. Answer: When the profession is *in* you so completely that you can't get *out* of sales.

**The best-paying hard work in the world is selling, and the poorest-paying easy work in the world is selling!**

Lack of commitment is a primary reason that the sales profession has earned the reputation for having a high turnover rate. Fortunately, this is changing, and the public is rapidly gaining respect for the true sales professional. Training methods are improving, and selling is attracting a higher caliber of recruit today than ever before. The benefits for joining the greatest profession in the world are growing on an almost daily basis.

Now I know you appreciate that last sentence—a completely unbiased statement from a man who is proud to say he has been a salesman all his life. I have a deep love for the sales profession and the selling professional, a sincere belief in the value of our profession, and an unquenchable thirst for knowledge about becoming even more professional.

## JOURNEY TO SALES SUCCESS

My sales career didn't begin in 1947. That was my first "official" sales call. I actually started in childhood when I sold vegetables on the streets of Yazoo City, Mississippi. I also had a paper route, and early in my sales career, it was my good fortune to work in a grocery store for several years.

At the University of South Carolina, I sold sandwiches at the dormitory in the evening to finance my marriage and education. I later moved into direct sales that has included stints in the securities business, life insurance, and home care products. I entered the world of personal growth and corporate development in 1964 and have been selling training and motivation since then.

**OPPORTUNITY IS BORN OF INDEPENDENCE HANDLED IN A RESPONSIBLE MANNER.**

Obviously, your experiences are not going to be exactly like mine. I would venture to guess that not many of you will have your spouse with you on sales calls. You will probably not be selling sandwiches in a dormitory, and you probably ride more elevators than knock on doors. But before you discount these experiences, let me remind you that we are both on a pilgrimage. You and I are working together, and to repeat what I said in the Introduction, our challenge is to learn from the past without living there, live and grow in the present, and look to the future with hope and optimism. Rarely a day goes by that I do not learn something new to help me become an even more effective sales professional for the 1990s. Come with me and learn with me on this journey.

## THE BENEFITS ARE FOR YOU!

As you enter professional sales (whether this is your first experience or you are rededicating yourself to a new level of professionalism), you must stop to realize that choosing to be a sales professional is a *daily* task. As a matter of fact, let me encourage you to make this first entry on your "to do" list: "Today I will be a successful sales professional, AND I will learn something today that will make me even more professional tomorrow." If you will begin each day with this commitment to our great profession, there are MANY benefits that await YOU—the successful sales professional! Best of all, this procedure helps you make certain your tomorrows are better than your yesterdays.

## INDEPENDENCE

One of the MANY great things about our profession is that you are truly your own boss. You are in business, as the saying goes, "for yourself but not by yourself." When you stand in front of the mirror each morning, you can look yourself right in the eye and say, "My goodness, you're such a nice, efficient, effective, hardworking, and professional person—you deserve a raise!" and the board just met. I might add that the raise will become effective as soon as you do.

## OPPORTUNITY

The reality is that as a salesperson you are the chairman of the board, the general sales manager, the chief financial officer, the executive vice president; and yes, you're the janitor, chief cook, and bottle washer. In short, with the independence of being your own boss comes a tremendous responsibility, and this is the exciting part of the profession! OPPORTUNITY IS BORN OF INDEPENDENCE HANDLED IN A RESPONSIBLE MANNER, and in the sales profession, your opportunities are unparalleled.

Although it's true that you do have to be versatile, strong-willed, organized, disciplined, enthusiastic, and motivated and you need a great attitude, these characteristics fall into place for the professional salesperson who has the most important characteristics of them all—the servant's heart, a humble spirit, and a willingness to grow.

## PROBLEM SOLVING

With the possible exceptions of medicine and the ministry, no one is in as good a position to solve problems as you, the professional persuader. There is virtually nothing on earth that brings as much personal satisfaction and gratification as being able to empower another human being to become more efficient, effective, and successful because of the goods, products, or services you have to offer. How much does it mean when you save another human being a considerable amount of time, money, frustration, and/or anxiety? Nothing is so rewarding as receiving those "hero" letters from your clients telling you about the dramatic difference you made in their lives.

## SECURITY

Of course, I'd be less than honest if I didn't confess that the high income potential offered in the profession of selling is a tremendous lure to those who are ambitiously dissatisfied with having low ceilings established on their worth and activities. I'll also confess that this adds to the security of being in sales. Security, according to General Douglas MacArthur, comes from your ability to produce; in other words, it is an "inside" job. In sales you don't have to wait for things to happen; you can make things happen. When business is slow, you can go out and stir the marketplace and get it into action.

Your attitude, discipline, willingness to work, and organizational skills bring you a security that is not found when you're dependent on the whims of other people who are frequently incapable of making objective evaluations about your worth. As a salesperson, you can tip the scales in your own favor by getting up earlier, working later, becoming more professional, and learning how to better serve and persuade. All these things simply mean you have greater control of your life and your future, and THAT is a secure feeling!

## FAMILY

The family benefits are also enormous. As many of you know, my wife is a decided redhead, meaning one day she just "decided" to be a redhead, so when I talk about her, I call her "The Redhead" (and she enthusiastically encourages me to do so). When I talk to her, it's "Sugar Baby." Her name is Jean.

From the beginning of my marriage to The Redhead through the rearing of our children—Suzy, Cindy, Julie, and Tom—each has been intimately involved in considerable detail in every aspect of my sales career. They have shared the excitement, the glory, the benefits, the fun, and yes, the frustrations and anxieties that come with the profession of selling. My family has been privileged to go on trips to beautiful convention areas, share in the rewards when performance was extraordinary, and reap the benefits of sharing the limelight when trophies and awards were earned. They were also there when I was in a sales slump and needed their support and encouragement. Actually, those times drew us as close as (if not closer than) the times when things were going wonderfully well.

Message: Be honest with the family. They want to "feel" and "be" a part of trials and triumphs. They can be a source of strength and encouragement, and in the process their own growth into maturity will be enhanced. This great profession enabled us, as a family, to have more shared interests, develop more mutual friends, and broaden our scope of life and living by associating with other people who were excited about selling and the products and services they were able to offer.

Enjoying a profession where your success is specifically measurable and your performance is recognized based on results is tremendously satisfying. Having your spouse and children hear from the boss about what a great job mom or dad is doing has significant benefits for the entire family.

The growth, training, and development received in the sales profession combined with the independence, confidence, discipline, assertiveness, and caring for other people make that truly professional salesperson a better wife or husband AND parent.

## COMMUNICATION

The profession of selling soon teaches you that people do things for their reasons, not yours. This principle helps you be more effective in communicating not only with members of your family but with members of your community as well. Professional salespeople learn to put themselves in the other person's shoes, and this is always a comfortable fit, regardless of shoe size!

The communication and persuasion skills learned in your career benefit family and community as you go about helping others to be all that they can be.

## MOVING UP

Salespeople consistently move into the executive suites. I believe this is going to be even more prevalent in the future than it has been in the past because of the increasing depth and breadth of skills the successful entrepreneurial salesperson of the nineties must acquire. As a group, we must be creative and open as well as flexible in our thinking. Traditionally, salespeople have had to come up with a creative way to solve problems almost *as* they have made their presentation and have had to adapt to fit the prospect's needs and desires. This training is perfect for the executive office.

As salespeople, we encounter people at every emotional level—when they're happy, excited, and enthusiastic; and when they're irritated and down in the dumps. We learn how to deal with the extroverts, the introverts, the procrastinators, the optimists, the pessimists, the detail oriented, the impetuous, the loudmouths, the big shots, the ego maniacs, and a host of others. This is tremendous preparation for a spot in the executive suite, and the better we get at those "people skills," the more likely we are to move into the upper echelons of management.

In sales, we learn to persuade people to our way of thinking rather than order people to do the things we want them to do. Effective persuaders are going to be in great demand for leadership roles in the 1990s! After a period of time, persuasiveness and creativity become second nature.

Obviously, we must know how to persuade others if we're going to convince people to buy, and these skills transfer to corporate headquarters. Considerable skill is required to encourage people to cooperate, to work with other people in the organization, and to persuade them that even when they feel their idea is best, once that idea has been rejected and someone else's inserted, the good, ambitious employee will lay aside personal whims and cooperate for the good of the team. And believe me when I say this task requires great persuasion skills!

# MANAGEMENT

Successful salespersons of the nineties are also excellent managers. They have to manage time, territory, personal habits, and life in general. The better they manage their lives, the better they will be able to manage their business.

Successful sales professionals learn to keep a balance. This area is where many people drop the ball because they think balance means giving equal priority and the same amount of time to everything. That simply is not the case. You know you should eat a balanced diet, but for it to be balanced, you definitely do not want or need as much fat as carbohydrates. The same is true of your schedule. You don't spend as much time eating as you do sleeping. Separate priorities and balance—"priorities" relate to chronological order; "balance" relates to variety.

Priorities and balance can be confusing. For example, most people will spend more time working than any other single activity. If you work eight hours a day, surely you would not expect to play eight hours a day, but you will do what is necessary to maintain the physical, mental, and spiritual aspects of life. You will also want to maintain social relationships and family relationships.

The key is understanding that when all is said and done, you must be able to answer the following question: Are you happy, healthy, and reasonably prosperous and secure, and do you have friends, peace of mind, and good family relationships? As you examine each of these areas, let me challenge you to look at your activities and daily tasks. Do the results of the tasks you are working to take action upon yield the results you are looking for? If not, why not? If not, what are you going to do about it? These are the questions individuals who would have their names on the doors for the executive suites of tomorrow must answer.

This doesn't mean that every day everything is going to be in balance. Sometimes rush projects throw you out of kilter, and for a brief period of time you work longer and harder. But you ultimately must bring your activities back into a reasonable balance, or you will short-circuit some areas of your life and end up with less of what you're seeking than you otherwise would have.

## ARE YOU WITH ME?

If I haven't "sold" you on the concept that selling is a magnificently rewarding, exciting, AND demanding career—and not a stopgap job until something better comes along—and you honestly believe you can live without selling, be about it!

And if you can't imagine living without enjoying all the wonderful benefits our great profession offers, CONGRATULATIONS! You just joined the profession that has the power to dramatically affect and empower our society in a way that many other professions cannot. The current paradigm shift that the sales professional of the 1990s will address is the true importance of sales as a profession.

## THE SALESMAN

Salesmen are a big problem to their bosses, customers and wives, to credit managers, hotels and sometimes to each other. Individually and collectively they are cussed and discussed in sales meetings, conventions, behind closed doors, in bathrooms, bar rooms, and under one's breath from many angles, and with much fervor.

They make more noise and more mistakes, create more cheer, correct more errors, adjust more differences, spread more gossip, explain more discrepancies, hear more grievances, pacify more belligerence, and waste more time under pressure, all without losing their temper, than any class we know—including ministers. They live in hotels, cabs and tents, on trains, buses, and park benches, eat all kinds of food, drink all kinds of liquids—good and bad, sleep before, during and after business with no more schedule than the weather bureau, and with no sympathy from the office.

Yet salesmen are a power in society and in the public economy. In many ways they are a tribute unto themselves. They draw and spend more money with less effort, and with less return, than any other group in business. They come at the most inopportune time, under the slightest pretext, stay longer under more opposition, ask more personal questions, make more comments, put up with more inconveniences, and take more for granted under greater resistance than any group or body, including the U.S. Army. They introduce more new goods, dispose of more old goods, load or move freight cars, unload more ships, build more factories, start more new businesses, and write more debits and credits in our ledgers than all the other people in America. With all their faults, they keep the wheels of commerce turning, and the currents of human emotions running. More cannot be said of any man. Be careful whom you call a SALESMAN, *LEST YOU FLATTER HIM.*

*The Salesman was sent to me by Donald Benenson of Levittown, New York, and I think it says a great deal about our proud profession.*

CHAPTER TWO

# SELLING IN THE MODERN MARKET

## *The Decade of Technology*

"My husband, Joe, is a police officer in a small town. He receives many phone calls at home about his work and decided to get an answering machine to screen them, especially the threatening or harassing ones. This is the greeting he prepared:

" 'You have reached the home of a police officer. You have the right to remain silent. If you wish to give up this right, leave your message after the beep. Anything you say can, and probably will, be held against you.' The phone calls became much friendlier."*

Yes, the calls got friendlier because in the 1990s, the "decade of technology," the officer used modern methods to help "sell" the importance of courtesy.

## "SALES TECHNOLOGY" BEGINS WITH *SALES*!

In 1943, I was a junior in high school. World War II was going full force, and patriotism in America was high. My goal was to become a naval aviator, help win the war, and return to Yazoo City, Mississippi, as a conquering hero.

Realizing that even with the classes I would be taking my senior

---

*Reprinted with permission from the April 1991 Reader's Digest. Copyright © 1991 by The Reader's Digest Assn., Inc. Contributed by Susan Escujuri.

year in high school, I would still be deficient in the math and science fundamentals necessary to be successful in the Naval Air Corps, I made the decision to attend summer school at Hinds Junior College in Raymond, Mississippi. Then I could graduate from high school educationally equipped to qualify for the V-5 flight training program. Despite the fact that it was one of my first ventures into the area of goal setting, the plan seemed sound.

Well, of all the seemingly idiotic things to have happen, the school required me to take a history course. What possible good was it going to do me to know what happened a hundred years ago? I needed math and science so I could get in the air corps, fly those airplanes, shoot down the enemy, and come back home to Yazoo City and have a ticker tape parade!

However, I needed my graduation certificate to make application to the navy, so I decided to "suck it up and tough it out." As you might suspect, I walked into that history class with a chip on my shoulder, which is a pretty fair indicator that there is "wood above." My attitude was, "O.K., I'm here. Now teach me enough to get out of here and get on with my life. I'll go along with your ridiculous policies just enough to get my diploma. Let's get this over with!"

The teacher was Coach Joby Harris, who turned out to be one of the most incredible salesmen I have ever encountered. He spent literally the entire first class selling me on why I had to know my history. Oh, I guess he was talking to the others, too, but he seemed to be speaking directly to me. He did such a beautiful sales job that I walked out of that class having made the decision to become a history major in college—and history was the only course I consistently made *A*'s in while I was in college. In addition to selling me on history, Coach Harris sold me on something else that day.

Coach Joby Harris sold me the idea that if you have an ability that goes beyond providing for your own needs, you have a responsibility to use that ability to reach down and help those who do not have that capacity. He turned out to be something of a prophet when he said, "As a matter of fact, if you don't reach down and help pick up those less fortunate, the day will come when due to sheer weight of numbers, those less fortunate will reach up and pull you down." This generation is the first with a lower educational accomplishment than the preceding generation; it is also the first generation with a lower standard of living. Coach Harris's words must be heard by all.

A primary reason I have worked so hard to grow The Zig Ziglar Corporation into an internationally respected training company is so that we can SELL each other on the importance of building our lives on the foundation stones of honesty, character, integrity, faith, love, and loyalty. When we build on these foundation stones, we can build a business, a life, a family, a friendship, and a professional selling career while making a difference in the world in which we live.

## THE COACH IS A SALES PROFESSIONAL

Not only did Coach Harris prove my point that each of us IS in the business of selling, regardless of our daily activities; he also showed that we must get the person right before we can get the salesperson right.

**"If you don't reach down and help pick up those less fortunate, the day will come when due to sheer weight of numbers, those less fortunate will reach up and pull you down." This present generation of high school graduates is the first with a lower educational accomplishment than the preceding generation; it is also the first generation with a lower standard of living.**

When Joby Harris was a youngster, he was a Boy Scout. His scoutmaster was Thomas B. Abernathy. Mr. Abernathy was the first scout official and scoutmaster in the state of Mississippi. Even though

Joby had a dad, Mr. Abernathy took a special interest in him and became a mentor and teacher. Joby learned scouting skills, but his education didn't stop there. He learned a sense of responsibility and honesty that developed into character and integrity—because Thomas Abernathy took the time necessary to help a little boy named Joby Harris.

Incidentally, Mr. Abernathy had four children, three daughters and a son. His youngest daughter's name was Jean Abernathy. For over forty-five years now, her name has been Jean Abernathy Ziglar. There is no way that Mr. Abernathy could ever have known that when he was spending time with little Joby Harris, he was spending time with the boy who would become the man who would have such a dramatic impact on his future son-in-law. The man who would help make Zig Ziglar a better man, husband, and father to Thomas Abernathy's yet unborn grandchildren.

Major Point: When you make a "sale" and service the sales properly, there is no way you can possibly know what will happen as a direct AND an indirect result of that sales. Career-minded professionals make every effort to "follow through" in EVERY sales and service opportunity.

**Being ethical is not only the RIGHT way to live; it is also the most practical way to live. True selling professionals don't only talk about ethics; they LIVE ethically!**

Although the war ended before I was able to get into the flying phase of the training, Joby Harris influenced the man whose training programs are being used by the naval aviators (as well as many others on the base) in Corpus Christi, Texas, and other bases across the U.S.

## HONESTY AND INTEGRITY IN SELLING

One of the buzzwords for the nineties is *ethics*. It has become a buzzword because of its lack of visibility. Politicians from Washington, D.C., to California with stops in South Carolina, Texas, and Arizona have been and are continuing to "sell out." The most talked about names in the business community have been Charles Keating, Ivan Boesky, and Michael Milken. You would be hard-pressed not to have heard about the tragedies in our religious community regarding Jim Bakker or Jimmy Swaggart. Unfortunately, the list goes on and on in all areas and all industries. The American public (and the world, for that matter) is saying, "Please give me someone I can trust."

My point in "The Ultimate Handbook for the Complete Sales Professional" is exactly this: Being ethical is not only the RIGHT way to live; it is also the most practical way to live. True selling professionals don't only talk about ethics; they LIVE ethically!

## INTEGRITY, HONESTY, AND ETHICS PAY OFF

Robert Davis is an outstanding salesman and sales manager in Baton Rouge, Louisiana. He works with Terminix Pest Control, and when asked what he does for a living, he simply responds, "I kill bugs." His healthy self-esteem and belief in his company's services allow him to excel personally and professionally.

Recently, Robert had a new salesman who got a little overzealous. Late one Friday afternoon, a client called with a serious problem. Bees were swarming around his home and placing the family in distress. Robert assigned his new man to the seemingly simple task, but as the salesman headed out the door, he called back, "Has anyone ever sold a $200 'bee job'?" The others smiled at his "bravado" and said, "No."

When the new man returned in less than thirty minutes with a check for $225, everyone was quite amazed. The telephone interrupted the excitement that bringing in a check for the largest "bee job" ever was generating. Robert answered, and the man who had signed the check was on the phone.

"I just wanted to call and thank you for responding so quickly and getting rid of my problem," the man began. "Those bees were a real concern, and your man certainly did the job.

"But I was wondering," he continued, "if $225 was normal for a fifteen-minute job."

"Are you going to be home for the next few minutes?" was Robert's immediate response. When he got an affirmative answer, Robert put the salesman and the check in his car. When they arrived at the man's home, Robert walked right up to the man and said, "Sir, I'm afraid we got a little carried away with our enthusiasm. Since I had not clearly explained the parameters of this job and how it should be billed to our new salesman, we overcharged you. (Notice that he did nothing to embarrass the salesman, though he had in fact explained exactly how to do the job and that it was a $125 job at the most.) So this one's on us." With that, he handed the man his check.

"Well, that's mighty kind of you," the man said, "but I still have this problem with roaches and ants. Can you do that for me at no charge, too?"

They all laughed, even as Robert wrote out the contract for the $300 sale that resulted from his ethics, integrity, and honesty. Had they kept the check for the "record" (and unfair) bee job, they would have had a client who wondered if he had been "ripped off." By their returning the money and doing the right thing, Terminix was rewarded with a larger sale AND a long-term client.

When you are honest and ethical and live with integrity, your rewards are guaranteed. They may not happen as quickly as they did for Robert Davis, but just like putting money in the bank guarantees a return, demonstrating the qualities of honesty, integrity, and ethical behavior will guarantee a positive return in your career.

This book is designed to guide you toward the balanced, ethical life that will help you become everything possible personally and professionally. Every sales technique, concept, formula, and principle can assist you as you build your career on an ethical foundation with the foundation stones of honesty, character, integrity, faith, love, and loyalty.

## THE NEW ORDER OF SALES PROFESSIONAL

Today's sales professional is not the plaid-coated, white-belted, snake oil-selling carnival barker or the outdated stereotype of the fast-talking, back-slapping, joke-telling used car salesman. Today's sales professional has the appearance of the Harvard MBA, even if he or she didn't complete high school. Today's sales professional is educated in what is necessary to be successful in the modern world—from computer literacy to market knowledge.

**Build your career on an ethical foundation with the foundation stones of honesty, character, integrity, faith, love, and loyalty.**

The sales professional of today clearly understands that you can finish school, but you never finish your education. You might have finished school with ease, but continuing your education is seldom easy. Education is a lifetime experience. Many men and women who have not earned a degree are brilliantly educated because they never really left school.

Interestingly enough, two of my Ph.D. friends, with whom I've done a considerable amount of work, shared an intriguing thought with me. They are convinced, though they have no scientific data, that an individual who has an earned Ph.D. will have accumulated less than 1 percent of the total knowledge in a formal educational environment. The rest of that knowledge was acquired at the mother's knee; by learning the lessons of life; by having interchanges with people; by observing; by reading books, magazines, and newspapers; by taking correspondence courses; by attending seminars; by listening to cassette recordings; by watching video training tapes; and by taking advantage of a host of other educational opportunities. This is completely believable to me because many studies have shown that a child has acquired 60 to 65 percent of the working vocabulary by the age of three!

## FORMAL EDUCATION

In no way is this intended as a put-down of formal education. A real joy of my life is hearing about, through the number of letters I receive and the conversations I have, the people who went back to school and got their degree after reading one of my books or listening to one of my presentations. I'm in favor of acquiring as much formal education as possible. I just want you to understand that if you do not have that degree, you can still make it and make it BIG in the world of selling . . . IF you will take advantage of the learning opportunities (like reading and applying the principles in this book) all around you.

Actually, some of the best educated people I know had a limited amount of formal education, but their unlimited curiosity, drive, and ambition enabled them to acquire a tremendous amount of knowledge and a broad general education. One trademark of an "educated" person is the commitment to growth and keeping pace with the rapidly changing technology of the times. The words we hear most in today's selling world are *change* and *technology*. The salesperson who refuses to adapt to the changes and capitalize on the technology of today is going to be left at the starting gate and will have a limited career that will not be nearly as productive as it otherwise could be.

## AN INCREDIBLE EXAMPLE OF CHANGE AND TECHNOLOGY

Perhaps one of the most startling articles I've ever read appeared in the *Dallas Morning News* on January 5, 1991. For a long time we've been hearing about the "paperless" world that is ultimately going to be ours due to the advent of computers and other business machines. However, even with the proliferation of computers, 95 percent of the nation's information is stored on paper, not magnetic disks, microfiche, or any other source. But the change is coming.

In Irving, Texas, at the Westinghouse Security Systems Division of Westinghouse Electric Corporation, you won't find any paper or anything that suggests the use of paper. No paper clips, trash cans, staplers, or scissors. There is no copying machine. The employees have desks, but the desks have no drawers. There are conference rooms but no conference tables. You won't see any letters, bills, magazines, or other publications. If it is paper, it is not there! What you will see are innumerable computers and other pieces of electronic equipment.

## FUTURE SHOCK

Most of us would be terribly uncomfortable and really have to work at accepting and working in that environment. I'm sure the culture shock would be something. However, as I said earlier, the sales professional of the nineties who is going to be a top performer has to be capable of adapting to change and using the current technology. Our adaptability is directly dependent on our attitude, and when I think of adaptability, change, and technology fueled by the right attitude, Louise Padgett of Forest City, North Carolina, comes to mind.

Louise and her late husband, "Fifty," became friends of mine back in the early 1950s when we worked in the same division of a direct sales organization. I recently corresponded with her, and what an inspiration she is!

Louise joined the Avon organization over twenty-six years ago. In 1990, at eighty-four years of age she was in the President's Club, received an award (a six-foot bevel-edged mirror in a gold frame and a gold marble-topped table) for recruiting, and consistently placed in the top ten of her division. Over the last quarter of a century, she has had three hip replacements and two heart attacks—without missing a single order! As Louise says, "Where there's a will, there's a way." And coming from a top performer like Louise Padgett, the quote is far from a cliché!

## "NEW" TECHNOLOGY?

At this point, you might be asking, "But, Zig, what does this have to do with the new technology you are talking about?" Well, as most of you know, Avon for years and years has had a reputation for their ladies ringing those doorbells, but when you're eighty-four and living in the 1990s, there are some changes that can be made. So Louise Padgett learned to use electronic equipment to handle her business. It is better known as the telephone. As far as I know, she is one of the only women in the country selling Avon in this manner, but for her situation, it has been a must. Why, Louise even has the ability to persuade most of her customers to come by her home to pick up their orders!

Many direct sales businesses like Avon are taking technology forward and working at allowing corporate computers to interact with field sales staff computers to facilitate orders—through the telephone.

## WORTH REMEMBERING

Based on people like Louise Padgett, all of us can be successful when the modern technology is combined with "old-fashioned" positive thinking, charm, persuasion, persistence, and commitment.

To me, people like Louise point out what is most exciting about our great profession. Change and technology cannot pass us by unless we allow them to because each of us is restricted only by mental and emotional attitudes. As long as we control our attitudes, we can be as productive as we choose to be—in whatever we want to do. In Louise's words, "Zig, you know yourself that it takes enthusiasm, hard work and, as the old saying goes, 'a lot of guts.' I keep my clock of enthusiasm wound up real tight, and I always try to think positively." That is great advice for all of us as we deal with change and technology!

## TELE-TECHNOLOGY

In 1990, the J. C. Penney Company relocated its corporate headquarters from New York City to Dallas, Texas. While working on a training project for the company, some of our staff toured the facilities. Penney stores across the nation make inventory decisions based on information they receive over Penney's television network! In 1985, buyers thought it impossible to make decisions without "touching the material" and "seeing the items" in person. Today, with this tele-technology, orders can be placed directly with manufacturers, time is saved (shipments can come directly to the stores instead of having to stop at inventory management warehouses), and profit margins can be increased. An outgrowth of this activity is Penney's Training Network, which allows the expert training staff to train "associates" (as all employees are called) across the U.S. and around the world.

Mobil Oil accounting executives here in Dallas have also used our training services, and while we were customizing the program we developed for them, they revealed that key executives have a portable laptop computer that attaches to the system used in their building, which can be detached and used at home in the evenings. If they need to "plug in" to the main system, they need only call in on "dedicated" telephone lines. Instant access to information is a must in the selling profession.

Even as we are finalizing the manuscript for this book, Oliver-Nelson Books and the Thomas Nelson sales staff under the direction of Publisher Bruce Barbour and Sales Manager Bob Zaloba are in the process of doing a feasibility study to determine the practicality of having their sales representatives work with laptop computers. They currently report sales results on a daily basis from their portable facsimile machines.

## THE 1990s SALES OFFICE

*Success* magazine releases an annual issue devoted completely to selling. In May 1991 (the fourth annual sales-focused issue), writer Dan Gutman, a "cutting edge" technology writer whose syndicated column "I Didn't Know You Could Do THAT with a Computer!" is worth reading, reported on an unusual and interesting office of the future.

Salesman Perry Solomon (who is also the CEO of High Technology Distributing in Van Nuys, California) will often set up an appointment from his cellular car phone, pull over to write a proposal on his laptop computer, fax the proposal from his car to the client, receive feedback via fax, and walk through the client's door ready for a signature on the contract. No problem if he has to wait for a few minutes outside his client's office because the portable phone in his briefcase keeps him in constant contact with other clients.

"The office of the future," Solomon is fond of saying, "has four wheels, not four walls."

## SCIENCE FICTION OR SCIENCE FACT

Fact: Laptop computers weigh less than eight pounds and are smaller than most briefcases. They have more power than machines ten times that size from five years ago and cost less than $1,500. Pocket organizers (phone number storage, notes, "to do" lists, calculators, and calendars), "palm" top computers (computers that will fit in a purse or coat pocket and have the capacity to upload and download Lotus 1-2-3 files), and computer notebooks (the size of this book, with hard drive and easy to read screen) are realities today.

Fact: Portable printers for your laptop computer are small, comparatively inexpensive, and of such quality that for less than $800 you can get a unit capable of producing printouts almost indistinguishable from those done by laser printers.

Fact: Cellular telephones have reception that is as clear as home telephones. The size of the unit gets smaller and smaller—and the cost per minute is declining.

Fact: Facsimile machines have become a way of life on the road as in the office. "Fax it to my car phone" is no longer a joke but a necessary reality.

Fact: The pager is keeping up with technology quite nicely. In addition to getting smaller and lighter, it is getting less expensive. A pager can save you money on your cellular phone bill by allowing you to determine which calls to return in what order. This also can be a great time saver.

## THE MORE THINGS CHANGE . . .

The old adage, "The more things change, the more they remain the same," is still valid. Despite the fact that we must all deal with change and technology, some basic truths must be consistently considered.

If you are going to be successful in the 1990s as a sales star, you MUST (there is no option) understand the changes and the new technology. You must also understand that in some ways the "old" work force is similar to the "new" work force.

## THE NEW WORK FORCE

The one thing that customers have ALWAYS rated highest in the sales world is TRUST, which also is called dependability because it is a direct reflection on the integrity of the individual. The primary reason people will choose NOT to buy from you is lack of TRUST. When you make a serious promise to the prospect or a "casual comment" involving a promise, the prospect takes both as gospel. This is especially true if there is any difficulty during the sales process and even after the sale. If the person has any trouble in any phase of the relationship or use of the product, there is the distinct possibility that any "lack of follow-through" will be blown completely out of proportion. Even the tiniest matters become "deal shattering."

**The primary reason people will choose NOT to buy from you is lack of TRUST.**

In the new work force of the 1990s, women sales representatives are getting an ever-increasing portion of the business—a portion of the business that goes beyond the number of women involved in the selling profession. There are several excellent reasons. Number one is the fact that women are more dependable. No, this does not mean that every female in sales is completely reliable or that all men in the selling profession cannot be depended upon. It does mean, however, that by and large when a saleswoman says she will send you the report on Thursday, she will. When a salesman says he will send it on Thursday, he is less likely to keep that commitment. The saleswoman who says she will service the machinery on Friday is generally more dependable than the salesman who makes the same commitment.

Now before you accuse me of being abusive to men or patronizing to women, let me say that right is right, truth is truth, and success is success. Any objective observer will verify what I am sharing with you now, and many wise observers will tell you, "Those who don't learn from history are doomed to repeat its failures." As you and I study success in the sales profession, we can "learn from the successful and repeat their successful principles." We must analyze HOW and WHY so that we may learn from failure and build upon success.

## THE WOMAN'S PERSPECTIVE

Sheila West (author of *Beyond Chaos,* a classic book I encourage you to read) is an extremely successful entrepreneur and sales professional. As a household executive and mother, she gained valuable leadership and management skills. She also gained extensive insight into human nature ("people" skills). During this part of her career, she made literally thousands of management decisions and demonstrated leadership skills as well as persuasion skills. In 1981 she entered the archery business full force. Her husband, John, handles the retail side of the business, and Sheila handles the wholesale portion of Archery Center International in Monroe, Michigan.

In a conversation, I made the observation that in America, women are instinctively trusted more than men and that people are inclined to take them at face value and act on their suggestions. Men and women prospects are willing to "trust" the saleswoman more than the salesman and take action according to her recommendations.

Sheila agreed with that and asked me if I knew why. I admitted I did not. She explained, "Well, women are far more open than men. This makes them more vulnerable, but it generates trust on the part of the people with whom they are dealing. The prospects do not feel they're being sold and certainly not 'conned' by someone who is willing to be so vulnerable."

She elaborated and said that ego is far less likely to "muddy the waters." Where salesmen might get involved in one-up-manship, saleswomen will be far more inclined to let the *prospects* be the center of attention and listen to what they are saying. This is due in large part to women's ability to listen. All successful sales professionals utilize listening skills to their fullest. Thus far in my career, I have never heard of anyone missing a sale because of listening to the prospects' needs, wants, and desires. Interestingly enough, the more salespersons know about the prospects' needs, the better position they are in to meet those needs. Not only that, but the trust factor goes up, up, and up when the prospects see salespeople intensely listening to their needs and desires.

Listening is just *not* as difficult as we make it. When we are NOT talking or PREPARING to talk, we can listen. There are many steps and even week-long courses in developing listening skills, but for our needs here, we can use the old saying, "Talking is sharing, but listening is caring."

## LISTENING WITH YOUR EYES

When you listen, you do more than listen with your ears. If humanly possible, turn directly toward the person speaking and forget forms, data, product samples, or anything else. Look your prospect in the eye and watch for those nonverbal clues that give insights into the person speaking. Notice the gestures, the way the person sits or stands, the smile or frown—anything and everything indicating the frame of mind at that particular moment.

---

**Talking is sharing, but listening is caring.**

---

Listen to "the way" the person is speaking: the speed as well as the tone of voice and intensity. Listen empathetically, always asking yourself how you would feel if you were in the prospects's shoes. And listen with an open heart as you carefully observe the speaker's emotional involvement in the words chosen.

Most important, DO NOT INTERRUPT, and NEVER FINISH A PHRASE, THOUGHT, OR SENTENCE when your prospect pauses.

**You can finish school, but you can never finish your education.**

## RECIPROCITY

Another factor involved in being a good listener is the "Law of Reciprocity." When we carefully "listen" to the prospects elaborate interests, desires, hobbies, and other thoughts, we are putting them in debt to us. They then have a feeling they "owe" us something, and consequently, they are more willing to "listen" to our story since we have given them the courtesy of listening to them. This skill, I hasten to add, is not the exclusive domain of saleswomen and can be learned by anyone. The real professional salesperson—whether male or female—will develop the skill and get more sales as a result.

## COMMUNICATION SPECIFICS

Most people like to listen at the same speed they speak, so whenever possible adjust your speech patterns to conform to those of the prospect. Some exceptions to this policy are the following:

1. The prospect "loses his cool" and gets loud and abusive. When anger enters the picture, lower your voice and slow down your rate of speech.
2. The prospect uses crude or profane language. Keep your language clean and professional. Chances are excellent that the prospect will judge you by a higher standard than he judges himself. The higher the level of moral dignity and integrity,

the higher the level of trust and respect. The higher the level of trust and respect, the better your chances are of making the sale.

3. The prospect speaks so quietly you must strain to hear every word. Keep your voice level at a comfortable volume so you are certain you are being heard. The prospect will not work as hard to understand you as you will to understand him.
4. The prospect speaks so agonizingly slow or so incredibly fast that if you emulate him or her completely, the distraction would be obvious. You should make some adjustment in the direction of the prospect's speech pattern.
5. Never conform to speech accents, bad grammar, slang, or speech impediments.

## DEPENDABILITY AND CREDIBILITY

Sheila West helped me understand even more about the woman's perspective in sales when she said, "The most difficult part for a woman in sales (or many other fields) is to gain credibility. It is impossible for women to do this without being dependable. Therefore, the ones who do not have this trait are washed out of the field quickly. In other words, their dependability gives them credibility. Their credibility makes them believable. With credibility and believability comes confidence, and with confidence comes success!"

## YOUR SALES PROSPECTS

In addition to having a dramatic impact on the profession of selling, women are a significant factor in the consumer area. Some experts believe that women control (directly and indirectly) the single largest amount of "dollar buying power" of any group in the history of the world. Forty percent of all videocassette recorders are purchased by women. Women also purchase 41 percent of all compact disc players and 58 percent of all component stereo systems. For years, women have bought more books and clothes than men have. The clothes were bought not only for themselves but also for their children and, in many cases, their husbands. And women generally have more say-so in the purchase of homes AND the thousands of consumables in those homes than do the men. For that reason, women deserve more of the attention than they are getting.

Unfortunately, in many ways, the female consumer has been abused. Far too many men are treating women with disrespect when it comes to purchases that involve significant dollar amounts or technical knowledge. Jokes abound, ridicule exists, disdain is shown, and 1,001 subtle put-downs take place. And lest you think these remarks are just for the men, think again! Many women report that female sales representatives treat them more rudely and with less respect than the men do.

One particular area where women have been abused is the automotive industry. To be candid, many have been taken advantage of in some situations. This is especially true of young single women, older women who are widows or divorcées, and women of a minority race. The old saying that "somebody saw them coming" applies to too many cases.

But this situation is changing—and changing rapidly. The increasing number of single and working women has made becoming more knowledgeable a necessity. The areas chauvinistic thinking labeled as "for men only" (mechanics, finance, law enforcement, electronics, and construction are examples) are being studied and mastered by women. Women are excelling in all industries. In this computer age, women clearly understand that having the proper information is a vital necessity to survive and move forward. The bottom line is that in today's world any woman who is taken advantage of or abused in a transaction will be highly unlikely to do business with the incompetent and unprofessional salesperson again.

Prediction: These salespeople are on their way out since they never should have been in sales in the first place. Second Prediction: The successful sales professional will recognize and utilize this incredible market by working to meet the needs of this portion of the marketplace, which just happens to be the fastest growing segment of the market by far.

The same qualities that women sales representatives are using to become successful in sales are the qualities that make them excellent prospects for goods and services: trust, listening skills, dependability, integrity, growing confidence, and ego security—just what the ethical, professional sales representative of the nineties would hope to find in all buyers. By treating women with the respect they deserve, we are better serving all people.

## TODAY'S SALES PRO

Today's sales professional is the consummate professional in every sense of the word. The sales pro understands the importance of the proper balance between home and career and understands that to be successful in only one area of life is the biggest failure of all. The successful sales professional of the nineties knows that happiness is not pleasure, it is victory; that when you do what you need to do when you need to do it, you will eventually be able to do what you WANT to do when you want to do it. And most important, the successful sales professional of the nineties KNOWS and UNDERSTANDS the sales credo: YOU CAN HAVE EVERYTHING IN LIFE YOU WANT IF YOU WILL JUST HELP ENOUGH OTHER PEOPLE GET WHAT THEY WANT!

Please understand, that sales credo is a philosophy, not a tactic. To help others get what they want, you must first understand what they want. So what do people want? The answer is simple. From you, my selling friend, they want the best solution to their "problem." And you provide this solution by persuading them to use your goods, products, or services. Do this often enough, and you will build a beautiful sales career!

CHAPTER THREE

# FINDING SOMEONE WILLING TO BUY

## *How to Stay in Business in the Profession of Selling*

"Once, when her car hit a large pothole and no road repairs were made despite her repeated calls, Sheila painted a huge white circle around the hole, lettered the word *Pothole* and dabbed a giant arrow below it. Next she called the local newspaper and told them of a photo opportunity on Route 22 near Sun Valley Road. The pothole was repaired the same day the picture appeared in the paper."*

## THE GREAT DEBATE

An ongoing debate at every sales get-together (meaning when two salespeople start talking) is this: "What is the most important part of the selling process?" A disproportionate number believe that "closing sales" more effectively would solve all their selling problems; some say that the only way to sales success is to sell the proper product; others say that handling objections is the key to success;

---

*Excerpted with permission from "Unforgettable Sheila Petersen" by Barbara W. MacInnes, Reader's Digest February 1991. Copyright © by 1991 by The Reader's Digest Assn., Inc.

one group claims that making a powerful presentation is the most important area; and still another group believes determining the specific wants and needs of the prospect is most important to sales success. The reality is, if you can't handle all phases of the sales process, you will not sell enough to stay in the profession.

## PROSPECTING

However, regardless of how good your closing skills, your product, your ability to handle objections, your presentation, or your skills at determining wants and needs, you are out of business if you don't have a prospect! The consensus among outstanding salespeople and sales trainers is almost unanimous: Prospecting is the most important key to sales success! Without prospects you are stillborn as a sales professional—dead before you get started. It is true that a journey of a thousand leagues begins with but a single step, and it is equally true that until you have a prospect, you have no chance of making a sale.

Someone once facetiously remarked, "The only problem with making a sale is the fact that you just lost your best prospect!" Obviously, this is true, but when you replace that prospect with several more, you have actually won twice.

Without prospects, you are out of business. With prospects, the professional salesperson has a chance to change the world—starting with your own! So let's look at this most important area of sales—prospecting!

## WHAT?

What is a prospect? A prospect is an individual or a group capable of making the decision on the product or service the salesperson is selling. There is obviously a difference between a "prospect" and a "suspect." A "suspect" is a name that *could* be a prospect, so the name offers hope. But unless that hope has a solid foundation, you have only a suspect. A "prospect" has a need for the product, a possible desire to own that product, and the financial capacity to implement that decision. You "spend" time with suspects; you "invest" time with prospects.

## WHEN?

So the question becomes, When do people prospect? The answer is, ALL THE TIME! Prospecting is not an eight-to-five job. Prospecting, when done graciously, can be done in virtually any environment—in social situations, on an airplane, in an airport, at a luncheon or a club meeting, or WHEREVER PEOPLE ARE PRESENT.

## THE PROSPECTING ATTITUDE

Once again, the best-paying hard work in the world is selling, and the poorest-paying easy work in the world is selling! Your chosen field is not an industry that allows you to "coast." When you get in the business of professional selling—or more important, when the business gets in you—you will discover that prospecting is not a chore; it is truly an exciting opportunity for success!

My friend Cavett Robert has a little saying: "You've got to circulate before you can percolate." How true it is! There's no denying that ACTIVITY (making contacts and calls) in the world of sales is critical. Alert salespeople are constantly in the state of "awareness," with eyes and ears open for business. This doesn't necessarily mean they approach everybody at a social function or corner the people on the driving range or golf course; nor does it mean they approach every person at the post office or supermarket. The successful prospecting attitude does mean, however, that when great prospectors pick up the newspaper, there is a sensitivity to local events or news stories that contain leads or prospects for the business. The successful prospecting attitude means tuning in to conversations that would directly or indirectly involve the use of the goods or services the salespeople offer.

Becoming successful at finding buyers means knowing when a new business opens or a new family moves to the neighborhood, practicing good neighborliness, and being a good citizen by welcoming them. Oftentimes business is born from such relationships. As the old saying goes, "You never trip over anything while you're seated."

## HOW?

The best way to begin prospecting is to display a genuine interest in the other person, which brings us back to an oft-made point. When you're the right kind of person, your chances of becoming an effective salesperson are much, much better. Here's what I mean. My mother and my wife would rebel at the thought that they could be very successful salespeople since neither ever "officially sold" any goods, products, or services. Yet each of them would have been superb because they're the greatest natural "friend makers" I've ever seen.

My mother could get aboard a bus for a trip, and by the time she reached her destination, she would have made a lifelong friend of the person seated next to her. They would correspond with each other for years. She had a *genuine* INTEREST IN and CONCERN FOR other people. The same is true of The Redhead. When we're aboard an aircraft or, for that matter, waiting in a line at the airport, in a hotel to check in, or in a restaurant to be seated, the chances are excellent, SOMETHING will happen—the conversational door will be opened, and thirty seconds later The Redhead will be engaged in a conversation that would lead you to believe a lifetime friendship was inevitable. I am fascinated and in awe of the way this happens.

## WHO?

Under normal circumstances, with a genuine interest in people, it's quite natural to weave what you do into the conversation by inquiring of the other person what he or she does. Then because you are trained to do so and are interested in doing so, you can gently direct the conversation to what you do. Often the individual with whom you're talking is not a prospect, but because of your sincerity and your genuine interest in people, the individual will not only refer you to a prospect but will even call on your behalf because you're such a nice person.

My point is simple. You are thinking prospecting all the time, and when you do, it's amazing how potential buyers will pop up in the most unlikely places. It's somewhat like buying a blue, red, green, black, purple, orange, or almost any color automobile. Suddenly it seems that everybody in town has bought the same color and the same model you have chosen.

## PROSPECTS COME C.O.D.

In the minds of most people, C.O.D. stands for "cash on delivery," but in the world of prospecting, C.O.D. has an entirely different meaning. The *C* stands for "communication." Every time you communicate with anybody who remotely resembles a prospect or one who might know a prospect, in some way you communicate the business you are in and your interest in sharing the excitement of what you have to offer with the prospect.

The *O* stands for "observation." You watch and listen to what's going on around you, whether it's in an elevator, on a bus, in a crowded store, at a club or social gathering.

The *D* stands for "dedication." You need to be dedicated to the concept of making the contacts and getting those references.

Let's do a more detailed analysis on C.O.D. and see what we can learn about finding more prospects.

## COMMUNICATION

May I ask you a few questions? With whom do you communicate most often? With whom do you communicate most effectively? Why do you spend so much time selling everybody but the people you know best?

When first asked that question, I was stumped for an answer. After giving it some thought, I reacted by saying, "Well, I wouldn't want my friends and family to think I am pushing my product on them."

The question I had to answer then, and you must answer now, is, If you think your product is good enough for all those strangers, why isn't it good enough for your friends and your family?

If what you are selling is not good enough for your friends and family, then why are you selling it? If it is good, then why would you want to keep it from those you care about most? I understand that there are organizations that encourage you to sell friends and relatives and then drop you like the proverbial "hot potato." But you are mature enough to know (or you wouldn't be reading this book) that you are not going to sell for an organization of this type.

## WHAT SHOULD I DO?

I often receive letters from people in sales asking how to determine what company to join. Many considering selling as a profession write to me to ask how they can be sure they are getting into the right field. The answer is discovered in the area of family and friends. What product or service would you want to offer to your parents, brothers and sisters, friends, acquaintances, and others with whom you come in contact? I strongly encourage those in the world of selling to deal with a product or service THEY CANNOT HELP TALKING ABOUT! Frankly, the product or service becomes something of an obsession, and instead of having to be reminded to tell someone about it, the great sales professionals have to remind themselves to "tone it down." They love what they do so much, they are ALWAYS selling and prospecting.

I believe this is obvious, but let me say that it is important to never take advantage of a friendship to make the sale. You should remind friends and family that you're offering your product or service because you sincerely believe their interests are best served by buying. This must be done with tact, but the key is your conviction that you really are offering something that will strengthen the friendship or relationship because of the value of your offer.

An additional advantage to offering your services to close friends and relatives is that they will have a serious interest in your success and will be delighted to open doors for you to the best prospects of all.

## FOR YOUR CREDIBILITY

I cannot emphasize the following information too much, so please READ CAREFULLY. Offer your product one time and one time only to your friends and relatives. At the conclusion of the presentation simply say, "Now, Paul (Sally, John, or whoever), I'd like to emphasize that the next time this product or service is mentioned, it will be because you bring it up, not me. In other words, I don't want you to even harbor a thought that when we bump into each other as a family or in a social gathering, I'm going to be talking about my services. It just won't happen."

This approach removes the tension, if any should exist, and certainly puts your prospects at ease that you're not going to be on their backs. Then stand by your commitment and wait for *them* to bring up the product.

**I strongly encourage those in the world of selling to deal with a product or service THEY CANNOT HELP TALKING ABOUT.**

You offer the product because you are friends. However, you don't expect them to buy (and won't permit them to buy) because they are your friends and want to "help" you. You don't build a career that way, and you *do* kill friendships. Expect your friends to buy for the same reason you expect all other prospects to buy—because it is in their best interests.

## CENTERS OF INFLUENCE

Family and friends can become great "centers of influence" in your career, but you are not restricted when developing this prospecting technique. For many years the center of influence has been a favorite source of prospects for the professional salesperson. The sales professional will seek and find people who are influential in a certain community, area, market, or organization and cultivate a relationship. By encouraging those people to introduce you to friends and acquaintances, you can acquire a large number of very good prospects.

While I was in the cookware business, one lady conducted eleven dinner demonstrations for me, and each one was extremely successful. First, the lady believed fervently in the product (and eventually became a close friend). Second, she literally knew everyone within twenty miles of the little community where she lived. Third, she was an elderly widow and basically enjoyed having her friends around. Fourth, she considered the evenings a social occasion and took full advantage. Fifth, she loved to entertain but, financially speaking, simply could not entertain very many of her friends—certainly not six to eight couples—at any one time with a full meal. Sixth, she was able to get a number of beautiful items for her home and kitchen (as a result of the complimentary gifts our company offered) that she otherwise could never have afforded. Not only did I conduct those eleven product presentations for her, but the circle was almost endless as her friends who had been to the demonstrations also had demonstrations of their own, so the "radiation method" of prospecting was going full-swing.

A friend related the story of a man selling copiers in Chicago who never leaves Michigan Avenue. Within a six-block area, he has developed centers of influence that allow him to do well over $1 million worth of business and service over 350 clients.

## A WORD OF CAUTION

When you're getting referrals over a period of time, those referrals weaken. Someone sends you to someone, who sends you to someone, who sends you to someone. . . . This is true regardless of industry. The reason is simple: Prospects or clients tend to refer you to people who are on the same social or business level or perhaps a notch below. Seldom do you find an hourly wage earner who can successfully send you to prospects who occupy a spot in the upper echelons of management—unless the prospect referred is a family member or special and unique friend. There are obvious exceptions, but generally, prospect strength diminishes over time.

So what do you do? I encourage you to remember your ABP's—that is, "*A*lways *B*e *P*rospecting." Regularly get out of the circle you're in, and start another circle or another chain. Use all your resources to keep those prospect lists long and diverse so that your career is not dependent on one individual or one specific group of individuals.

## SPECIFIC "HOW TO'S"

Professionals have been asking their prospects and clients for many years, "Mr. Smith, if your best friend were to walk in here at this moment, would you introduce him to me?" The odds are about four thousand to one the answer will be yes. "Then, Mr. Smith, let me get you to do this. Why not introduce me to your best friend who has a need for our services by giving me his name and a little information about him?" You have just taken step one in developing a center of influence.

Step two: If the person who is your center of influence is thoroughly sold on what you do and has benefited from your services, ask him if he will introduce you to the friend via the telephone. A nice alternative to the phone call is a short note saying something like, "John, my friend Bill has something that will benefit you."

Step three: My personal experience tells me that when I am prospecting, I should never place several prospect cards (information cards with a place for name, address, etc.) in front of the client and ask for names. Many times the customer gets a mental block. Always start by asking for one prospect, and *you* write that person's name on a card. At that point do not attempt to get any information concerning that particular prospect. Go for the second, third, fourth, and fifth names. When the "referrer's" well has apparently run dry, go back to prospect number one and get the vital information about addresses, employment, phone numbers, responsibilities, general interests and activities.

Oftentimes as the person is giving you information on the prospect, he will remember other people who work at the same place, go to the same church, or live in the same neighborhood. Your list of prospects will grow substantially.

CAUTION: At this point be conscious of the prospect's or client's time. This prospecting procedure can drag out the interview too long, so if you see the mildest hint of nervousness (prospect glancing at watch, beginning to shift papers on desk, etc.), you need to terminate the interview and get back at a later date for additional prospects.

Step four: In prospecting please remember that all of us frequently need a little memory jogging. You can accomplish this by asking a few questions: "With whom do you jog, play bridge, work, go to club meetings or church? Who are your neighbors, classmates, etc.?"

Step five: Once you've gotten your prospects, ask the "referrer" which person you should call on first, and work with the client to establish a priority list for your names. You will also obtain some "qualifying" information (knowledge about the prospect's ability to buy).

## A WORD TO THE WISE

CAUTION: Many times salespeople believe that just because a customer has given them a few good referrals, there are no more. Actually, the person who has given you a few good prospects is more likely to give you a few *more* than the customer who has never given you a prospect. Message: Don't assume that the well has run dry.

**The sales process is something you do *for* or *with* the prospect, and not *to* the prospect.**

IMPORTANT REMINDER: The key to continuing to get good prospects from satisfied clients is to report back to your "referrers" and let them know the results of your calls. Whether the results are positive, negative, or pending, let them know what happened. Keeping satisfied clients informed is good public relations and good selling, and it makes good sense. In most cases, after you left they remembered other prospects they should have given you. They will likely not call and give you those names, but if you display real professionalism by getting back to them with the results on their previous prospects, they'll be glad to give you more.

## FROM SATISFIED CLIENTS

My friend Walter Hailey says that the best lists of prospects you can possibly get are the accounts payable of your clients. Use your imagination just a bit. You're calling on one of the biggest customers of the person you have just sold. This prospect has a vested interest in maintaining a good relationship with your new client, so when you go in and use the name, the odds are long that you will at least get a courteous reception. Whether or not the prospect buys depends on specific needs and your skills, but the door is open, and that's the first step in the sales process.

## YOUR SERVICE "VALUE"

One key in prospecting is to always remember that the person with whom you've already established a relationship is probably your best prospect for additional goods, products, or services. If you represent a company that has an extensive line of products, or if it has come out with new items, you certainly want to offer them to your customers. You've already covered the major obstacles in the sales process. You've built a relationship, developed confidence and rapport, established the fact that you're a person who can be trusted, and convinced the prospect that what you offer has value. Under these circumstances it's natural that these customers are your best prospects to sell additional items.

Returning to existing customers enables you to increase your value to them by offering them additional problem-solving or money-saving items and sparing them the process of having to shop with strangers. After all, the sales process (assuming you're a person of integrity selling a product of value) is something you do *for* or *with* the prospect, and not *to* the prospect.

# OBSERVATION

Suppose you're brand-new. You picked up this book and your sample kit on the same day, and you don't have Prospect Number One. Where do you start? Answer: You begin by opening your eyes and observing *everything* around you! You will notice that in your office there are customer files with which you can begin working. Chances are excellent that your trainer and your company will be willing and anxious to share this information with you so you can start making those contacts on the service and referral concept as your beginning point.

Beware of the most common "rookie" error: incorrect activity. As important as it is for you to be reading this book, if you are doing so in a time period where it is possible to be face-to-face (or voice-to-voice) with a prospect, you are making an error in judgment. In my "observation" of successful sales professionals, each makes excellent use of time. Each task yields the desired outcome. If your primary goal is to make sales, then get with a prospect. Read during downtime, listen to tapes between calls or while traveling, but focus on desired outcome when making choices regarding activities.

## KEEP AN EYE OUT

Whether beginning or experienced, professional salespeople use a technique known as "eagle-eye prospecting." By carrying a tape recorder as you drive around, you can "sight" possible prospects. Billboards, store fronts, auto advertising—anything that looks like a legitimate prospect can be recorded. Later you can look up details (addresses, phone numbers, etc.).

Reference sources like Dun & Bradstreet provide data about the basic business, CEO's name, number of employees, and the approximate volume of business.

The library has a source book called *Contacts Influential,* which will have the names of companies listed by streets. If you are going from one business to the next, you will have the advantage of knowing the name of every business on that street, plus the name of the CEO.

The Chamber of Commerce and the Better Business Bureau also have sources of pertinent information. If you are an "in-home" salesperson, you can get information from many power and light companies about the new services they've installed. The newspapers print announcements that will provide prospects if you will carefully screen them. New births indicate a need for baby products and additional insurance. Weddings-to-be open the door for bridal services, clothing, furniture, insurance, travel services, and hotel or motel accommodations for the upcoming event. Executive promotions could mean prospects for larger homes, expanded wardrobes, club memberships, investment programs, automobiles, personal computers, and numerous other items. The possibilities are limited only by your imagination—and your powers of observation.

## RELATED INDUSTRIES

Remember the related industries that are companions TO and prospects FOR the products you sell. Computer sales representatives often meet with maintenance or service engineers who are excellent sources for prospects. By probing, the professional can uncover frustrations, dated equipment, problems, needs, and many other things that lead directly to sales!

Networking with other salespeople is also available to many salespeople. Some firms specialize in computers, others in the software that goes with them. It's a natural relationship to establish and can be mutually advantageous to form a marketing team, supplying each other with prospects. A communications systems sales associate of mine began networking with another person who was also selling communications but offered a completely different service. They were a great complement to each other—regardless of who saw the client first. Bottom line: This procedure enabled both to actually double their sales in just six months' time. That's professionalism and networking at their very finest!

## PROFESSIONAL SALESPEOPLE ARE GOOD CITIZENS

As you are practicing your powers of observation, you will notice that many professional salespeople are very much involved with their community. This includes those sales pros like the architects, CPA's, merchants, motel managers, doctors, teachers, and others who realize the importance of selling skills in what is traditionally perceived as a nonselling role.

Dave Liniger, the founder of Re/Max, is a firm believer that salespeople should get involved in civic activities. However, Dave stresses that your objective in joining worthwhile civic organizations should be service oriented. He feels that if your major objective in joining the organization is to market to the membership, you are probably going to alienate many of the people you want to influence. I concur with that assessment because, in essence, that has to do with manipulation and not motivation. If you're in the group, organization, or club with a "what's-in-it-for-me?" attitude rather than a "what-can-I-do-to-help?" attitude, you are doing the group, and yourself, a great disservice.

**Prospects are perishable—handle with care.**

If you love the city you work in and want to give something back to your community and help make it better, you should get involved. Dave points out that your spirit and attitude will make a favorable impression on the people you're with. As a result, friendships will develop, and the members will want to do business with you.

Once relationships are established and the conversation turns to what you're doing, it is permissible to share with these friends that you do have something to offer and that your goods or services can be of value to them. That way you've created a friendly "win-win" environment that can be beneficial to all concerned. *Intent* and *integrity* are the key words.

## DEDICATION

"Pressure" selling (selling where you MUST make the sale to survive) is caused by lack of prospects. If you're making a call on your last prospect, the feeling you transfer is one of desperation and personal need and not value for your product or service. Add to this the fact that if you don't sell this prospect, you're out of business. That is enormous pressure and will ultimately cripple and eventually kill any sales career. This is especially true if the cupboard is bare, the bank account has been emptied, and the indicator on the gasoline gauge is pointed toward "E."

## THE "SIN OF THE DESERT"

An individual who knows where the water is in the desert but will not share the information with others is committing the "sin of the desert." The successful salesperson learns to feel that a customer who is completely sold on the product but will not share the names of other prospects for the product is guilty of the "sin of the desert."

The "sin of the desert" for the sales professional is not actively prospecting every day, especially with the people for whom you make presentations. Selling is a transference of feeling, and to transfer feeling you must have strong feelings. Once you truly believe in the "sin of the desert" as a salesperson, you will be infinitely more capable of persuading your customers and prospects that they in turn should refer you to other people who will benefit from your goods or services.

## PROSPECTS ARE PERISHABLE—HANDLE WITH CARE

What do you do when you get a prospect from a customer, direct mail, advertising, or a friend? How long do you wait before you go to see the new prospect? Psychologically, the instant you get that prospect on a referral, or any other method, that prospect is the best prospect he will ever be. There is something about the psychology of a brand-new prospect, especially is he's just been given to you by an enthusiastic customer. I encourage you to go with all possible haste to see that individual. A week later you won't be nearly as enthused about the prospect. Even though the prospect's needs might not have changed and he might have no earthly idea that he's even on your list, the fact is that you will be less enthused about him, which means you will be less effective in your presentation to him.

The message is short, sweet, and clear. When you get a prospect's name, proceed with all possible haste to make the contact.

Obviously, I'm going to assume you have now come far enough in the profession that you get all the information about the person when you get him as a prospect (or immediately thereafter) so you will be prepared to make the best presentation based on the prospect's needs.

What about the prospect who calls in? It's even more important that you respond to that call with all haste. You've already crossed the first bridge on the way to making the sale; you've gotten action from a prospect who is interested in your goods or services. Now all you really have to do is handle the rest of the presentation, and if your services meet the needs and finances can be arranged, you're in business. The fact that the prospect called indicates an interest now, but it does not guarantee an interest at a later date. And another salesperson selling a similar (but obviously inferior) product may get there first and sell YOUR prospect. The farmer spoke for all salespeople when he said, "Those who desire the milk should not seat themselves on a stool in the middle of a field in hopes that a cow would back up to them." It won't happen—and prospects won't seek you out to buy although they are literally all over the field.

## IN CLOSING

Now that you know how to find those "willing buyers," what are you going to do? If you said, "Make the sales call," you answered properly. However, some fail to take action. The following chapter on overcoming call reluctance will help you follow through on your "good intentions."

## PROSPECTING METHODOLOGY

1. **Develop the prospecting attitude.** Prospecting is a way of life and should be done constantly and consistently.

2. **Develop a GENUINE INTEREST IN AND CONCERN FOR other people.**

3. **Communicate.**
   A. Share with family and friends.
   B. Find "centers of influence."
   C. Ask for a list of your client's accounts payable.
   D. Go back to existing customers.

4. **Observe.**
   A. Become an "eagle-eye" prospector.
   B. Use resources: D & B, *Contacts Influential*, the Chamber of Commerce, the Better Business Bureau, newspapers, the power company, and your imagination.
   C. Observe related industries.
   D. Network with other salespeople.
   E. Get involved in community projects, and maintain a "what-can-I-do-to-help?" attitude.

5. **Dedicate yourself to success.**
   A. Never commit the "sin of the desert."
   B. Handle prospects with care.
   C. Go out and "make it happen."

CHAPTER FOUR

# SELLING IN THE REAL WORLD

## *Dealing Effectively with Call Reluctance*

Question: Do you honestly and sincerely believe there is something you can do within the next twenty-four hours as a professional salesperson that will make your personal, family, and sales life even worse?

Next question: Do you honestly and sincerely believe there is something you can do within the next twenty-four hours (and every twenty-four hours after that) that will make your personal, family, and sales life even better?

Obviously, the answer to both questions is yes, and since you are busily reading, it's even more obvious that you ARE doing something to make your personal, family, and sales life even better. Congratulations to you! (And thanks to psychologist Bob Wubbolding for sharing those questions with us.)

## BRENDA BECOMES BETTER

Brenda was new to the sales profession. She had been in the work force for a few years and had observed people with less talent than she who were doing extremely well. Her first job was as an assistant in the accounting department in one of the Fortune 100 companies that specializes in computer products. There she found that the sales staff earned four, five, and even six times as much as she was earning. Subsequent jobs had similar findings. Brenda determined she had to "give sales a try."

Outside the office of Smythe, Dithers, and Dathers, Inc., she was trying to summon the courage to walk in. The questions raced through her mind: "How could I do something as foolish as getting into sales. . . . I'm gonna need the extra money for heart surgery when mine bursts from beating so fast. . . . I'll just come back later when these people aren't so busy. . . . Actually the money I was making before wasn't so bad. . . . I wonder if I can get my old job back?"

Brenda faces a crossroads in her new career. She is at the same point I reached (mentioned in chapter 1) at the end of Adelia Drive in Columbia, South Carolina. She is not going to make any ultimatums to herself about staying in sales based on the prospect's attitude or actions, but what should she do? What would you do? Before you answer, let me share an important point with you: THOSE WHO KNOW "WHAT" AND "HOW" WILL ALWAYS WORK FOR THOSE WHO KNOW "WHY." As you analyze each of the anecdotes and examples in this handbook, please look for the answer to the question, "Why?" And then think of ways to adapt and adopt the ideas and principles so they will work for you in your specific area of persuasion.

## A NATURAL PHENOMENON

Brenda's feelings, as described above, are not unusual. Professional persuaders like stage and screen actors, professional speakers, managers, teachers, doctors, and sales professionals have many things in common, not the least of which is anxiety at "the moment of truth." Whether that moment comes in front of an audience, a camera, a crowd of people, the office staff, students, patients, or prospects, anxiety is real.

## AVOIDING ANXIETY

Few who join the proud profession of selling avoid the anxious and excited feelings that accompany the sales call. In fact, according to a study done by George W. Dudley and Shannon L. Goodson (coauthors of *The Psychology of Selling*) who have been studying the subject of "fear in performance" since 1970,

> In 1986, sales people struggling with call reluctance averaged $40,000 in commissions per year while those who had overcome the problem averaged over $200,000, despite the fact that both groups were essentially equal in talent, ability, motivation, intelligence, preparation and experience. To add insult to injury, the call-reluctant group had invested far more time and money in learning what to do. They were just emotionally unable to allow themselves to apply what they knew.

## THE MOST IMPORTANT FACTOR IN CALL RELUCTANCE

The good news is that YOU can join the group of achievers who overcame call reluctance by using the feelings of anxiety to work *for* you instead of against you. I can assure you that those earning $200,000 in commissions also felt apprehensive. The difference was an ability to direct the nervous energy. As my friends in the outstanding speaking organization Toastmasters International are fond of saying, "You will not get rid of the butterflies, but you can get them flying in formation."

As a matter of fact, if you feel no anxiety in making the sales call, your chances of success will be greatly diminished. When healthy and functioning properly, the human body is equipped with an endocrinological system that provides every chemical necessary to be successful in life. The anxiety we feel when making the sales call is a biological response to a stressful situation. The pituitary gland secretes adrenaline, which increases our mental and physical capacity. Scientists have proven beyond doubt that when our adrenaline is flowing properly, we respond more quickly, more accurately, and more enthusiastically to the situation. Simply stated, when you get your "butterflies" flying in formation, you are directing the adrenaline positively—making it work for you instead of against you. Realizing that your anxiety is a positive factor, not a negative factor, allows you to focus on the most important factor in call reluctance —YOU!

## BRENDA IS NOT ALONE

According to sales experts, 84 percent of all salespeople have call reluctance to some degree. This fear is manifested in 1,001 different ways, but PROCRASTINATION is the number one indication that a problem is developing. When the salesperson creates nonessential tasks that must be done before going out to face the public, call reluctance is setting in.

In many ways, fear of facing the public has a great deal to do with self-image. If the salesperson stands in fear or awe of the prospect, making an effective presentation is extremely difficult. The salesperson who thinks, "Who am I to tell this person my product, goods, or services will be helpful?" is not going to have the level of enthusiasm, forcefulness, and confidence necessary to be successful.

Until the salesperson learns to "look up to" or "down upon" no person, fear will prevail. Regarding your product or service, YOU ARE THE EXPERT! You have more experience, more knowledge, and more expertise than the prospect will ever have in your area. Mediocre performance is the order of the day until the salesperson becomes a sales professional by realizing that each individual has strengths.

## BUILDING CONFIDENCE

One of the best ways to recognize your strengths is to replay the tapes on your mind's "video player" of the times you were successful. Go back to any and all successful experiences: a big sale; a good grade at school; a winning performance in the orchestra, the band, or athletics; a great shot on the golf course or tennis court; a time when you and your family experienced a feeling of love and togetherness; an event when you were recognized for exceptional performance. Focus on one time in particular and recapture the sights, smells, and feelings that accompanied success. The next time you feel self-doubt creeping up on you, replay this vivid, positive tape.

Next, recognize that no matter how successful, wealthy, or powerful your prospect may be, the person makes mistakes just like you and I do. No one has been 100 percent successful in life. As a general rule, my experience is that the more successful the person becomes, the more obstacles, mistakes, and hurts have been overcome. When you realize that the prospect is human, you are less likely to be intimidated.

Learn as much as possible about your prospect. The more you know about your prospect, the more respectfully you will be treated by the prospect. In addition, your knowledge about the prospect translates to the good feeling the prospect has about you AND your business. The respect your prospect shows you is quite a boost to your self-image.

## THE HEALTHY SELF-IMAGE

High self-esteem and a good self-image are vital because salespersons with these qualities will always consider themselves to be self-employed and will act accordingly. Selling professionals with high self-regard accept responsibility for sales results, never falling back on the old "I just got lucky" comment. They realize that RESULTS FOLLOW EFFORT when the effort comes from a competent, confident salesperson. You seldom, if ever, get lucky sitting down.

The person with high self-esteem loves to sell and is eager to get face-to-face with a prospect, anxious to become an "assistant buyer," and deeply concerned about customer satisfaction because "aiming to please" is not enough in today's market. When you "hit the target" in satisfying customers, your self-concept grows even more, which makes you even more effective, which gives you even more self-esteem, which . . . I think you get the idea!

Sales professionals with healthy self-respect like themselves and get along with themselves. They are sold on their profession, their product, and their company.

You can begin to make anxiety work for you instead of against you by focusing on the one factor you can control—YOU! Accept personal responsibility for building self-confidence and self-esteem, and you have taken the first step in overcoming call reluctance.

## THE PROPER FOCUS

The second step in alleviating anxiety is understanding that SELLING IS A TRANSFERENCE OF FEELING. After learning to focus on YOU so that you may improve your self-concept in a positive manner, you need to recognize that the most successful sales professionals make sales calls with the PROSPECT as the center of their focus. I have read the books and even had a brother who taught that there is only one reason to make a sales call—and that is to get the money. And please believe me when I say that getting the money can be a motivating (and necessary) factor. After all, if you don't get the money, you don't stay in business. But when you go into the sales call strictly for the money, you will leave that call without the sale more often than not.

**RESULTS FOLLOW EFFORT when the effort comes from a competent, confident salesperson. You seldom, if ever, get lucky sitting down.**

Even my brother, who took such a firm stand in saying that the prospects had "his" money in "their" pocket, clarified the statement by saying that was O.K. because he had "their" product in "his" inventory. And he never sold a product he didn't believe in 1000 percent.

Here is the danger. When you place the focus ONLY on the money, or if you're in the financial position of HAVING to make the sale, you will instinctively press too hard or become overly conscious of your need, putting undue pressure on yourself and increasing your feelings of anxiety.

## THE BURDEN OF FINANCIAL PRESSURE

Ultimately, financial pressure will take a toll on the strongest of us, so I say without fear of error that if you want to reach your peak as a professional salesperson, you must become a good manager of money. As my friend Fred Smith says, "Money is option. With money, you have many options. Without money, you have very few options." I might add that without money you are in the "hope" business: "Hope I don't have a flat tire on those 'bald eagles' I'm driving; hope this car doesn't break down again; hope the kids don't get sick; hope this suit holds up with being worn three days per week. . . ." We all need to have positive hope, but this negative kind of hope is a miserable way to live and will seriously curtail your effectiveness.

For those suffering from financial woes, I have put together some specific steps and ideas on how to overcome money problems, and these principles and techniques are included in chapter 14, "The Successful Sales Support System." The key in the short-term (until you get to chapter 14) is twofold. In the first place, start a savings account immediately. Even if you put in a minimal amount, begin today. Even if you have to go back tomorrow and remove the money, get in the habit of saving by starting today! In the second place, avoid the indiscriminate use of credit cards. The old saying, "The borrower is servant to the lender," is certainly true. To quote Fred Smith again, "If you don't have savings, you're going to be an economic slave to the boss." And in the world of selling, your boss is the prospect.

## THE GOOD NEWS

You will be absolutely astonished by how much more relaxed you become as a persuader when your financial future is not at stake and you can focus on the prospect instead of your own problems. Selling truly is a transference of feeling. If you transfer the feeling that you MUST make the sale for YOUR benefit, the chances of making the sale are greatly negated. If you transfer the feeling that you want to make the sale for the prospect's benefit, your chances for success are dramatically increased.

## PRESSURE SELLING

Now I understand that there will be times when you must sell under pressure. When our first daughter was born, it cost $64 to get her out of the hospital. The only problem was, I didn't have $64. I had to sell two sets of cookware to bring my own daughter and wife home from the hospital—and that is selling pressure!

I have a friend who through a series of unmanageable events (including a failed business and a personal bankruptcy) fell behind in his taxes and owed over $80,000 to the Internal Revenue Service. When he was faced with the bill, he could have collapsed from the pressure. Instead, for two years he sold more effectively than ever before in his career. But let me emphasize that in both situations the salesperson put the circumstances out of the mind and focused on the prospect's needs and wants—and not the personal problem.

**Fred Smith: "If you don't have savings, you're going to be an economic slave to the boss." And in the world of selling, your boss is the prospect.**

Successful sales professionals make the sales call for the benefit of the prospect AND for their personal gain—IN THAT ORDER. You see, YOU CAN HAVE EVERYTHING IN LIFE YOU WANT IF YOU WILL JUST HELP ENOUGH OTHER PEOPLE GET WHAT THEY WANT. Keeping this statement in mind is the third step in overcoming anxiety.

## TELEPHONE TERROR

The salesperson who is COMPETENT in the use and understanding of the telephone and is CONFIDENT of having that competence is going to be a far more EFFECTIVE salesperson than the one who is "afraid" of the telephone. Let me put your mind at ease. In the history of telephone sales, no salesperson has lost his or her life by using the telephone to get an appointment or make a sale.

Since billions of phone calls have been made in the pursuit of our profession, it is comforting to know that the telephone is a safe tool for a salesperson to use.

One of the greatest causes of phone fear is failing to set an objective for the call. Are you going to do a market survey, make an appointment, or get the sale? Until you have that clear-cut picture in your mind, your *willingness* to "smile and dial" is going to be seriously limited. Please don't look past this seemingly simple but significant point: DETERMINE WHY YOU ARE MAKING THE CALL! Start by asking yourself: "What am I going to say? Which person am I going to ask for? What is the purpose of the call? Do I have a clearly defined procedure I will follow, regardless of who answers my call?"

Once you've made your objective clear as to whether you're going to be prospecting, qualifying, making appointments, or seeking the sale, you can approach the call with much more confidence.

## HAVE SOME FUN ON THE PHONE

In all the years I've been in selling I don't remember ever looking forward with excitement to what many salespeople have come to refer to as "the cold call." Whether knocking on the door or picking up on the telephone, almost everyone I have ever met (who has been successful) has felt some fear and trepidation regarding the first sales call of the day—and I am no exception. However, I knew that once I got into the swing of things and made several calls, I was getting closer and closer to the sale. With that in mind, I gave no further thought to making the call. I set my time to get started, and at precisely that time I started.

By all means I encourage you to do exactly the same thing. After the third, fourth, or fifth call, you will discover that you're enjoying the process more and more; you know that for each call you are being paid, regardless of results, because each call is bringing you closer to the sale.

In the case of the telephone, you can have some fun by figuring out just what each call is worth to you. At the end of your sales week or sales month, take the total dollar volume sold and divide it by the total number of calls you made—whether busy, unanswered, or disconnected. Divide the number of calls into the total dollars and you will see exactly how much you were paid for each time you dialed the numbers.

For example, one of our telemarketers had a very good month in May 1991, selling $58,500. During the month, she attempted 682 calls, meaning she dialed 682 numbers of prospects (31 per day for 22 selling days worked). So, for every time she lifted the receiver and dialed a number, she generated $85.77. She completed (made a presentation) to 264 prospects (12 per day for 22 selling days worked), which meant that every time she *talked* to someone she generated $221.59. Now obviously each conversation didn't result in a sale, but one $5,000 sale makes up for several "no" responses. By playing this little numbers game, she reminded herself to be excited every time she picked up the receiver—and you know how excited she got when someone actually answered!

**One of the greatest causes of phone fear is failing to set an objective for the call. DETERMINE WHY YOU ARE MAKING THE CALL!**

Incidentally, when you meet resistance—and sometimes rudeness—on the telephone, you've got to know that in many cases telephone rejection is easier on you than rudeness in person. After all, you can remind yourself, "If the prospects saw what a fine person I am, they would have opened their home or office and warmly invited me to come in." Please understand that even when prospects are rude and "reject" you on the phone, they really are not rejecting you. They are refusing to listen to you. Odds are extremely high that they would not have listened to anyone else, so don't get down on yourself. Be realistic. After all, anyone who really knows you would never reject you. And if that is not 100 percent true at the moment, it will be totally true if you will apply all the principles advocated in this book.

## REJECTION FROM THE RECEPTIONIST

In using the telephone you often need to get through a switchboard operator or an administrative assistant. You must not think of that person as a "screener" or a "gatekeeper." You are talking to an INFLUENCER, and you want to use every legitimate means of making that person feel important because that's the truth! The influencer who has a positive attitude toward you is more likely to say to the person you're calling, "Here's somebody you will enjoy talking with."

You should know and use the influencer's name. When you can start the conversation with, "Hi, Betty, this is Hillary with The Zig Ziglar Corporation," you show a real interest in the person, and you help with her responsibility, which is to get your name and company. Then without hesitation, add, "May I speak with Mr. Jones?" You are often going to be asked, "Who's calling?" and "What company are you with?" If you give this information "up front," you have a much better chance of getting through without any delay.

Once you've gotten through to the decision maker, you need to make a general benefit statement or a direct benefit statement. Here is one example: "Hi, Ed, this is Hillary. If you recall, we visited last week concerning a new sales seminar. As I indicated to you, we've been able to increase closing ratios over 27 percent by following some very simple procedures. When would it be most convenient for me to talk with you concerning this?" And another: "As you recall, we discussed the reduction of personnel turnover, and I have an article with me that I promised to put in your hands." And another: "I'm calling concerning the article in your publication about reducing overhead, and I have an idea how you can utilize not only that but an additional benefit. When would be the best time for us to get together?" Chapters 9 and 10 address the ways you can develop benefit statements that will help you close more sales more often.

## HANDLING OBJECTIONS

Whenever possible, objections need to be anticipated. You can build in power phrases that overcome key objections before they occur. And here is some really good news for the beginning salesperson: Objections are almost always predictable! If you've been in the business more than six months, through your company's training program and your personal experience you should encounter no more than one or two "new" objections each quarter. There will be the "standards," but not many you will not have heard. Consequently, with careful planning and forethought, you can have reasonable answers ready to present. Chapter 11 addresses overcoming objections in quite a bit of detail.

Many times when you call your prospect and reach the influencer, the three most popular reasons given for not putting you through are these: "She's on the phone," "She's busy," or "She's in a meeting." At that point you ask, "What is the best time for me to call back?" In most cases the answer will be something like, "She's always in the office from two until four in the afternoon." With that information you respond, "Would you please tell her that I called and I'll call back at 2:35 this afternoon?" Generally speaking, establishing a specific time for the return call gives you the best opportunity for getting through next time. The influencer often feels some responsibility in putting you through to the party you're calling because she feels her word is on the line.

Another good question to ask is, "What is the best time to catch her when her schedule is not likely to be quite as hectic or busy?" This indicates consideration on your part and scores points with the influencer.

A "tip" you might find helpful when you are having extreme difficulty in reaching your contact is to make your calls early in the morning. Many times the decision makers will answer the phone at 6:30, 7:00, or 7:30 in the morning. Their energy level is high, and generally speaking, they're more gracious and willing to listen. Equally important, they respect—even admire—someone with a work ethic similar to their own.

## TIME SENSITIVITY

On occasion you will reach a person who will respond to the question, "Do you have a few moments we can talk?" with, "I really don't, but go ahead and tell me what's on your mind." I encourage you not to rush into the presentation because you will probably have to speed through and leave out some relevant details. This leads to a snap decision, and in many cases, it's not the one you want. If the person indicates being busy but still wants you to proceed, respond by saying, "I really think it would be better for both of us if I caught you a little later because with less than the complete information, it would not be fair to you and would not be the best use of time for either of us. With that in mind, when would be the best time for me to call back?"

What you have to say and the value of your product to your prospect should be too important for you to be willing to give out incomplete information that would not adequately prepare your prospect to make a decision.

Along these same lines, if you hear a lot of paper shuffling while you're in the process of making a presentation, the prospect is giving indication of moving around, and there's undue noise in the background, obviously he's not giving you his undivided attention. Please remember that you would not make a serious presentation in the lobby of a busy hotel or theater and expect maximum results. The same is true over the telephone. Be sensitive to what your prospect is saying and is *not* saying. The first few seconds you're on the phone will set the stage, mood, and atmosphere of the presentation, so have a plan.

## DRESS FOR SUCCESS—OVER THE PHONE!

Even if you're working from home or a spot where you know you will not be seen by anyone, are you properly dressed? Did you take a shower this morning? Shave? Apply your makeup? In short, did you really get physically dressed for the call? The evidence is overwhelming that to be mentally sharp you need to be physically sharp. The old Gillette razor commercial is true: "Look Sharp—Feel Sharp—Be Sharp!" And, yes, they all do go together. Even though the prospect is not in front of you, your dress will make a difference in your willingness to begin making calls. There's also a difference in the expression on your face and the expectancy in your mind, and there'll be a difference in your voice.

Are you ready to make those calls? By ready, I mean have you given yourself a good sales self-talk? Have you reminded yourself that you're a winner, that you're on an important mission, that as you dial people they will eagerly anticipate your call? Do you visualize them responding favorably to what you're going to say? Do you clearly see in your mind that you're making the appointment or making the sale? When you do these things, your results will be spectacular!

### A GREAT SALES TOOL

As a practical matter, the expenses of travel and ever-increasing traffic problems mean that the dollar and time costs per sales call get higher and higher almost by the day. If we can efficiently use the telephone, our sales effectiveness and net income will increase substantially. I don't claim to be an expert at telephone usage, but I do have a significant set of experiences developed in using this most important instrument through the years. Telephone tips are interspersed throughout *Ziglar on Selling*. I have tried to place the ideas and concepts in the chapters where they best fit the subject matter. In my opinion, this subject deserves a book solely devoted to it. So if you have some ideas, write me at the address listed in the back of this book and be a "contributing expert" on a future book.

The fourth step in overcoming call reluctance is to "TAME THE TELEPHONE" and make it work for you instead of against you.

## INTRODUCING A WINNER!

I sincerely believe that no matter who you are, where you live, or how good (or bad) your career has been to this point in your life, YOU were Born to Win in the profession of selling! You might well ask how I could make that statement without knowing who might read this book. I make the statement with complete confidence because I know from training and experience (my head and my heart) that when you understand and apply the following statement, you are WINNING!

To be the winner you are allowed to become, you must PLAN to Win; you must PREPARE to Win; and then you have every right to EXPECT to Win.

Planning and preparation begin with the simplest of ideas. How are you starting your day? Are you properly dressed? I'm not talking about the style of outfit you are wearing. I'm talking about something as simple (and important!) as a SMILE. No matter how sophisticated your selling arena, you're never completely dressed without a smile. An old Jewish proverb says, "He who is without a smile should not be a merchant."

Now you're ready to consider your physical appearance. Are you "dressed" appropriately for the job? Regardless of industry, your attire must be neat, matched, first class, and in good taste. Do your clothes blend with your clientele? Obviously, a fertilizer salesman calling on dairies and large farms is going to be dressed for the environment and in a style that makes his prospects comfortable. The business machine sales professional and the financial advisor are going to be attired in an entirely different manner. Appropriateness is the key! In less than three seconds the prospect makes a decision about you based on three basic parts of your "look."

1. Your smile
2. Your shirt and tie or blouse
3. Your shoes

One saleslady I know has more shoes than Imelda Marcos! She seems to have two pairs for every outfit. She says that her shoes give her a feeling of confidence, and some days when she is near home, she will change shoes at noon for a "lift"! One salesman we work with gets his shoes shined every day. He doesn't necessarily need the shine, but he uses the time as an attitude adjustment period. He says he feels like "pickin' 'em up and puttin' 'em down" with that little extra feeling of confidence after his shoe-shine start.

## WHAT ABOUT YOUR PLAN?

What are your plans for the day, week, month, year, career? Have you ever noticed how much better you feel about yourself when you have a plan of action? You must remember that the will to win is nothing without the will to prepare to win. I have never met a salesperson who would not want to sell more with less time and effort. Selling more is only possible when extra effort is expended in the area of preparation. All of us have heard about the woodcutter whose production kept going down because he didn't take time to sharpen his axe (prepare).

Preparing for the day involves more than a quick run-through of this book (or any other book) or a fast listen-to of a sales training seminar or recording. Preparation and training include taking the information you receive from an outside source and adapting it to fit your situation, learning it so thoroughly that it becomes your own, and then applying those procedures and techniques in the field.

**To be the winner you are allowed to become, you must PLAN to Win; you must PREPARE to Win; and then you have every right to EXPECT to WIN.**

I have included examples in this book from people who wrote to me saying they had adapted and adopted ideas from my books (as well as those of other authors). As you read, notice how using thorough preparation allowed these men and women to transfer the principles to their specific field.

Step five in overcoming call reluctance is this: PLAN TO WIN, PREPARE TO WIN, AND EXPECT TO WIN IN THE WORLD OF SELLING.

# EXPERIMENTAL SYNDROME

Many years ago, while conferring with a direct sales organization, my friend Fred Smith learned that the turnover rate of the sales team was extremely high. The primary reason was call reluctance, which generally resulted from what the sales staff called "rejection." Sound familiar to anyone?

Fred's solution to the problem of sales professionals feeling so rejected that they quit their job was to TURN AN *EXPERIENCE* INTO AN *EXPERIMENT,* step six. *Experiment* by definition is limited in life span—and based on the *experiences* of some of the sales staff, the more limited the life span, the better! The good news for you is that if you will try this experiment, your life span as a sales professional will be increased.

The concept is valid in all type contact situations, so regardless of what you sell or how you sell it, this principle can work for you. Don't be fooled by its simplicity. It works!

Here's how the "Experimental Syndrome" works: When you approach a prospect (whether by phone or in person), you are to remind yourself that you are conducting an experiment to determine the way the prospect acts toward you. You will keep a chart of all people and all responses. For example, you may encounter a "young man/door slammer," or your prospect might be an "older woman/friendly welcome." Basically your prospects will be younger or older than you, and men or women. Their response (or reaction) can run from "door closer" to "door slammer." On the phone, you might encounter a "mumbling male" or a "finicky female." In a one-on-one business call you might visit a "grouchy, Type-A male" or "an aloof female." (Use your imagination with the categorization.)

When you approach the prospect, instead of taking the negative reaction as a "personal rejection," you simply note on your chart exactly what you observed. This approach causes the prospect's actions to have minimal effect on YOU! Your concentration and focus are on the "experiment," not the "experience." After all, you are a nice, cheerful, friendly, optimistic, helpful person with a beautiful presentation and a tremendous product. The "nasty prospect" is the one with the problem! Let the prospect keep the problem, and you continue with the experiment.

## THIRD-PERSON OBSERVATION

When you call on the "not interested" prospect who "exercised no curiosity or good judgment," you observe through the eyes of a third person—YOU! This "experiment" allows you to detach yourself from the feelings of rejection or "presumed failure" because now you can understand that this prospect would not have been interested, regardless of who made the sales call.

Here's the really exciting part. As you adapt, adopt, and make this procedure your own, your confidence will grow substantially, and you will become much more effective in your approach and presentation. Over a period of time, you'll encounter fewer negative reactions and more positive responses. And therein lies the danger. The fewer negative reactions you receive, the more likely you will be to stop using this procedure, which could cause negativity to increase. Keep this book handy so that every three to six months you can review this principle (and others) to maintain a high level of effectiveness.

Pull this together by making summary notes at the end of your day—recording each "experiment" conducted. As you watch your records, you will notice an ever-increasing number of pleasant results overwhelming the negative ones. In addition, when you review your "experiments" for the day, you will look forward to new "experiments" on the following day!

# THE KEY TO OVERCOMING CALL RELUCTANCE

I have saved the most essential step in overcoming call reluctance for last. Based on personal experience and professional observation, I can say without reservation that if you will follow the ideas outlined on the next few pages, you will NOT be held back by procrastination or any other manifestation of call reluctance. There are few guarantees in life. What follows comes as close to being a "sure thing" as most salespeople will ever experience.

When I was a fledgling salesman, my major problems were those of organization and discipline. Until I began my formal sales career, being on a specific time schedule had not been a problem. Organization and discipline had been provided for me.

In high school, I worked in a grocery store, with close supervision. I went almost immediately from there into the navy and experienced close, direct supervision. From the navy I was back in the grocery store for two months until college started. In college, I had a strict schedule, at least for the working portion of my life. I sold sandwiches around the dormitories at night and quickly learned that there was little, if any, need to start my rounds before 9:00 P.M. By then the students had all returned from dinner and had studied for a couple of hours and were ready for a break.

When I began my full-time sales career, we moved fifty miles from anyone else in the company. My only contact with my manager was the Monday morning sales meeting and an infrequent phone call. In essence, *everything* was up to me! I really enjoyed my freedom. NO set time to go to work, NO set time to finish, NO direction in between. The only problem with that was—NO sales and NO money!

In those initial years I also suffered from a serious self-image problem and took it quite personally when anyone would refuse to allow me to make my presentation. A personal rejection, which is what I interpreted the prospect's resistance to be, meant that I would then have to spend time rethinking my situation and alternating between pouting, meditating, having a "pity party," and planning what to do next. Put all these misperceptions together and you get a terrible combination of procrastination and call reluctance.

How much I wish at that point someone had explained to me that when people refused to let me make my presentation or turned down my marvelous offer, they were not rejecting me. In their minds it was a simple *business refusal*. The prospects really had no interest in my offer or did not possess the financial resources to make the purchase. They would have said no to anyone.

My friend Fred Smith, whom I so highly regard, says even those people who are mean, rude, ugly, and nasty to you are not that way because they want to hurt you but because *they* are hurting. Had I understood this concept in those early years, my production would have been considerably higher and a great deal more stable. Additionally, my self-image would not have taken the beating it did.

## GETTING ON SCHEDULE

After I had been in the world of professional selling for two and a half years, an experience with Mr. P. C. Merrell made a dramatic difference in my life. Mr. Merrell was the sales executive who had developed the training programs and set many of the sales records, and he was a marvelous role model. In a nutshell, Mr. Merrell convinced me that I really did have ability and worth. He persuaded me that I could, in fact, be a national champion. He also persuaded me that to realize my potential and stabilize my production, I needed to GET ON AN ORGANIZED PROGRAM FOLLOWED IN A DISCIPLINED MANNER.

**Those people who are mean, rude, ugly, and nasty to you are not that way because they want to hurt you but because *they* are hurting.**

He specifically suggested that regardless of what time I finished my work in the evening, I should make an appointment with myself to call on my first prospect at precisely the same time the next day. He emphasized that it really did not make that much difference (within reasonable limitations) what that time was, but I should follow through on that commitment, despite any other little "obstacles" or "interruptions" that came my way. I recognize that this sounds like simplicity itself because that's exactly what success in life and success in selling is all about—doing the little things that make the big difference. But for salespeople who are away from the direct supervision of management, failing to work at a regular time on a regular basis is one of the biggest reasons for failure. Organization, discipline, and commitment make for consistent high-volume production.

If you get nothing else out of this chapter (or maybe this book), please hear me on this key point. STEP SEVEN IN OVERCOMING CALL RELUCTANCE IS THIS: GET ON A REGULAR SCHEDULE AND MAKE AN APPOINTMENT WITH YOURSELF TO BE FACE-TO-FACE WITH A PROSPECT AT THE SAME TIME EVERY DAY!

### DO IT NOW!

Courage has been described as an action you take not because of the absence of fear but because you know that taking the action is the RIGHT (and in most cases the desirable) thing to do! As I have already said several times, for all the years I have been in the world of selling, I have rarely looked forward with excitement to making that first phone call or face-to-face contact. But by making an appointment with myself to start every day at exactly the same time, and KEEPING THE APPOINTMENT, I defeated procrastination and call reluctance. And you can, too!

Make the appointment with yourself, and when the time comes, without fail head for that telephone or that prospect. When I made that adjustment, the sales results were dramatic! There is a simple yet profound psychological reason: LOGIC WILL NOT CHANGE AN EMOTION, BUT ACTION WILL! Call reluctance is an emotion, and it will not be overcome consistently by logic. Get into action, support the action with logic, and sales success is sure to be yours!

## READY TO SELL

So now you're all dressed up and ready to sell! You have on a sincere smile that definitely increases your face value; you are appropriately attired; you feel good about yourself; you are mentally knowledgeable concerning the basics of your product or service and how to best present your information to the right prospect at the proper time.

You've taken the enthusiastic approach by developing the right mental attitude while building your life and career on a foundation of integrity. You're armed with confidence, based on product knowledge and people knowledge. You're loaded with the right intent—

which is to do whatever is in the prospect's best interests. You're convinced that your product fills a real need or satisfies a desire for the prospect. You know what you bring to your prospect offers real value for every dollar in price it carries. You have a missionary zeal as a problem solver and have learned to AIM your anxiety to make it work for you by believing in yourself and going to work on a regular schedule.

**Courage has been described as an action you take not because of the absence of fear but because you know that taking the action is the RIGHT (and in most cases the desirable) thing to do!**

You are truly ready, willing, and able to sell! So let's get going! Regardless of whether this is your first day of your first year or the last day of your twentieth year, you now understand more than 90 percent of the people who have ever sold a product or service. You are ready to make a career for yourself in this decade. You are ready for professional persuasion in the 1990s!

REMEMBER: THE SECRET OF GETTING AHEAD IS GETTING STARTED!

## TO OVERCOME CALL RELUCTANCE AND UNDERSTAND THAT ANXIETY IS A POSITIVE FACTOR IN PROFESSIONAL SELLING, REMEMBER:

1. Take personal responsibility for building self-confidence and self-esteem.

2. Selling is a transference of feeling.

3. You can have everything in life you want if you will just help enough other people get what they want.

4. Tame the telephone. Make it work for you instead of against you.

5. To be the winner you were born to be, you must Plan to Win, Prepare to Win, and Expect to Win.

6. Use the "Experimental Syndrome" to overcome feelings of rejection by making each call a positive "experiment" instead of a negative "experience."

7. Get on a regular schedule and make an appointment with yourself to be face-to-face with a prospect at the same time every day!

CHAPTER FIVE

# SELL BY DESIGN, NOT BY CHANCE

## *The Formula for Successful Selling Skills*

Sales professionals are open-minded (not empty-headed) and willing to change. Nonprofessionals are so narrow-minded they can look through a keyhole with both eyes at the same time!

## BUILDING ON THE PROPER FOUNDATION

Table tennis was a very popular recreational sport during my high-school years. One of my buddies taught me to use the "three-finger" grip on the paddle. Being a better than average player allowed me to have lots of fun. I often competed with a friend whose physical talent and competitive spirit were similar, so we alternated in the win-loss column.

One day a new kid came to town, and he used the "handshake" grip and absolutely slaughtered me. Needless to say, I was somewhat chagrined at the experience, but I could immediately see that he could do things with that grip that I would never be able to do with the way I was holding the paddle—regardless of how long or how often I practiced.

I immediately changed the way I was gripping the paddle, and for the next few weeks the level of my performance dropped considerably. As a matter of fact, for about six weeks my regular playing partner won virtually every game. However, as I mastered the new concept, we played closer and closer until the day came that I won. From that point forward, my table tennis improved remarkably. I'm proud to say that I won the championship tournament we held at Yazoo City High School. Now when you understand that there were forty-two students (including the boy who taught me the new grip) in my senior class, that was no mean feat.

Here's my point: Sometimes as you change and learn, you might not make immediate progress, but if the fundamentals are correct (and the ones in this book are), you can rest assured that as you "drill for skill" and start to own the procedures, your career will definitely move to new heights (and so will your personal life).

## A NEW "GRIP" FOR SOME OF YOU!

In 1987, Bryan Flanagan and Jim Savage took the concepts from my book *Secrets of Closing the Sale*, as well as information from all my audio and videotape albums, and combined my research and experience with their own research and experience to develop a sales seminar for our company called Sell by Design, Not by Chance. Bryan had been a national sales instructor for IBM and had been a successful salesman and sales manager before joining our company as a speaker and trainer. Jim, who is our senior vice president and publisher, has a background in education as well as sales and sales management, which allowed him to help shape the program and preserve the educational integrity. The goal of Sell by Design, Not by Chance was to shape a sales training program that would function as a BLUEPRINT for success in the world of selling. Much of this book has evolved from the Sell by Design, Not by Chance seminar.

## CANNED VS. PLANNED

Today's successful persuader must have a specific plan of action. If we had to stop and develop a plan for each sales call, there would be more planning than selling. Since there is a direct correlation between "money earned" and "time spent with a prospect," we can eliminate unnecessary planning by examining a "formula" with CONCOMITANT value.

*Concomitant* is a seventy-five-cent word that means "transferable skills." For example, a person who is a good table tennis player will probably have some skills that will transfer to badminton or racquetball. In the world of selling, we need a plan of action that will transcend product line and situational differences.

Our planned selling process consists of a four-step formula that we will overview here and develop in detail in the following chapters. The first step is Need Analysis, second is Need Awareness, third is Need Solution, and finally, Need Satisfaction.

## PAVLOVIAN SELLING

In 1904, Russian physiologist Ivan Petrovich Pavlov won the Nobel Prize in medicine for his research. Pavlov did research on digestion and the nervous system. He included experiments with dogs in which he rang a bell just before feeding time. In subsequent experiments, he would ring the bell, and the dogs would salivate—whether the food was present or not.

**Four-Step Formula**

1. **Need Analysis**
2. **Need Awareness**
3. **Need Solution**
4. **Need Satisfaction**

In today's sophisticated selling market, getting in front of a client with a brochure and saying, "Stop me when you see something you like," just won't make it. You can make an occasional sale, but you can't make a living—and you certainly can't build a career.

Too many salespeople are ringing a bell and hoping the suspects will salivate when in fact just the opposite happens. If your actions come across as what some perceive as stereotypically "salesy" in nature, the prospects are turned off.

As an example, at one time, cafeterias put the desserts at the beginning of the line. This is done less frequently today because the public has "marketing savvy" to a much larger degree than at any time in the history of the world. The dinosaur is extinct, and so are the career hopes of any salesperson who comes across as the fast-talking, high-pressure used car salesman who has a model that his grandmother drove only to church (and she must have gone quite often since the odometer has been around twice).

Of course you will see items next to the cash registers in some grocery stores and some retail outlets because impulse purchasing is an important part of sales and marketing, but the sophistication level of the buying public prevents Pavlovian selling to any large degree. Add-on sales can be made using this technique because when you buy a dress suit, a shirt or blouse is a natural addition. However, Pavlovian selling is selling by CHANCE.

Successful sales professionals use a process or design—a blueprint. And the good news is that there is a single blueprint for sales success regardless of product or service. I know this may seem hard to believe, but read on!

## PROCESS

The following is a four-step formula that you can plug into your sales efforts. The time spent on each step may vary, but if you are successful in sales, you will be involved in some form of each of these steps.

## STEP ONE: NEED ANALYSIS

Customer-driven (wants) and need-oriented (needs) selling begins with the sales professional doing a Need Analysis. Even if the prospects are coming to you and asking for your product or service, it is entirely possible that they have not properly identified what they are really looking for.

Let me give you a specific example. It is a fact of life that everybody who is breathing is getting older. And when you consider the alternative, getting older isn't all bad! It is equally true that our population consists of more and more senior citizens, and over the next thirty years or so the number will increase significantly. There is a tremendous market for goods and services among those senior citizens, but I might point out that many of the products of today were completely unknown just a few years ago. As simple as telephone answering machines, computers, and mobile telephones might seem to some, these "gadgets" can be quite bewildering to others. The 'in-tune" salesperson of today will do well to become "tuned in" to the thinking, fears, concerns, and interests of all prospects, including the senior citizens.

The following example from *Agewave* by Ken Dychtwald and Joe Flower indicates the importance of properly identifying the need of the prospect and utilizes the senior citizen to make this major point.

**Customer-driven (wants) and need-oriented (needs) selling begins with the sales professional doing a Need Analysis.**

Robert Beck is currently executive vice-president of Bank of America and was the director of benefits at IBM during its phenomenal growth years in the late 1970's and early 1980's. Because of his work involvements, Beck, who is middle-aged, has become very capable at using a wide variety of computer and electronic technologies.

It should not have been surprising to him when his 78-year-old father commented one day that he wished he could have a VCR (Video Cassette Recorder) like his son's.

"You can, Dad—all you need to do is go out and buy one," said the younger Beck. "Easy for you to say," replied his father. "First of all, even though I'd like to own one, I wouldn't know which one to buy. Second, I could never carry it into my house. Third, I wouldn't know how to set it up. And fourth, I'm not sure that I could follow the instructions on how to use it, and I wouldn't want to buy something I couldn't use." For the elder Beck, money wasn't the issue; the real concern was the inconvenience of purchasing, setting up and use.

As a solution, the son went with his father to an electronics store and helped him buy a good, easy-to-use VCR. Then they worked out a deal with the store manager whereby one of the technicians would deliver and set it up. For an additional $25, they arranged for the technician—now Mr. Beck's "personal customer service representative"—to give him three lessons, spaced one day apart, on how to use the VCR. Once he got the feel for the new technology, Mr. Beck quickly became a big fan of prerecorded videos and now boasts the largest collection of movies on his block. In fact, he has begun a weekly movie-watching club for his retired neighbors and friends.

He has come to enjoy his VCR so much that he recently returned to the electronics store and worked out similar arrangements for a stereo, cordless phone and coffee pot. For him, making the purchase more convenient and being taught to use the equipment was every bit as important a part of the sale as the product itself.

I hope the point is obvious. The Norwegian word from which *sell* is derived is *selje,* which means "to serve." In order for you to serve your prospects, you must clearly understand THEIR needs before you can proceed.

## LOOKING INSIDE THE PROSPECT

In Needs Analysis, the goal is to X-ray the prospect. The sales professional develops the skill and talents necessary to look within the customer and find the needs of the customer—to uncover existing needs. These needs may be on the surface or just below the surface, but they definitely exist. Your duty (and opportunity) as a sales professional is to get those needs out into the open—to discover needs.

As you are searching for needs, "wants" and desires will surface. Don't make the mistake of discounting these wants as frivolous because prospects take action on their "want to's" as well as their needs.

Please understand that I did not say you INVENT or CREATE the needs and wants. That's not selling. You uncover a need that is already there and, in the process, render a real service.

Recently, I had difficulty with one of my tires so I went to the tire store to get it replaced. Much to my chagrin, the service attendant identified a small problem with another tire, which indicated the front end was out of alignment. He explained that if I did not correct the alignment, I would soon be replacing yet another tire. Needless to say, realigning the front end of my car cost money, but the *investment* actually saved me additional costs in the future. The attendant (salesperson) did not cause the problem; he simply identified the problem and offered a solution, which is exactly what the professional does. We don't create problems; we identify them and offer solutions through our goods and services.

## NEEDS AND WANTS—REASONS AND EXCUSES

Today's successful salesperson is CUSTOMER DESIRE DRIVEN AND NEEDS ORIENTED! The days of product-driven, product-oriented sales are gone forever. So, regardless of the product or the service, the customer has needs and wants that must be met. If your product or service meets a need or desire, then you have a chance to make the sale. If no needs or desires are met, no sale!

Basically, people buy because they either NEED or WANT something. If we can give persons a reason for buying AND an excuse for buying, the chances are rather dramatically improved that they will buy.

Many years ago, I was privileged to be part of an organization that raised more money in the state of Georgia than any organization had ever raised. By selling stock in a direct marketing effort, we raised over $40 million to build a paper mill in Blakely, Georgia. In many, many instances, when I sold one member of the family a few shares of stock, virtually every other member of the family bought. They often made me promise not to tell how many shares (some would invest only $50 or $100), but all were able to say they were stockholders with their family, and they were very happy about that fact.

The same principle worked in the cookware business. Many sets of cookware were bought because other family members had bought, and family pride can be a tremendous motivating factor. The *reasons* people bought were (1) they wanted the cookware and (2) the other family members had the cookware. The *excuses* people had for buying the cookware were (1) savings on fuel bills, cooking oil, and electricity and (2) less food shrinkage and increased nutritional food value. Each "excuse" was legitimate, but the overwhelming factor in buying (just as was the case in the stock sales) was "want to."

Today, home computers and cellular telephones are bought similarly. The *reasons* people buy are (1) they want these high-tech products and (2) other family members and peers have the products. The *excuses* people have for buying P.C.'s and portable phones are (1) convenience and (2) communication improvement. Again, each "excuse" is legitimate, but the overwhelming factor in buying is "want to" (which is enhanced by others' ownership).

**If we can give persons a reason for buying AND an excuse for buying, the chances are rather dramatically improved that they will buy.**

People invariably will buy what they want, even above what they need. How many times have all of us seen families literally living in poverty and yet every family member is smoking, drinking soda pop, and watching TV? How many fur coats do we really need in Dallas, Texas? People certainly don't buy them primarily because they need them; they buy because they want them. When you start looking at needs and wants, just how many suits of clothes do we really need? How big a house do we need? How many shirts, dresses, blouses, sweaters, or pairs of shoes? Fortunately, for those of us in the world of selling, our job is NOT to determine *only* needs (in the strictest sense of the definition of the word *need*) because people buy more than they need.

I suspect that if you and I were to stop a thousand people on the streets of Any City, U.S.A., and ask them point-blank, "Do you need . . . (a new car, air conditioning, a new computer, more life insurance, or any other products, goods, or services)?" very, very, very few would say, "Well, as a matter of fact. . . ." I'm also even more convinced that if we were to tell our sales story in a persuasive manner, out of the one thousand people there would be at least fifty—and maybe as many as three or four hundred of them (depending, of course, on our product)—who would buy.

What happened to those people who didn't "need" our product? Let me remind you that people often have no idea what their needs may be because they don't know what is available. Fifty years ago we didn't realize we needed air conditioning in our cars, computers in our homes, extensions on the telephone line, and 1,001 other things. We don't make people unhappy by revealing new "needs" to them. The reality is, we can bring a much more enjoyable lifestyle to them, help them enjoy ease of living, provide more effective and efficient operations, or offer significant savings through the use of our products. The basic question is not, "Do you need a new computer?" The question is, "Would you like to reduce errors in expensive promotional mailings as well as time spent entering names?"

If you are fortunate enough to sell a product or service that people want and need—and you believe they need and want it, even if they are not yet convinced—you are on your way to sales success!

A salesperson armed with INTEGRITY, a strong BELIEF in the product, and the DESIRE to get the product into the hands of as many people as possible is a POWERFUL FORCE with which to deal. And even more powerful when you add persuasion skills to the sales arsenal.

For our purposes, *wants* and *needs* are basically used interchangeably throughout this book.

## EXPERIENCE SPEAKS

Many years ago when I was in direct sales, selling cookware, I made a presentation to a family that desperately NEEDED my cookware. I had the opportunity to inventory their kitchen utensils while preparing the demonstration meal, and they had NOTHING. Because their need was so great, I spent nearly two hours attempting to close the sale. The lady and her husband had the same level of intensity in their ability to persevere as I did because they continued to say, "No money, too expensive, can't afford it!"

As I was packing my sample case to leave, the husband, his wife, or I mentioned "china." To this day I can still remember the way that dear lady's eyes lighted up. She said, "China? Do you sell fine china?"

"Yes, ma'am," I responded. "We sell the *finest* fine china in the whole world!"

Less than thirty minutes later, I left that household with an order worth substantially more than the entire set of cookware. Now think with me. If she couldn't afford the set of cookware she so desperately needed, how could she afford the china she didn't need? The answer is, she *couldn't* afford a set of cookware she didn't want, but she *could* afford a set of fine china she did want.

Here is the key point: PEOPLE BUY WHAT THEY WANT WHEN THEY WANT IT MORE THAN THEY WANT THE MONEY IT COSTS.

How do you uncover wants and needs? I'm glad you asked.

## PROBING

With the proper probing effort, you can discover the needs of the prospect. Each of us living and breathing human beings has a bundle of needs and wants. Often these are masked by symptoms. The salesperson who sells to symptoms fails to make sales and does not understand why or has sales *fall out, come back,* or *returned,* whichever term you might use for losing sales, commissions, and the chance to help a prospect.

Andrew Downie of New South Wales, Australia, shared the following story with me, which explains how he probed for the root need of the prospect without getting caught up in the symptom of the problem. It also shows a great deal of creativity in adapting ageless principles to his specific situation (remember "concomitant" value?).

Andrew concluded his presentation by saying, "And so the total investment is xx amount, and most people take care of it by cash, check, or credit card. Which particular method suits this family best?" The prospect had the countenance of a person who was totally overwhelmed as he said, "It's not the money that's the problem. There is just so much to consider."

Andrew immediately picked up the signal that the prospect was sending: THERE IS A PROBLEM HERE, AND I AM NOT BUYING.

## PROBING PSYCHOLOGY

Andrew used one of the oldest probing devices available to the professional salesperson, the Ben Franklin Close, and immediately went to work. Folks who live in New South Wales, Australia, may or may not know who Ben Franklin is—and even if they know, his name probably wouldn't have the same impact there as in the United States. So Andrew adapted the idea and used the phrase "great statesmen and stateswomen."

**PEOPLE BUY WHAT THEY WANT WHEN THEY WANT IT MORE THAN THEY WANT THE MONEY IT COSTS.**

"Mr. Prospect," he began, "great statesmen and stateswomen from all countries have found themselves in a similar situation to you. They want to make sure that they make the right decision and not the wrong decision. Is that pretty much how you feel at the moment?" Mr. Prospect acknowledged this with an affirmative, if somewhat suspicious, nod of his head. And with the ease of a true master of his profession, Andrew moved to the prospect's side of the table. No, he didn't physically walk over and pull up a chair next to the prospect, though some salespeople do. As a matter of fact, some chess masters will get up and stand behind their opponent for a moment so they can look at the board from their side of the table to gain a different perspective. What Andrew did was to move to the prospect's side of the table by looking at the situation from the prospect's perspective.

"What great statesmen and stateswomen do in this situation, Mr. Prospect, is to take a clean sheet of paper and draw a line across the top and down the middle. On the left-hand side they write all the reasons in favor of the decision and on the right-hand side all the reasons against the decision, and then they make their decision based on the number of reasons for as opposed to the number of reasons against. Why don't we do the same?" Again, Andrew received the affirmative and now less suspicious nod of agreement.

Working together, Andrew and the prospect came up with twelve reasons for moving forward with the decision. When Andrew asked what the prospect didn't like about the program, he got a one-word response, "Money."

## A GENTLE CHALLENGE

"So, Mr. Prospect, the only reason you wouldn't go ahead today is the level of investment. Is that right?" And this time Andrew got a positive head nod and a strong "yes" reply. Now remember, earlier the prospect had said that money was not a problem; "so much to consider" had been his concern. Andrew had helped him analyze the situation with the Franklin Close, so the prospect had all the information he needed. Andrew clarified by asking, "But you said earlier that money wasn't a problem, didn't you?" After the briefest of pauses, the prospect agreed, so Andrew continued, "Therefore, there's no reason not to complete the paperwork today, is there?" And the prospect responded with the kind of "no" that Andrew was pleased to get, the one that says, "Write it up. I'll buy!"

## IMPORTANT LESSONS

Andrew was tremendously excited after completing the sale, and so was the prospect because both had gotten what they wanted. As Andrew left, he reviewed the successful sales presentation in his mind (great sales professionals constantly "play the tapes" of successful sales presentations before, during, and after sales calls).

Andrew understood that there were many lessons to be learned. He had gotten on the prospect's side of the table; he got the prospect involved in the process with the Ben Franklin Close; he committed the prospect to taking action by asking questions properly; and Andrew closed decisively, getting the results that benefited the prospect and the salesperson. However, the sale would not have taken place had he accepted the prospect's original, "No, I can't buy today."

The root problems were lack of information and procrastination. Andrew solved these by providing the needed information (not just the stated reasons for not buying) and by asking the questions that encouraged the prospect to take action.

## WHO DO WE PROBE?

Many times needs and wants may be discovered by selecting the proper market to probe. For years, the Zig Ziglar Corporation has worked with Dunn's Marketing in purchasing direct mail lists with specific SIC (Strategic Industry Code) information that allows us to penetrate markets prone to have specific needs.

Outstanding sales professionals do their homework and discover background information on companies—and often do this before making the sales call—especially if they sell a high ticket item or specialize in significant repeat business. My friend Jerry Aull sells training products and seminars in the Atlanta, Georgia, area. Jerry has an assistant who goes into an organization and requests information ranging from the annual report to the administrative assistant's name who works for the decision maker... and the assistant is telemarketing! He is making thousands of dollars' worth of sales, and his only face-to-face contact is done in a research mode.

Jerry Aull, who is truly an outstanding speaker and trainer as well as a supersuccessful sales professional, takes the information and makes face-to-face calls for the necessary accounts. Jerry and his assistant make a great team that is setting records for the company while helping thousands of people to be more efficient and effective in their lives.

Regardless of how you do your homework or how much homework you might do, the probing is eventually done WITH the client or prospect. Again, no matter what product or service, the same basic "probing principles" apply.

## QUESTIONS ARE THE ANSWER

Probing begins with asking questions. You must develop an attitude of curiosity and sincere interest in the answers to your questions. Let the little child out. Studies have shown that children from the ages of two to twelve may ask as many as eighty questions per day. When they get to high school, those questions are down to thirty-five to forty per day. In the business world, we are asking only ten to fifteen questions per day. We need to ask questions like a child does.

My friend Bryan Flanagan, whom I will mention several times throughout this book, is not only an outstanding speaker and trainer but also an excellent role model as a family man. His presentations are liberally sprinkled with examples from his family. He and his wife, Cyndi, have two beautiful children—Patrick and Quinn—and like many of us, Bryan and Cyndi are continually learning from their kids.

Several years ago when Patrick was seven years old, we had one of those rare days when it snows in Dallas, Texas. Bryan and Patrick were in their front yard building a snowman as Cyndi and Quinn watched joyfully (and wisely) from the warmth of the living room. Later in the day, the sun came out. As the snowman began to slowly disappear, Patrick asked his dad one of those great "little child" questions that we all need to emulate. He asked, "Dad, where does the white go when the snow melts?"

Well, Bryan has taught the importance of asking the right kinds of questions, and he is also well schooled in the techniques of answering questions properly. After only the slightest of pauses, Bryan responded with the only possible answer to a question of such magnitude when he said, "Go ask your mother."

## THE RIGHT KINDS OF QUESTIONS

You want to ask questions to gather information, not to gather facts. Although you want factual information, facts alone won't help you discover the needs of the prospect. Chapter 6, "Questions Are the Answer," contains the details on the right kinds of questions. The P.O.G.O. formula in chapter 7 will help you carry a comfortable conversation and not "grill" the prospect.

## STEP TWO: NEED AWARENESS

In the Need Awareness step, there are two distinct parts. In the first place, the salesperson must have identified one or more specific needs that can be clearly articulated. In the second place, the prospect must understand that there is a need AND the specifics of the need. The "light bulb" must first come on in your mind and then in the prospect's mind.

### TUFF STUFF

You get started in Need Awareness in the same way you began Need Analysis—by asking questions. But Need Awareness is difficult because to ask questions that cause both you and the prospect to understand the needs and wants, you are required to THINK! Now the reason this is difficult is that "us sales folks" are often so intent on getting the sale that we stop thinking—or we think about the result we want to the detriment of the process we must go through to achieve that result.

Even if prospects are coming to you in a retail environment, and especially when they are not coming to you, developing Need Awareness is vital. I know some of you will find this hard to believe, but some prospects will actually tell you that they want to buy and then change their minds! (Yes, that lump in my cheek is my tongue.) The truth is, when confronted with the fact that you are asking for an amount of money that resembles (to the prospect) the national debt, some people are going to get cold feet. Your product or service may cost only a few dollars, but you must be sensitive to the fact that your perception of the dollar may vary enormously from the prospect's perception of that price tag. If you have not identified the proper need AND made that need perfectly clear to the prospect, either the sale will not be made, or it will not stick.

## REAL CONCERNS

A successful salesperson must be able to listen carefully to what the prospect is saying. For example, the real estate prospect might say, "I do not like this location. It's too far from my job, it's in the wrong neighborhood, it's too close to (or too far from) the school, it's the most expensive house on the block," or a variety of other things. But the prospect might really be saying, "I know very little about the real estate market. I'm not tuned in to what financing is available, or I frankly cannot tell if the home is really well-built or simply appearance-built." The sensitive and knowledgeable real estate salesperson would gently probe and discover the obvious as well as the "not so obvious" objections. The professional would supply comparable costs or sales prices of similar homes sold in that neighborhood during the past few months. The professional could make possible financing avenues as well as rates of interest known to the prospect.

Perhaps one of the great unspoken objections is the "fear of loss" factor that enters the mind when someone is contemplating a major purchase—and for most people a home is the biggest individual purchase they will ever make. The salesperson could reassure the prospect by either sharing the very latest building inspection on the property or encouraging the prospect to have another inspector look over the property.

The peace of mind, which incidentally is one of the things the prospect is buying with ownership, would certainly be worth the small amount invested for a thorough inspection when the total home investment can run from $100,000 to several hundred thousand. In short, probe (ask questions that show a sincere interest in the prospect) until you find the real concern. Missing a sale and not knowing why is extremely frustrating.

In chapter 8, "Making the Lights Go on," you will learn the details of how to help the prospect understand that there is a real and specific need by upsetting the "homeostatic balance." You will learn how to get the person back in balance before a competitor comes along and makes your sale.

## STEP THREE: NEED SOLUTION

Step three in the four-step formula that fits all sales products and services is Need Solution. In this step you present your product. Now is the time to stop asking questions and begin presenting solutions to needs.

You have spent two phases of the professional sales process discovering and tuning in to needs and wants, so don't lead with your product at this point. Now I can just hear some of you saying, "Wait a minute, Ziglar. In the last paragraph you said it was time to present the product. I have spent months learning my sales presentation. I read this book, and you devote all these pages to telling me that I've got to find the prospect's needs, become aware myself, and make the prospect aware. We finally get to the part where I can present my product (which is, after all, the reason I am making the sales call), and now you tell me not to lead with the product??? Explain yourself, man!"

---

**We never lead with product;
we lead with need.**

---

All right, I will. Let me ask you a series of *trick* questions. Now, I did say they were designed to be misleading, so consider yourself warned. Have you ever purchased a bed? A new outfit? An automobile? An insurance policy? A copier for the office? A training program? A set of audio tapes? A book?

Let me submit to you that not one of you reading this book has ever bought any of these items.

What you bought was a good night's sleep; the way you look and feel in a particular outfit; transportation; protection for your family with savings and investment advantages; increased communication and organization for the office; added productivity; more information; a fundamental sales program that will help you be even more successful in your sales career.

None of us buy products. We all buy products of the product—which are called benefits or need solutions. In short, we don't buy what the product is; we buy what the product DOES FOR US.

### LEAD WITH NEED

We never lead with product; we lead with need. Everyone listens to the same radio station according to my friend and fellow sales trainer Don Hutson. Don says, and I agree completely, that every one of us listens to radio station WII-FM—and those call letters stand for *W*hat's *I*n *I*t *F*or *M*e? We must relate to the prospect in terms of need, not in terms of product.

Communication consultant Nick Dalley has done some contract work for our organization. It had been several months since any of us had seen him, and several people noticed that there was something different about Nick when he returned to help us with a particular project. We eventually realized he was wearing braces on his teeth. Finally, someone's curiosity led him to ask Nick why he wanted braces.

Nick's answer contains a valuable lesson about WII-FM and leading with need. He responded, "I don't want braces. I want straight teeth."

Please don't waste your time and the prospects' time telling them what the product IS. Tell them what it can DO and why it will do it for them.

In chapter 9, "Selling Solutions to People's Problems," you will learn how to tell people what you are selling, what it does, and why it will do what it does for them better than anything else!

## STEP FOUR: NEED SATISFACTION

The fourth step in the process is Need Satisfaction. Here is the most important step the salesperson can take when it comes to helping others. If you truly have a desire to help other people; if you truly believe in your product or service; if you truly want the prospect to benefit; if you truly want to benefit financially from your hard work and effort; then you must remember:

A.A.F.T.O.
ALWAYS ASK FOR THE ORDER!!!!

As silly as this may seem to some of you, we sometimes freeze up, burn out, or just "blow it" when the time for the close is near. This is such a common mistake that I wrote an entire book called *Secrets of Closing the Sale*. It has sold hundreds of thousands of copies because we all want to close more sales more often.

## A "ROOKIE" AT WORK

I have truly been blessed in my sales career, but lest you mistakenly think it's always been that way, let me share a story that will bring you some insight (and hopefully some encouragement).

In my earliest days of selling, I did something that only a few companies were doing at that time—a group demonstration. Getting several prospects together to give a presentation once instead of six to eight times makes sense, wouldn't you agree? At any rate, my first group demonstration was one I will never forget. Mr. and Mrs. M. P. Gates and Mr. and Mrs. Clarence Spence gathered at the home of Mr. and Mrs. B. C. Moore in Columbia, South Carolina. Mr. and Mrs. Moore already owned the product but were struggling with proper use, so in return for their inviting their neighbors over, I agree to give them some ideas on how to better utilize the product. And at the risk of sounding immodest, I gave quite a demonstration. After finishing, both of the prospects gave a dozen reasons why they should not and could not buy. Yet to my great delight, both ended up by saying, "I'll take it."

Now my dear reading friend, let me ask you this question. Knowing that if it didn't take but fifty cents to go around the world, my financial situation would not have allowed me to get out of sight, and knowing that it had been a significant time since I had actually closed a sale, what would you have done if you were in my place? I have got to believe that 99.9 percent of the salespeople in the world who could get out of a phone booth without written instructions would have written the order. Guess what "Ole Zig" did? I looked at my watch and said, "Folks, as much as I would like to write the order for you, I have another appointment, and I'm running late." And with that, I packed my sample case and left.

With two prospects, money in hand, literally asking me to take it, I in essence said, "No, I have something more important to do." On your greenest day, YOU will not make that mistake. I did. All of that is just to say that regardless of how new and inept you might be (or perceive yourself to be), there IS hope for you.

Now the good news is, I did return the next day, but Mrs. Gates was not at Mrs. Spence's home as she had agreed to be. Mrs. Spence had her check already written and was glad to get the product. As I was about to leave, Mrs. Gates came hurrying up the hill with her check in her hand. When she reached me, she handed me her check and, after pausing to catch her breath, said, "Whew, I thought I was gonna miss you again!"

### LEARNING YOUR ABC'S

In chapter 10, "The ABC's of Closing Sales," you will learn how to ask for and get the order.

## FOUR STEPS TO SUCCESS—FOR YOU!

In this chapter, "Sell by Design, Not by Chance," you have been presented a teaching lesson for the beginning salesperson and a review of fundamentals for the experienced salesperson. If you are in a slump in selling or are not getting off to as fast a start as you had hoped, these pages will help you identify a basic error.

WARNING: The next five chapters should be read only by those who want to sell a WHOLE LOT because they are the how-to, nitty-gritty details of each of the steps that make up YOUR blueprint for success!

## THE SUCCESSFUL SALES FORMULA

1. **Need Analysis**
   A. Customer-driven (wants) and need-oriented (needs) selling begins with the sales professional probing to understand the prospect's wants and needs.
   B. During Need Analysis, the sales professional will "X-ray" the prospect.
   C. Professional probing is done with questions.

2. **Need Awareness**
   A. The "light" (understanding) must go on for the sales professional.
   B. The "light" (understanding) must go on for the prospect.
   C. Prospects often address symptoms rather than root problems; root problems are discovered by probing.

3. **Need Solution**
   A. Lead with need.
   B. Prospects don't buy products; they buy what the products do for them.
   C. Remember: WII-FM = *W*hat's *I*n *I*t *F*or *M*e? (the prospect).

4. **Need Satisfaction**
   A. A.A.F.T.O. = *A*lways *A*sk *F*or *T*he *O*rder.
   B. Belief in your product or service DEMANDS that you ask for the order.
   C. When the selling professional satisfies needs and wants, future clients are guaranteed!

CHAPTER SIX

# QUESTIONS ARE THE ANSWER

## *Beginning with Need Analysis*

The salesman got the address from another sales professional and made the call late one afternoon. As The Lady of the house answered the door, he was standing back several feet to show that he was not a threat to her when she opened the door. The first words out of his mouth were, "Mrs. Prospect (he had gotten the family's name from his friend who had given him the lead), I understand that you have a swimming pool and that Mr. Prospect is having to take care of it all by himself. Is that true?" The Lady smilingly acknowledged that he had identified the situation correctly, so the salesman continued. "Well, Mrs. Prospect, if I could clean that pool for you and supply all the chemicals needed for about $2.50 per day, would it be worthwhile to have your husband freed of that responsibility, which would give the two of you about three extra hours per week to do what you want to do instead of doing what needs to be done?"

With those powerful questions, the sales professional began a very meaningful and beneficial sales presentation (meaningful because he got the sale and the commission; beneficial because the prospect got a very important need met).

I had a similar experience in the Lubbock airport. The skycap gave me a hand with my bags, which included a very heavy golf bag. Being anxious to get home to Dallas after several days away, I immediately became engrossed in conversation with the ticket agent and forgot about the gentleman who had so courteously assisted me. His sales expertise manifested itself in one very pleasant, enthusiastic question: "Sir, is there anything else I can do to help?"

That ten-word "sales talk" was just a question, but it produced the desired results. I promptly gave him the gratuity he so richly deserved. Now, that's selling!

## IN THE BEGINNING

What is the best way to begin the sales presentation? With questions! What is the purpose of beginning with questions? Questions allow us to gather important information, which enables us to help our clients, AND just as important (maybe more important), when we ask questions in a professional manner, we establish the most important aspect of the sales process—TRUST!

Even though the pool cleaning service salesman thought he knew our needs, he asked questions. His questions showed his insight into our needs and his concern for helping us and encouraged The Redhead to believe we could trust him.

## THE FIRST STEP IN THE SUCCESSFUL SELLING PROCESS

The successful sales presentation will always begin with Need Analysis. Regardless of product or service, you must analyze the needs of the prospect. As I have already stated, even if the potential client is coming to you with the need seemingly obvious, the professional salesperson will still ask enough questions to verify that the need truly is what it appears to be.

## ASK YOURSELF

If you were to ask me a series of questions in a professional manner that showed a SINCERE interest in me and my company, what would I think of you? If you handle this portion of the sales presentation in the proper manner, I would learn that you are not "just another salesperson out to separate me from my money." Instead, I would discover that you are truly interested in helping me! The

BEST way to discover the true needs of a prospect or client is with proper questions.

Since questions are the subject, your question should be, Why does asking the proper questions lead to trust? Answer: Questions demonstrate that the purpose of our call is to find the prospect's needs and interests while gathering information, so that TOGETHER we learn how our goods or services meet the prospect's need (solve the problem). We communicate this message: "Let's work together to discover the need (problem) before we offer a solution."

Psychiatrists, physicians, attorneys, marriage counselors, and others in the "helping" professions all carefully listen before they make any effort to diagnose problems and prescribe solutions. Prospects like to be heard in order to have the confidence that we really do understand that their situation is "different." In reality their situation might not be different, but reality, like beauty, is in the eye of the beholder. We can never gain the trust of prospects until they believe we are really interested in solving their "unique" problem.

The sales professional of the nineties must clearly understand that the sales prospect of the nineties is better informed and more cynical than any consumer in history. There has been so much marketing emphasis (through the media—radio, TV, and print) that today's consumer is very sophisticated. Questions ARE important, but a series of obvious questions designed to lead the prospects "through the hoops" and manipulate them to the point of reaching into "deep pockets" to dig out their hard-earned dollars for you or me is not unlike a root canal without Novocain—it will not be tolerated! As professionals, we need to "motivate" the prospects to share their needs, wants, problems, and interests with us so we can "motivate" them to use our services to solve their problem.

## MOTIVATION OR MANIPULATION?

This brings us to an ethical question, and ethics is the foundation upon which we must build a career. What is the difference between motivation and manipulation? Unfortunately these terms are often confused, but comparing motivation to manipulation is like comparing kindness to deceit. The difference lies in the intent of the person. Motivation will cause people to act out of free choice and desire while manipulation often results in forced compliance. One is ethical and long lasting, and the other is unethical and temporary.

Thomas Carlyle said,

> A great man shows his greatness by the way he treats the little man. The value you place on people determines whether you are a motivator or a manipulator of men. Motivation is moving together for a mutual advantage. Manipulation is moving together for my advantage. That is a substantial difference. With the motivator everybody wins. With the manipulator only the manipulator wins.

**Motivation will cause people to act out of free choice and desire while manipulation often results in forced compliance.**

To those thoughts I might add that the "win" or "victory" for the manipulator is temporary and the price is prohibitive. This tainted, hollow victory certainly shortcuts the relationship and in all probability means that you've just closed your one and only sale with that prospect. This may make you look good in your sales manager's eyes, could show up well in the report, and temporarily brings you financial reward, but it definitely short-circuits your move to the top and is a self-destructive approach to a sales career.

## THIS KID CAN SELL

Leonard Harvison tells the story of how, after a tough day of working in the yard, he received a call from his seven-year-old nephew, Robert Gibson. Here's how the conversation went:

ROBBIE: "Uncle Bubba, do you have company?"
LEONARD (Uncle Bubba): "No, I sure don't."
ROBBIE: "Am I bothering you by calling?"
UNCLE BUBBA: "No, not at all."

ROBBIE: "Are you as bored as I am?"
UNCLE BUBBA (thinking Robbie wanted to spend the evening with his favorite uncle): "Yes, I am bored, Robbie."
ROBBIE: "Hey, I just got an idea. We could go fishin'."

All Leonard wanted to do was take a shower and get some rest, but Robbie had boarded up all logical escapes beforehand. "I was the biggest fish caught that day," Leonard said, "and I loved it!"

Under no circumstances would I accuse seven-year-old Robbie Gibson of being a manipulator because he probably doesn't understand the word. However, he knew exactly what he wanted, and in a natural childlike way he asked some significant questions. I might also point out that the love between uncle and nephew is obvious. The heart of the story is contained in Leonard's last four words: "And I loved it!" A clear-cut, motivated (win-win) sale.

## THINKING VS. FEELING QUESTIONS

You do yourself and your prospect a real service when you ask, "How do you feel about . . . ?" questions in the early part of the Need Analysis segment of the sales process. When you learn how the customer feels, you are far more likely to find out what the person thinks. Most of us claim to make logical decisions, but the reality is, we make primarily emotional decisions.

The classic example is the seat belt. Most people "fussed" when their states passed the seat belt laws—claiming this was a "free country, what would the government try to get us to do next?" And this complaining was despite the odds of about three to one that in case of an accident a seat belt would help prevent injury or death. On the other hand, I have flown over four million miles, and I have yet to hear even one passenger get unhappy about being asked to buckle the seat belt. All of us meekly and even enthusiastically comply. I might point out that if the plane crashes, the odds are about one thousand to one that the airline seat belt will do us any good at all. Yes, we are emotional, not logical, people.

However, as salespeople, we must understand that if we use only emotion-creating questions, we might well get the prospects to take action, but what happens when the emotion of the moment fades?

"Buyer's remorse" may set in, and we can lose sales that appeared very solid at the moment of closure. On the other hand, if we use only logical questions (which the prospects answer out of their intellect), we might well educate them about their needs and the benefits of our product or service, but there is a strong likelihood that they will go down the street and buy from someone who gets them emotionally involved in the benefits of the product. Therefore, it behooves us to combine emotion and logic. Emotion makes the prospects take action now, and logic enables them to justify the purchase later. This is important because many sales must be explained to friends and family members.

Have you ever had to (or wanted to) explain a purchase to a friend or family member? You might be like the man whose wife asked him so many questions about the used car he bought, he returned to the dealership. When the salesman saw our "hero" coming, he rushed onto the lot and immediately began explaining the car company's return policy.

"Oh, I don't want to return the car," the man stated emphatically. "I was just wondering if you would go through your sales presentation one more time?"

Understanding and utilizing the emotional AND the logical aspects of the sale will help all sales professionals become even more effective.

## SEEING, HEARING, AND BELIEVING

Generally speaking, when we see something (charts, graphs, demonstrations), we are more likely to respond logically. When we hear a message, especially if it is sincerely and/or enthusiastically delivered, we tend to become more emotionally involved. From birth we are told, "You can't believe everything you hear," and "Seeing is believing." Conclusion: Let the prospects see so they will believe, and let them hear so they will take action.

## COMBINING EMOTION AND LOGIC

Let's presume you have a product or service that saves your prospect money. At the end of your demonstration or presentation, when you have conclusively shown that your product or service does indeed save the prospect money, you should ask three questions:

- "Can you see where our product would save you money?"
- "Are you interested in saving money?"
- "If you were ever going to start saving money, when do you think would be the best time to start?"

One of the strongest emotions we face is FEAR. And you probably have heard the old sales adage, "Fear of loss is greater than the desire for gain." Obviously, you are trying to help the prospect by taking away the fear of losing money. (You didn't create the fear; you are helping eliminate it.) Your first question ("Can you see where our product would save you money?") begins the "fear elimination" process. You are now speaking to your prospect on an *emotional* level.

The second question may seem quite obvious, but it must be asked. This direct question ("Are you interested in saving money?") brings the prospect from the world of emotion into the world of *logic*. "Of course, I'm interested in saving money; any sensible person is interested in saving money" would be the mental response, even if the oral response is simply yes.

Now, by the prospect's own admission, your product saves money, and the person is adamant in the desire to save money. Question three ("If you were ever going to start saving money, when do you feel would be the best time to start?") calls for immediate action! It also is a reminder (emotionally) that failure to take action might result in further losses of money.

## BUT WILL THAT WORK FOR ME?

If (and that is a BIG "IF") you have made your presentation in such a way that you can expect an affirmative answer to question one, then the process will work for you. The principle works in many other areas as well.

If your product or service has a health benefit, you may use the same three-question process to tie emotion and logic together. In the areas of exercise equipment, vitamins, health club memberships, or physical therapy, the questions might be:

- "Can you see where this would be beneficial to your health?"
- "Are you seriously interested in maintaining (or regaining) good, vibrant health?"
- "Under these circumstances, when do you think it would be best to start really taking care of the health that you obviously cherish so highly?"

Let me challenge you to stop here and determine the number one benefit of the product or service you are involved in selling. What is the primary reason you might move people to take action on your product or service? Now develop your personalized version of the three questions that tie emotion to logic.

My primary benefit (what my product or service does for others) is:
________________________________________

My "customized" three questions are:

"Can you see ______________________________

________________________________________?"

"Are you interested in __________________________

________________________________________?"

"When do you think ___________________________

________________________________________?"

If you didn't take the time to write out these questions, may I ask you a few questions? Can you see where tying emotion to logic in the sales process would help you to close more sales? Are you interested in closing more sales? When do you think would be the best time to begin closing more sales?

## PAINT THAT VIVID AND EMOTIONAL PICTURE

Outstanding sales professionals are "word merchants" and "picture painters." As you carefully select the words for your logical and emotional questions, remember to paint vivid word pictures in the prospect's mind.

Greg Watt of London, Ontario, Canada, sells financial planning. He uses a simple analogy that he labels the Walk to Toronto Close. The idea is built around three questions using words that paint very special pictures for Greg's prospects. His objective is to help people see clearly that it is NOT futile to attempt a small savings program because small amounts saved regularly have a multiplying factor that turns $100 per month into a significant amount of money in time.

Greg paints the picture clearly with these three questions:

- "Mr. Prospect, if I offered you $100 to walk to Toronto, would you?" (Please understand that Gregg lives 120 miles from Toronto, so he doesn't get the affirmative response very often.)
- "If there was $1,000,000 waiting for you when you arrived, you'd start walking right now, wouldn't you?"
- "If I could show you how to arrive at the $1,000,000 city by saving $100 per month, you'd want to take the first step today, wouldn't you?"

The answer more often than not is yes!

## MORE VIVID WORD PICTURES

Connie Cox works with a major publishing entity, and she believes words are important. She teaches her people that asking for a contract is not nearly as effective as saying, "In order to reserve the space. . . ." The formerly intimidating contract becomes a form for space reservation, and the prospect is much happier.

Jay P. Curry of San Francisco, California, enthusiastically points out that instead of cold calls (or warm calls), he encourages professional salesmen and saleswomen to make "introductory" calls. He asks, "When you hear the word *introduction,* what word pops into your mind? When you are with someone special, don't you proudly introduce the person to your friends? When you go out with your mate and meet an acquaintance, you introduce your mate, don't you? When you go out to sell, you have to introduce yourself, your company and, most important, your product or service to your prospect.

"Since words are the colors of the paints we use to illustrate our pictures, we must use the best hue possible. We have a responsibility to paint the picture in terms that are easily understood and used."

**Outstanding sales professionals are "word merchants" and "picture painters."**

Words ARE the colors of the paints we use to illustrate our pictures of life. Isn't choosing the proper colors (words) a beautiful and exciting way to do exactly what we are trying to do—paint vivid word pictures?

## THE PROPER QUESTIONING PROCESS

So how do you ask the kinds of questions that allow you to do a proper Need Analysis to begin your sales presentation? Again, I'm glad you asked. Let me remind you of a statement I made earlier: Those who know "what" and "how" will always work for those who know "why." As we explore the kinds of questions professional salespeople ask and the way you develop questions to meet the needs of your clients and prospects, let me encourage you to work to understand the "why" behind the questioning process.

## OPEN DOOR QUESTIONS

Three basic types of questions allow us to discover the needs and wants of our clients and potential customers. And all questions—emotional or logical—fall into one of these three categories.

The first is the Open Door Question. Open Door Questions allow the persons being questioned to go wherever they like with their responses. After all, your purpose is not to close in the prospects—you want them to move freely in the areas of their choosing. With the Open Door Question, the wants, needs, desires, ideas, and opinions of the prospects are the focal points. You have imposed nothing and have shown a sincere interest in your clients.

Open Door Questions are identified as the "who, what, where, when, how, and why" questions. They may also begin with the phrases, "What do you think about . . . ?" or "How do you feel about . . . ?"

### For Instance

Let's look at some examples of Open Door Questions that will allow the professional salesperson to gather information while showing a sincere interest in the prospect.

1. What is the most exciting aspect of your job?
2. How do you see your responsibilities changing in the next five years?
3. What are your goals regarding your areas of responsibility?
4. What do you think are the greatest challenges facing you and your organization over the next six months?

Again, the purpose of the Open Door Question is to allow the prospects the freedom to take the answer where they want it to go. If you ask questions that have only "yes" or "no" answers, you allow the prospects to remain noncommittal and noninformational. Ask Open Door Questions.

### A Pet Peeve

A major error in asking Open Door Questions is supplying answers. You are not giving a multiple choice test! When you ask

Open Door Questions, there will often be a moment of silence. Although that can be terribly uncomfortable, a pause is often necessary for the person to form an insightful and intelligent response to your question. Please avoid offering answers to the question based on your discomfort or the desire to show your insights into the situation.

When you ask questions like, "How do you feel about your areas of responsibility? (pause) I mean are you feeling like these responsibilities are growing or being curtailed?" the person can answer, "Growing"; "Neither"; or "I feel good about my areas of responsibility." And none of these responses is what you are seeking with the Open Door Question. Ask the question . . . *then* LISTEN!

Salespeople are traditionally poor in this area. However, you will find there is a direct correlation between your commission check/dollar volume results and your ability to ask Open Door Questions and then LISTEN TO THE ANSWERS.

## CLOSED DOOR QUESTIONS

The second kind of question is the Closed Door Question. If an Open Door Question is designed to allow the prospects to move freely wherever their thoughts take them, then the Closed Door Question is designed to keep them in a certain area for clarification or embellishment. Closed Door Questions begin with phrases like, "Would you tell me more about . . . ?" or "That's fascinating. What do you mean by . . . ?"

Often, you can just repeat the prospect's words with a question mark at the end of the phrase or turn the declarative statement into a question. Now while this example won't happen for many of you, it makes a point: If the prospect abruptly stands up and firmly suggests that there is no interest in doing business with you and it would be "useless" to continue the interview, you might respond slowly and softly, "Useless, Mr. Prospect?" Then wait.

You have moved the ball back to his side of the court, and many times the reason behind the prospect's action will surface and your information base will be expanded. If this happens, you have moved to a more favorable position for future business, even if the prospect is not inclined or emotionally open to make a favorable buying decision at the moment. Even if the prospect doesn't respond, the old adage that "a soft answer turneth away wrath" is still true. Upon reflection, the prospect will recognize your professionalism, which means the door he invited you to exit may open for future calls.

### For Instance

Some samples of Closed Door Questions that would give you information to use in helping the prospect and building a trusting relationship are these:

1. How long did you teach before entering the business world?
2. How does your division compare in size to the other divisions in this company?
3. Since your goal is to increase profits, how would the company use those additional profits?
4. If worker absence is a major obstacle to productivity, what are you doing to cut down on absenteeism?

## YOUR MOST NEGLECTED SALES TOOL

Without reservation, one of the most important (and the least developed) sales tools is the salesperson's voice. Most speech therapists agree that only 5 percent of the people in our society have a naturally pleasant voice. Virtually all the rest, however, can be trained.

The Redhead fondly recalls a pleasant meeting with a young executive in Dallas. As they chatted, she inquired about where he was from. He identified a small town in the rural South. She expressed astonishment because his tone of voice and speech mannerisms could not be identified as being from any specific area, especially not the South. "Your diction is better than Zig's!" she told him. (Those of you who have heard me speak will understand this statement.)

The gentleman smilingly said that when he was a child, his parents had taken great pains to explain to him that a pleasant voice not identified with any area of the country would be a real asset. His diction was excellent, and his voice was pleasant to the ear. Realistically, he does have a brighter future due to developing his voice to its full potential.

Many executives and speech coaches believe that anyone can improve the voice, and I am in agreement. Many times laziness prevents people from taking the steps necessary for improvement, but more often they are simply unaware that their voices are "grating," harsh, shrill, or unpleasant.

Substantial improvement is not an overnight project. However, diction coach Gertrude Fogler says working on voice improvement is well worth the time and effort. People literally lose their jobs because of unpleasant voices (did you realize that many prospective employers will do at least one telephone check before the final decision to hire?); teachers and students irritate each other or fail to get favorable attention because of an ugly, rasping voice. I know a speaker who has an excellent stage presence, conducts a tremendous seminar, and is truly capable of helping many people. This particular person was turned down by a major audio production company due to voice quality. When confronted, the speaker reluctantly agreed to try to do something, took two lessons from a diction coach, and then used "time" as an excuse to drop out. Sad but true.

## Action Steps

What can the dedicated sales professional do to improve the voice? Let's begin with a double suggestion that will work wonders. Even as you read these words, I encourage you to get in a room by yourself and NOT ONLY read these words out loud but record them as well. Then, treat the rest of the book the same way. Not only will this substantially improve the tonal quality of your voice, but you will be planting memories and lessons of the book more deeply in your mind than if you just read normally. You probably won't record all of the book, but in those sections where memorization and the ability to recall ideas verbatim are beneficial, I strongly encourage you to read AND record. While you are driving or unable to read, you can review the contents of the key portions of this book, and you can evaluate your voice. Remember to ask this question while listening to yourself on tape: "Would I buy from this person?"

## Reading and Recording

I also encourage you to get involved in specialized reading and recording. Let me remind you again that though this sounds like a lot of trouble, your voice DOES reach your prospect at the emotional level. Since selling is a transference of feeling, what better way to begin than with the proper usage of your voice?

A truly outstanding passage in literature is the powerful speech that Mark Anthony delivered: "I come to bury Caesar, not to praise him!" As you read you will recognize one of the greatest sales presentations of all time. Notice how Mark Anthony changes that angry group of prospects to an entirely different crowd by his adept choice of words. As a salesperson you will face some hostile (or at least semihostile) prospects, and this sales presentation will give you many good ideas for dealing with them. With the added advantage of recording the information, you can learn much about your voice quality.

Another great piece of literature from which you can learn is the Bible. I particularly encourage you to get a New King James Version and read out loud the Psalms and Proverbs. The eloquence, for example, of the Twenty-third Psalm (which many authorities believe is the most beautiful single piece of writing ever put on paper) will move you and inspire you. Also read Lincoln's "Gettysburg Address" and read what Martin Luther King said in his "I Have A Dream" speech. If you will invest fifteen minutes each day in improving your voice, within three months people will begin to notice, and a year from now even you will be astonished at how much more effective your voice has become.

## Nervous Tension Leads to the "Squeaks"

Speech authority Charles Rondeau contends that most women's voices are too high pitched and can be dramatically improved and lowered with a conscious effort at doing so. For both men and women the key step is the ability to relax as they speak—concentrating on relaxing the throat muscles. When I'm conducting a seminar, I always have the person in charge of the meeting place a pitcher of hot water on the stage for my use. The hotter the better. By the time I drink the water it is pleasantly warm. Using ice water during a seminar is simply not thinking. Cold causes muscles to contract while heat causes muscles to relax, increasing the blood flow. I encourage you, as you do your voice recordings, to drink some warm water before you start recording. I also encourage you to make a conscious effort to open your mouth because many people with poor voices do not really open their mouths. Exaggerate the openness until you get the idea. Speak in front of a mirror to be sure that you are smiling as you speak and record. The smiling voice (whether in person or on the phone) is a warm, open, and friendly voice.

## Practice, Practice, and More Practice

My good friend and fellow sales trainer Peter Lowe says that many prospects use a number of universal phrases that are generally not true. He gives us some methods and words we can use to handle them if we use our voices properly:

PROSPECT: "All the people at our company are unhappy with the service we have received."
PETER (smiling): "All?"
PROSPECT: "No one trusts this individual!"
PETER: (smiling): "No one?"
PROSPECT: "You people never deliver on time!"
PETER (smiling): "Never?"
PROSPECT: "Every time we try something new, we are sorry!"
PETER (smiling): "Every time?"

These examples are universal, and you probably have encountered several others. If you will smile, pause, and repeat the primary words, you will handle the objection strictly with voice inflection.

Let me encourage you to take the questions you will ask hundreds of times and practice using the proper voice inflection. And if you are the true sales professional I believe you are, you will take the "extra step" and practice using the proper voice inflection for the ANSWERS/OBJECTIONS you deal with on a regular basis.

By using a cassette recorder to practice responses to client statements, you are becoming the consummate professional.

For example, if your prospect says, "We are very satisfied with our current vendor," your response might be, "You are satisfied with your current vendor?" (Note the question mark at the end of the sentence.) If you get a one-word response, just pause and nod your head. If you wait long enough, your prospect will explain why. Other common statements that you can turn into Closed Door Questions are:

PROSPECT: "Your price is too high."
YOU: "The price (pause) is too high?"

PROSPECT: "We don't need any more ———."
YOU: "You don't *NEED* any more ———?"

Would you take the time right now to think through your presentation for the two most common statements you deal with that might be handled with proper voice inflection?

______________________________________________

______________________________________________

What? You don't have TIME to stop now????????

## YES OR NO QUESTIONS

The third type of question is the Yes or No Question. This question demands a direct response. However, we will use this question only when we already know the answer. The danger of this kind of question is that if it is overused, it may be perceived as patronizing.

### For Instance

As we construct sample Yes or No Questions, remember to put them in your own words and the framework of your own personality.

1. Do you agree that this would save you money?
2. Is this the type product your organization might benefit from?
3. Would what I'm proposing fit into your goals?
4. Are we in agreement that this service is at least a partial solution to your problems?

Yes or No Questions allow you to "test the waters" and check on your progress in the sales process. Some trainers call these questions "trial closes" because they can tell you if you are getting "buy-in" from the prospect based on the response.

## He Just Couldn't Afford It

Art Lamstein of San Francisco, California, sells solar heating. Following one demonstration and presentation, the prospect gave the fairly standard "I just can't afford it" response. Art used Yes or No Questions to help the prospect.

"Mr. Prospect," Art began, "I appreciate your honesty in telling me you can't afford this system, but let me ask you this. You do like the system, don't you?" He got the expected answer. "Then if you could afford the system, you would get it today, wouldn't you?" Again the prospect answered, "Yes."

"Many of my clients initially felt they could not afford this system, but when they understood how much they would save over their previous utility bills, they found it was very affordable." Art then went to the "talking pad" (a legal pad that allowed him to let the prospect follow his words in print). He showed the prospect how the cost of doing nothing would be more than the cost of the solar heating system as utility prices rose. As he wrote the figures, Art continued to probe and got agreement from the prospect that the figures were reasonable and accurate.

Next, Art went back to the closing process, but he did not try to get the prospect to change his mind (that's a very difficult thing to do). He did encourage the prospect to make a new decision based on additional information. He did it with this statement: "Mr. Prospect, I'm not asking you to spend any more money than you are now spending. What I am asking is for you to change your habit of paying the utility company with these ever-increasing costs and start paying yourself with the savings from the solar system. Instead of seeing your money go up in smoke, you will have something to show for that money. In other words, Mr. Prospect, you're really deciding whether or not you want to pay yourself or the utility company, so that should be an easy decision. So the final question, Mr. Prospect, is this: Would you rather keep paying increasing amounts, which you might not be able to afford someday, or get a solar system that will keep your costs low and under control?" As you might suspect, the sale was made.

**USE YOUR OWN WORDS AND WORK WITHIN THE FRAMEWORK OF YOUR OWN PERSONALITY.**

Art used the Yes or No Questions very effectively. In addition, he taught us to get the prospect involved by getting him to agree; he got him involved visually by using the "talking pad"; Art used the Yes or No Questions to lead the prospect to a logical conclusion; and he did not try to get the man to change his mind but encouraged him to make a new decision based on additional information.

### Interview or Interrogation?

While I hope this next statement is obvious let me share with you that it is vital for you to USE YOUR OWN WORDS AND WORK WITHIN THE FRAMEWORK OF YOUR OWN PERSONALITY. Your job is to interview, explore, and uncover customer wants and needs, not interrogate.

Are you showing a sincere interest in the prospect? Are the questions based on what is being discussed (previous answers), or are you just going down your prepared list? The only thing more frustrating than the poor talk show host who asks questions regardless of the answer to the previous question is the nonprofessional salesperson who does the same thing.

One sales representative launched into the Need Analysis segment of his sales call, and the prospect interrupted to ask a question of his own. "I'm sorry. Did you say you were with BFI or the FBI?"

The importance of Need Analysis in the sales process cannot be overemphasized. However, before you can be comfortable with Need Analysis, you must be comfortable with the questioning process. Most professional salespeople don't want to give the appearance of FBI agents or poor talk show hosts. The obvious question becomes, How can you find out the information you need so that you and the prospect can be comfortable? Glad you asked, because that's the subject of chapter 7.

## PART I OF THE SUCCESSFUL SALES PROCESS: NEED ANALYSIS

1. **The proper questions enable you to gain the prospect's trust.**

2. **To combine emotion and logic:**
   A. Use "thinking" and "feeling" questions.
   B. Use the three-question close.
   C. Use a "talking pad" so the prospect can "see" the idea.

3. **The successful sales professional is a word merchant and a picture painter.**

4. **Probe the prospect with three kinds of questions:**
   A. Open Door Questions.
   B. Closed Door Questions.
   C. Yes or No Questions.

5. **The least-developed tool of the professional salesperson is the VOICE. To develop this important tool:**
   A. Practice, practice, and practice.
   B. Read and record this book and your presentation.
   C. Drink warm water before speaking.
   D. Exaggerate opening your mouth.
   E. Smile.

CHAPTER SEVEN

# THE CONVERSATIONAL "INTERROGATION"

## *Conducting the Comfortable Interview*

The 400-watt naked light bulb shined so brightly in Ralph's eyes that when he looked at his captor, he could see only a dim shadow with a red-and-yellow hue around the outline of the burly man demanding answers.

"I don't know," Ralph moaned, wondering if the torture would ever cease. "Well," his foe almost shouted, "if you don't know, then who does?"

Although this scene may sound like something from a movie originally shown in the late forties, it is in actuality the scene in many prospects' minds when YOU request an appointment. For some prospects, the sales appointment ranks right up there with a visit to traffic court or a meeting with auditors of the Internal Revenue Service. How can this attitude be changed? Only by your becoming the best and most professional interviewer possible.

## THE "INNER" VIEW

My friend and fellow speaker Jim Cathcart has a seminar he teaches on the "inner" view. Isn't the name terrific? Just thinking of doing an "innerview" instead of an interview will help paint the kind of picture in your mind that is necessary to be successful in gathering information in the Need Analysis segment of the sales process. If you will make conducting an "innerview" (with your prospect) your goal, your sales career will be greatly enhanced!

## THE P.O.G.O. FORMULA

Even some very successful sales professionals have difficulty "firing" off a series of questions to a prospect they are meeting for the first time. Still others struggle with asking for information without giving some first.

The P.O.G.O. formula will allow you to get involved in a conversational interview process that will be comfortable for you AND the prospect. P.O.G.O. gives you a track to run on and specific direction on how to best meet the "comfort-level" needs of the prospect.

## PERSON

The *P* in the P.O.G.O. formula stands for PERSON. The parameter for you as the salesperson who is interested in gaining trust and finding out wants and needs is to get (and give) information regarding the *people* involved in the sales process.

When you enter the prospect's office to make the call in person, look for visual clues (pictures, trophies, office design) that will allow you to establish a "common ground." When you enter the prospect's office via the telephone, a sincere compliment can be effective. "The person who answers your phone was certainly pleasant" or something as basic as a sincere (as opposed to cursory) "Thank you for taking my call" will help get you off on the right foot.

ANYTHING that expresses a SINCERE interest in the prospect will be valuable to you. While you are designing a series of questions relating to the person, remember that it is O.K. to share some personal information about yourself, but YOU already know about you. Give just enough about yourself to express common interests but not enough to monopolize the conversation. If you must have a rule of thumb, limit personal revelations to 25 percent of this part of the conversation. In other words, three parts prospect to one part salesperson.

The true professional, who really cares about prospects and clients, also gathers information for follow-up visits and calls. Casually asking how the big game turned out or where the prospect and the spouse decided to have their anniversary dinner can go a long way toward letting others know that you really do care about them and will treat them as the very important people they truly are. The key words to remember in the process are *brief, warm, sincere,* and *friendly.*

## FEED YOUR EGO OR FEED YOUR FAMILY

The Zig Ziglar Corporation sells training programs to all types and sizes of organizations. In 1990, we consolidated our sales efforts in our eighty-person organization, moving from eight divisions to four teams. As our company had grown, so had our lack of focus. We were failing to "keep the main thing the main thing." We took a decisive step in focusing our efforts by appointing Bob Alexander as our general sales manager, making him responsible for ALL sales efforts.

**Key words to remember are *brief, warm, sincere,* and *friendly.***

Soon after his appointment, Bob related to me that he accompanied one of our salesmen on a call where a veteran salesman made a rookie mistake.

While talking to the client about the *P* in the P.O.G.O. formula, our salesman determined that he had enough information and didn't need to go through the other three areas of P.O.G.O.—mistake number one! Then he began to solve what he perceived to be the client's problem by telling him how many presentations he had made to car dealerships and direct sales businesses (mistake number two!), concluding with, "And I think you can see where this level of experience would allow me to come in and really help you to build teamwork within this organization." The client's response wasn't exactly overwhelming; in fact, it wasn't even "whelming."

"No," the FORMER prospect began, "I cannot see how working with direct sales organizations and car dealerships could be of any benefit in dealing with the people on my production line here in this factory!"

Although the concepts to be taught were definitely transferable, our salesperson had put the emphasis on himself and not on what the program would do for the client—mistake number three, and he was out!

Thumbnail sketches of your experiences that are pertinent to the client are perfectly permissible—as long as they amplify the client's point, relate to the client's needs and wants, and establish your own credibility (without establishing your ego).

## DEVELOPING PEOPLE QUESTIONS

Questions persuade more powerfully than any other form of verbal behavior, so you should develop a set of questions that you are comfortable with and that allow you to work in your personal comfort zone in showing your sincere interest in others. My friend Gerhard Gschwandtner, the publisher of *Personal Selling Power* magazine, has a wonderful workbook called *The Sales Question Book,* which contains hundreds of sample questions arranged in specific categories. Get a copy of Gerhard's manual (address in the Bibliography), and take the time to adapt these questions to meet your situation and make the questions your own.

Here are some samples of the three types of questions that will help you learn more about the person while showing your sincere interest.

OPEN DOOR QUESTIONS—PERSON

1. How did you get into this particular business?
2. What part of the country do you come from originally?
3. What are some of your hobbies?

CLOSED DOOR QUESTIONS—PERSON

1. How long have you been a (golfer, tennis enthusiast, hunter)?
2. Would you tell me about your family?

3. Other than working here, what type career experiences have you pursued?

YES OR NO QUESTIONS—PERSON

1. Do you like living in Dallas?
2. Do you get to spend enough time with your family?
3. Are you enjoying your free-time activities?

## YOUR LIST

Let me strongly encourage you to write out your list of questions. "Won't that make my questions stilted or canned sounding?" you might ask. Absolutely! Until you (*a*) remember that the greatest actors and actresses who ever lived used "canned" presentations, but they had "canned" them so magnificently that the presentations came out fresh, alive, and vibrant; (*b*) take the time to practice these questions with friends, family, and new acquaintances; (*c*) record them on your cassette recorder; (*d*) listen carefully, asking yourself, "Would I buy from this person?"; and (*e*) repeat the process until you OWN the questions. Now if this sounds unnecessary or like the work isn't worth the time, let me ask you a question. Are you committed to doing everything within your power to be the best that you can be (Yes or No Question—and I hope I know the answer)? Since the little things really do make the big difference, why not start right here?

## PLAYING "TOPPER"

A danger point in the "person" part of P.O.G.O. is playing "topper." You know the drill: The salesperson notices the picture of the teenager in the basketball uniform and says, "It looks like you have an athlete in your family. How was their season?" (Open Door Question). "Well," the response begins, "last season we only won three games, but this season we are undefeated and . . ." Before the prospect can complete the sentence, the nonselling, nonprofessional salesperson has interrupted and takes off on a tangent about the time he played on a championship team in the seventh grade. The vivid details and exact scores from those games have the SALESPERSON completely enthralled. Rarely does he notice the "glazed-over" look in the PROSPECT'S eyes until he is being ushered from the office.

It's fine to tell about your championship season—AFTER the prospect finishes his story—and then in a brief statement that relates to the prospect such as, "I bet you felt like my dad felt when we won our first championship"; or "Our son played on a championship team when he was fourteen, and I can relate to how you must feel."

If you always have a better story (a "topper"), then you are feeding your ego but not your family.

## THE POWER OF OBSERVATION

When our general sales manager, Bob Alexander, was in the fund-raising business, he had a powerful experience that demonstrated the importance of knowing the person with whom you are dealing.

While watching the late news one evening, he noticed that the county recreation department in his area needed to raise money for new athletic fields. As the announcer mentioned the recreation department director's name, the "wheels began to turn" in Bob's dream machine. Like all successful sales professionals, Bob understands that goals are simply dreams we are willing to take action upon, so he made a note of the director's name and went to bed.

The next morning, Bob's first telephone call of the day went to the Columbia County Recreation Department. The director was in town and agreed to meet with him later that same day.

## IMPORTANT ALUMNI

As Bob shook hands with the director, he noticed a very impressive college graduation ring. One of the reasons he noticed the ring was that he understood the importance of being alert to any "signals" that might give him a clue about the "person" portion of this interview. The other reason he noticed the ring was that it was from the same university from which Bob had graduated.

Almost immediately after the handshake, Bob verified the fact that they both had attended the same university, and the rapport was instant. There were many mutual friends and geographical memories. Formal barriers that exist in most situations when we meet someone for the first time came tumbling down. Their mutual interests in athletics and raising positive children allowed the relationship to mature rapidly.

The director told Bob that fund-raising people were "coming out of the woodwork," and the board of advisors was having a difficult time in reducing the number of salesmen to a manageable-sized group for presentations. He recommended they give the chairman of the advisory board a call since he was going to be extremely influential in the final decision. The gentleman came over to the director's office, and the three men went to lunch.

During this time, Bob again worked on the *P*eople portion of the P.O.G.O. formula by making an effort to learn as much as possible about the advisory board chairman. By the end of lunch, Bob was invited to make a presentation to the board.

Please notice that Bob had to make a sale to get the chance to make a sale. First, Bob had to sell the men on himself and his sincere interest in THEM and *then* in their PROJECT. Without that first sale, there was no presentation to the committee. Without the presentation to the committee, there was no opportunity for the sale. The two prospects made it very clear to Bob that he was making the presentation to the committee because of his sincere interest in them and their program.

## THE ACTUAL PRESENTATION

On the evening of the actual sales presentation, Bob was the fourth of five presenters. Each was given thirty minutes to present their case and told that no decisions would be made until the following week. At the end of his presentation, Bob felt like he had given it his best shot and waited with the others to see if there would be any follow-up questions.

After the fifth presentation, the chairman stepped into the waiting area and asked if Bob would come back into the room. Though Bob didn't know it at the time, the director dismissed the other salesmen because Bob was about to be awarded the contract.

That was significant because the contract was for one of the largest recreation departments in the Southeast. In addition, Bob worked the account for the next four years, which resulted in literally thousands of dollars for the recreation department and Bob's organization. The crowning touch was when they put Bob Alexander's name on a sign at the primary baseball field in thanks and appreciation for what he and his fund-raising organization had done for Columbia County. And all this happened because a salesman took time to get to know the people involved in the sales process.

## ORGANIZATION

The first *O* in the P.O.G.O. formula stands for ORGANIZATION. As the conversation about the person draws to a close, move to the organization. Again, probe gently, and be willing to talk about your organization in the places you have positive common ground or you can sincerely compliment the prospect. The same rule applies as in the "person" aspect of P.O.G.O.—25 percent about your organization to 75 percent about the prospect's.

Now before I oversell that point, let me emphasize I am NOT saying you cannot talk about your company. Some prospects are very anxious to know about you, and you must give them enough information to build confidence that your company is solid and reputable. However, do not monopolize the conversation. Your objective is to give them enough information to build that confidence . . . and to gather enough information to make you effective (i.e., make the sale).

## DEVELOPING ORGANIZATIONAL QUESTIONS

Here are some sample questions that might be adaptable for you.

OPEN DOOR QUESTIONS—ORGANIZATION

1. Would you tell me something about your organization?
2. What about your plans for the future?
3. What part of your operation creates the most excitement in the business community?

CLOSED DOOR QUESTIONS—ORGANIZATION

1. How is the ——— department performing?
2. How would you rate the performance of support personnel?
3. What kind of training is the leadership of your organization receiving?

YES OR NO QUESTIONS—ORGANIZATION

1. Are you satisfied with your bottom-line profits?
2. Is your organization growing at the rate you desire?
3. Do you want to be able to promote from within?

## FAMILY CEO

Some people's organization is the family. When this is the situation, the Organizational Questions will sound similar to the Person Questions. Questioning statements like, "Tell me about your children," function as Open Door Questions because they give the prospect plenty of room for response. "What type recreational activities or hobbies do you and your family enjoy?" is another example.

# GOALS

The *G* in the P.O.G.O. formula stands for GOALS. This is the time for gathering information about personal and professional goals such as, "What do you plan to accomplish in the next six months?" and "What goals do you have in place for the next year?" (both Open Door Questions).

I would never accuse a prospect of "fibbing," but I have known a few who would say what they perceived the salesman wanted to hear. One of the greatest dangers in the Need Analysis portion of the sales process is to allow the prospect to throw up a "smoke screen" regarding true goals. In all fairness to each of us, our human nature is such that when we are probed about our goals, our first tendency is to tell the questioners what we think they would like to hear or what we think they expect to hear (or that our goals are none of their business).

Many nonprofessionals are so pleased to get a response that they hurry along to the next part of the process. The true professional will continue to probe. A useful probing question you will want to ask is, "Why would achieving that goal be important to you?" Another way of asking the same Closed Door Question (confining to a specific goal) is, "What would achieving that goal mean to you?" AND you may have to ask this question several times.

## QUESTIONS FOR DISCOVERING GOALS

Following are some sample questions that you might adapt for your goal "innerview."

OPEN DOOR QUESTIONS—GOALS

1. What are your personal/organizational goals?
2. How did you determine these were top priority goals?
3. What were your goals last year?

CLOSED DOOR QUESTIONS—GOALS

1. Which goal is the most important to you next year?
2. How are you currently tracking the progress of your goals?
3. What is your time frame to achieve your goal?

YES OR NO QUESTIONS—GOALS

1. Did you reach last year's goals?
2. Have your goals been realistic in the past?
3. You are using an established goal-setting process, aren't you?

## MONEY, MONEY, MONEY

Many times a prospect's goals will involve money. I want to submit to you that money is never a goal! The real goal revolves around WHAT CAN BE DONE with the money.

When you ask a prospect about goals and you get a money response, and you follow with, "Why would that be important to you?" you are beginning to discover true goals. In addition, you are helping the prospect discover true goals. Many will have given their goals very little thought. While this portion of the selling process must not digress into a counseling session, your goal must be for the prospect to "get real" with you.

## UNACHIEVED GOALS

Why do so few people actually achieve their goals? Primarily because they have never really identified the true goals. Once again: The people who think their goal is money are wrong. Their goal relates to WHAT THEY CAN DO WITH THE MONEY! Whether it's to build a monument to themselves (a beautiful home) or build a wing onto an orphanage, it is most important that the real goal be identified. Many sales "blow up" on even experienced sales professionals because they sold to the "smoke screen" and did not probe for the real goals.

## "TRACKING DOWN" A PROSPECT'S GOALS

In the goal evaluation process, you must move from the generic to the specific, from the abstract to the concrete. The questions here are designed to allow you to "track down" the specific goals. These sample questions will help you discover goals in the areas of finance, travel, education, home, vacations, and intangible goals.

### FINANCIAL INDEPENDENCE

1. How much money will you need to earn on a monthly basis to become financially independent?
2. What level of savings would be necessary?
3. How would you spend your time if you were financially independent?
4. What type investments would you like to have?

### TRAVEL

1. If you could go anywhere and everywhere, where would you begin?
2. How much traveling have you done?
3. Why do you want to travel?

EDUCATION FOR CHILDREN

1. What type preparatory schools would you like for your child to attend?
2. How would you finance these schools?
3. What university would you direct your child toward?
4. What does this university cost to attend per semester?
5. Have you saved any money yet?
6. How many children would you send to college?
7. What level of income increase would be necessary for you to send all your children to college?

HOME

1. What would be the square footage of your ideal home?
2. What type of exterior finish?
3. How many bedrooms, bathrooms, and living areas?
4. Why type amenities would you like (pool, acreage, fireplaces, upstairs, game room, creek)?
5. What color drapes, walls, and carpets?

VACATION

1. Where would you like to go on vacation?
2. What is the ideal length of time for the perfect vacation?

INTANGIBLE

1. Why do you want this goal to be a reality?
2. When do you want this goal to become a reality?
3. What will it mean to you when this goal is a reality?

At the risk of being redundant, be sure to personalize these questions; and after each one, you will normally want to ask, "What would achieving that goal mean to you?" or "Why would achieving that goal be important to you?"

## THE DOCTOR PRACTICES HIS SELLING SKILLS

John Leddo earned his Ph.D. from Yale. John is an incredibly bright psychologist, whose company, Innovative Thinkers, has developed software based on some of our products. After attending our Born To Win Seminar in Dallas, Texas, John wrote me a letter explaining how seeking someone's goals had been a benefit to him in the sales process. Let's let him tell the story:

"By applying what you have taught me about sales, I was able to make an important sale that otherwise would have been lost. I recently submitted a proposal for a seminar on decision making to a local organization that promotes professional seminars. The president of that organization called me to tell me that they couldn't use my seminar. Now, before I started studying your teachings, my response would have been something like, 'Well, thanks for your time in reviewing my proposal. I hope we'll have another opportunity at some future date.' I would have let the sale slip away.

"However, I remembered you teach (in your *Secrets of Closing the Sale* book and audio tapes) that when a prospect says no, what he's really saying is that he's not ready to trade his big stack of money for my little stack of benefits. But I know that my course is a good one, so I figured my task was to find out why he didn't see the benefits. So I began asking him questions about what his GOALS were in terms of attendance and what he was trying to accomplish with the seminars he promoted. It turned out that his goals were rather modest, so I asked him why he thought my seminar wouldn't meet them. He told me that he thought my seminar wasn't tailored to the highly technical people he markets to. At this point, I realized that I had been MISREADING HIS GOALS. I figured that since most people shy away from highly technical and mathematical approaches to decision making, I would do well to downplay those portions of my course—even though these were the ones he was most interested in. I told him why I wrote the proposal the way I did and explained that the material really was highly technical in nature and that I could structure the course to emphasize the technical aspects.

"At this point, he said, 'Well, maybe you don't need to change the course at all. Let me look at the proposal again and call you tomorrow.' At this point I was happy but I remembered that you teach that sometimes when the prospect says, 'I'll call you tomorrow,' he sometimes spends the day talking himself out of the deal. I prepared myself for this. When I CALLED HIM BACK I asked him, 'So do you think we need to modify the course or will we go with it as it is?' which is your 'alternate of choice' close. (Before I studied your material, I would have asked, 'Have you decided whether or not you want to go with the course?') The president replied that he'd leave the decision up to me. We began discussing the terms of our arrangement and the sale was closed.

"Thank you for helping me make this important sale. This is a case where your teachings literally made the difference between making and missing a sale."

John not only helped his prospect by probing for his true goals, but he identified the next *O* in the P.O.G.O. formula.

## OBSTACLES

The second *O* in the P.O.G.O. formula stands for OBSTACLES to reaching the goals just discussed. As Dr. Norman Vincent Peale says, "If you want to meet someone who has no problems, no obstacles in life, just go down to the cemetery . . . and come to think about it, some of them have a tremendous problem."

Everyone with whom we come in contact has problems. I once heard a man state, "You go up to anyone on the street and say, 'I heard about your problem,' and the person will ask, 'Who told you?' " The key doesn't lie in not having problems (once again, we all have problems); the key lies in finding solutions to those problems.

Jim Norman, the CEO of The Zig Ziglar Corporation (ZZC), made a sales call with one of our reps, and the prospect was adamant about not being able to use our services. As the two ZZC representatives neared the end of their allotted time, Jim asked, "As CEO of Zig's company, I know that we face our share of obstacles. Would you be willing to share some of the problems your organization faces?" Forty-five minutes later, they walked out with the sale.

### ZIG WHO?

People don't want to hear Zig Ziglar speak or read Zig Ziglar books. People want to hear that there is hope in their future and read that no matter how bad "things" have been, they still have a chance. People want "how to's" that are practical and applicable in their lives. People are seeking information, inspiration, and direction in their lives. People come to me because they believe that I may offer a solution to their problems . . . that I may help them overcome the obstacles. People will buy from you for the same reason.

## QUESTIONS FOR DISCOVERING OBSTACLES

Let's take some time to find the appropriate questions that will allow us to discover what obstacles stand between the prospect and professional and personal goals.

### OPEN DOOR QUESTIONS—OBSTACLES

1. What is preventing you from being where you want to be?
2. What are the obstacles you are facing?
3. What challenges must be met before you can achieve what you have worked so hard to achieve?

### CLOSED DOOR QUESTIONS—OBSTACLES

1. What are you doing to overcome ——— (a specific obstacle)?
2. Why haven't you achieved your goals?
3. Which obstacle is the most crucial to overcome?

### YES OR NO QUESTIONS—OBSTACLES

1. Are you making the progress necessary to overcome the obstacles you face?
2. Do you feel there are other steps you might take in overcoming obstacles?
3. Are you interested in overcoming the obstacles that seem to be holding you back?

## PREPARATION

It is impossible to be "too prepared" for a sales presentation. Preparation is vital to success. Think about it. Do you want to buy from the fumbling, bumbling, inept salesperson? Do you want to buy from the person who doesn't have a clue about you or your business? What do disorganized actions say about the company represented?

If you know precisely what you are doing, and you meet the distractions that will inevitably occur in some sales presentations, you CAN cope! When you are thoroughly prepared, the left brain (the carefully directed, organized, logical, and concretely sequential lobe of the brain) is already functioning at maximum capacity. This allows your right brain (the creative, freewheeling, visual lobe of the brain) to handle the interruption or distraction in the most effective manner possible.

The Rhodes scholar started out by learning to read and write. The great pianist Paderewski had to be taught the musical scale. When you learned to drive a car with a standard transmission, you struggled with the combination of movements required in manipulating the brake, clutch, gas, and gear shift at the proper time in the proper way. Early in your sales career, you may need to "struggle" through some of these tough learning processes. Preparation helps enormously.

## HOW MUCH TIME?

An integral part of preparation is time allocation. When you are involved in the P.O.G.O. process, you should have a solid feel for how much time you will be allowed to spend with the prospect. Once you commit to a length of time, be sure to exceed that time ONLY AT THE REQUEST OF THE PROSPECT.

I read about one salesman who has a special technique to make this important point. Before beginning the presentation, he takes off his watch and hands it to the prospect. Since he wears a Rolex valued at over $12,000, this is a significant move on his part. Next he says, "If I'm here longer than thirty minutes (the length of time it takes him to move from Need Analysis through Need Awareness and get into Need Solution) without your specifically asking me to stay, the watch is yours!" Yes, he does have a backup watch to keep from losing time.

However, he has much more at stake than a Rolex watch. A professional salesperson's most valuable asset is REPUTATION. When you deal with your clients and customers with integrity, your chances of making the sale are greatly enhanced.

## GET TO THE POINT!

Some prospects are incredibly impatient, and even as early as Need Analysis, they show their impatience. They are driven and impetuous and want "just the facts" without any "window dressing" along the way. When the prospect demands to know "what it will do for me and how much it will cost," you need to move immediately into benefit selling. Emphasize your most dramatic point—the reason the largest number of people buy your product or service—by asking a question: "Mr. Prospect, is ——— of any interest to you at all?" Insert "saving time, making more money, playing golf more often, traveling," or whatever your product's number one benefit may be. When you get an affirmative answer (and you will more often than not), simply say, "Then let me get right to the point . . . ," and continue your PLANNED PROFESSIONAL PRESENTATION.

**A professional salesperson's most valuable asset is REPUTATION.**

There is no need for you to get off track or panic or begin closing immediately. The prospect has sent you a definite signal: Get to the point. So get to the point in the manner that is best for the prospect. Stay with your plan and do an *abbreviated* version of each step. Each step is important or you would not have planned it, so stay with your plan. Just "move along."

## CONSISTENT INTERRUPTIONS

If the prospect continues to interrupt, stop and say, "Mr. Prospect, I really want to serve you in the best manner possible. Would it be better if we rescheduled this meeting for another time?" If the prospect says yes, set an appointment and leave immediately. As soon as possible, meet with your sales manager to evaluate the call. Some people must get to the bottom line more quickly than others, and some salespeople labor the presentation. Let your sales manager help you determine the cause in this situation.

## THE OTHER SIDE OF THE COIN

Obviously (at least I hope it's obvious), don't be like the salesperson who makes his presentation and after only five minutes is interrupted. The prospect says, "O.K., I'm sold. I'll take it," and the salesman says, "Oh, no, just a minute, I'm only halfway through my sales talk! When I finish, then I'll write the order."

## PERSONALITY "PLUS"

Much has been written about selling to personality types. I believe there is some valid information on the market, but let me caution you to be very careful when you "diagnose" the prospect. Psychologists who have spent years perfecting their skills cannot do what some salespeople are attempting to do.

Our company uses two basic personality analysis tools in seminars and in internal hiring and placement. These tools are the Activity Vector Analysis from Walter Clarke and Associates and the Personality Profile from Carlson Companies (addresses are in the Bibliography). We have spent an enormous amount of time and money in the past ten years studying this specialized area. Based on our experience, I would like to recommend that you consider the following information to help you make the prospect comfortable.

### CONSIDER ONLY FOUR AREAS

As you meet the prospect, be alert to clues and physical evidence that will give you insight. Listen with your eyes and ears, and be prepared to adjust your thinking if you are not getting the proper response. Concentrate on four basic personality styles, and look for the broad "brush strokes" rather than get caught up in "paralysis of analysis." Remember, at least some of the time, the prospect is trying

NOT to show the true personality, so don't get too enamored with these "hints."

## Bottom-Line Bob and Betty

You've called on Bob and Betty before. They have a very strong personality style that says, "Let's get on with it!" You deal with them first because they are impatient. The words that best "paint the picture" of Bob and Betty are *bold, confident, competitive,* and *direct.* They are RESULTS-ORIENTED people.

## Friendly Phil and Felicia

You will remember Phil and Felicia because they are some of the nicest folks you will ever call on. They think every meeting is a party, and if it isn't, it should be! Words that describe them are *friendly, outgoing, emotional,* and *social.* They are PEOPLE-ORIENTED people.

## Sincere Sam and Sarah

This duo will make you feel good about you! Sam and Sarah are stabilizing forces within every group they join. Words that describe them are *steady, loyal, good listeners,* and *cooperative.* They are TEAM-ORIENTED people.

## Competent Carl and Carol

Carl and Carol are perfectionists by nature. They want the job done right! Words that describe them are *cautious, analytical, by-the-book,* and *detailed.* They are QUALITY-ORIENTED people.

## DANGER—BEWARE

Please let me emphasize that you probably know someone by one of these names who doesn't fit the description. The names are for classification and differentiation.

If we were going to give specific examples of the styles by looking at the public persona, we would say that the BOLD category (results oriented) would be represented by people like Lee Iacocca ("If you can find a better car, buy it!") and Barbara Walters, the first female journalist to earn over $1,000,000 per year. These people have a reputation for bold, results oriented actions.

The names that come to mind for the FRIENDLY style (people oriented) are Bob Hope, who never meets a stranger, and Oprah Winfrey, who is always kind and cordial—even to the rudest of guests.

Examples of the SINCERE style (team oriented) might be Tonto, the Lone Ranger's faithful companion, and for the younger generation, Big Bird of Sesame Street fame. Both are highly loyal and stabilizing forces in life.

The COMPETENT style (quality oriented) might be seen in Mr. Spock if you are a Star Trek fan (I am not); the great coach of the Dallas Cowboys, Tom Landry, who was calm, cool, and collected; and Jane Pauley of "Today" show fame, who failed to get involved in all the hype and hoopla surrounding her leaving that show.

## WHAT'S IN A NAME?

From this point forward, let's divide our analysis into these four categories: (1) Bold; (2) Friendly; (3) Sincere; and (4) Competent. Please don't miss this point: Each person has SOME of all four qualities. The best sales presentation is Bold, Friendly, Sincere, and Competent. The purpose of sharing personality analysis information is to allow you to sell to THE STRONGEST ORIENTATION of the prospect.

## SELF-ANALYSIS

Before you can begin to look at the personality of the prospect, you need to take a look at YOU! Which of the following series of words BEST describes you?

1. **BOLD**
   Pioneer
   Initiator
   Outspoken
   Short fuse
   Likes measurement

2. **FRIENDLY**
   Extrovert
   Trusting
   Enthusiastic
   Persuasive
   Likes attention

Self-sufficient
Strong ego
Seeks responsibility

Good first impression
Articulate
Seeks variety

3. **SINCERE**
Systematic
Methodical
Service oriented
Long fuse
Compromiser
Consistent
Stable
Problem solver

4. **COMPETENT**
Neat
Humble
Sensitive
Apprehensive
Likes structure
Looks for backing
Suspicious
Reserved

As you can see, there is no right or wrong, good or bad. Most of us would like to have qualities from each list.

Once you have determined which of the lists BEST DESCRIBES YOU, check the Understanding Personality Differences chart.

## UNDERSTANDING PERSONALITY DIFFERENCES

| STYLE | STRENGTHS | WEAKNESSES | NEEDS |
|---|---|---|---|
| **Bold** | Problem solving<br>Decision making<br>Goal achieving | Finds fault<br>Lacks caution<br>Overruns people | Control<br>Authority<br>Prestige |
| **Friendly** | Communicating<br>Participating<br>Good-finding | Time control<br>Follow-through<br>Lack of objectivity | Recognition<br>Acceptance<br>To talk |
| **Sincere** | Loyalty<br>Listening<br>Patience | Overly possessive<br>Avoids risk taking<br>Avoids conflict | Appreciation<br>Security<br>Time |
| **Competent** | Analyzing<br>Accuracy<br>High standards | Rigid<br>Procrastinates<br>Overly critical | Precision Work<br>Time<br>Facts |

Remember: Our weaknesses are often extensions of our strengths.

## RECOGNIZING AND SELLING TO THE DIFFERENT STYLES

Following are some typical questions and statements that will make recognition of each style easier. Directly below are four "hints" or "tips" that will help you as you work with people who show strong personality characteristics.

The BOLD prospect will ask or say:
"I want it now or not at all!"
"How much?"
"When can I get it?"
"Have you ever sold anything before?"

Selling "secrets" for the BOLD prospect:
(1) be direct; (2) be concise—get to the point; (3) answer "WHAT," not "HOW"; and (4) be conscious of the "bottom line."

The FRIENDLY prospect will ask or say:
"What will my neighbors think?"
"Sorry I'm late. I was tied up at a long luncheon."
"Let's have some coffee and talk this over."
"Did you see the game last night?"

Selling "secrets" for the FRIENDLY prospect:
(1) spare the details; (2) socialize; (3) follow up; and (4) show "new" products.

The SINCERE prospect will ask or say:
"Why did you change the product?"
"Can I think about this and get back to you?"
"How can I be sure I am making the right decision?"
"I have a current supplier for your product."

Selling "secrets" for the SINCERE prospect:
(1) earn trust; (2) go slow and easy; (3) answer all questions; and (4) reassure.

The COMPETENT prospect will ask or say:
"Tell me about the warranty. Is it in writing?"
"Do you have any literature you can leave with me?"
"Will you be able to deliver on time?"
"We must follow company purchasing procedures."

Selling "secrets" for the COMPETENT prospect:
(1) show proof and share testimonials; (2) be prepared and structured in your presentation; (3) answer "HOW"; and (4) address any disadvantages early in the presentation.

## SELLING STYLE TO STYLE

The Selling Style to Style chart will give you some specific ways and means to deal with the prospect taking your style AND the prospect's style into consideration.

### SELLING STYLE TO STYLE

| | | | |
|---|---|---|---|
| ***Bold*** **selling to:** | Bold | = | Be yourself |
| | Friendly | = | Be prepared to socialize |
| | Sincere | = | Slow down; share information; don't push |
| | Competent | = | Provide proof/facts |
| ***Friendly*** **selling to:** | Bold | = | Be businesslike; don't initiate small talk |
| | Friendly | = | Remember to ask for the order |
| | Sincere | = | Earn trust; don't become overly friendly |
| | Competent | = | Stick to proof and facts |
| ***Sincere*** **selling to:** | Bold | = | Show confidence |
| | Friendly | = | Provide social time |
| | Sincere | = | Reassure |
| | Competent | = | Use evidence; answer all questions |
| ***Competent*** **selling to:** | Bold | = | Concentrate on "WHAT," not "HOW" |
| | Friendly | = | Hit high points |
| | Sincere | = | Give time to digest information |
| | Competent | = | Remember to take action |

## MOVING INTO NEED AWARENESS

And now is the moment of truth. Now that you know the Person, the Organization, the Goals, and the Obstacles to those goals, what do you do? You begin the next step in the sales process—Need Awareness.

CHAPTER EIGHT

# MAKING THE LIGHTS GO ON

## *Need Awareness for the Sales Pro AND the Sales Prospect*

Tony Ferguson is a successful salesman for a large department store in South Carolina. When a major tire manufacturer offered a free set of tires to the salesperson in his company who sold the most tires in a thirty-day promotional period, Tony set his sights on winning the prize.

To increase sales in an abbreviated period of time, he went to a print shop before the promotion started and had the following message printed on small cards:

> Hello,
>
> My name is Tony Ferguson. While passing your car, I noticed that some of your tires are dangerously worn. I represent a famous tire manufacturer, and we have quality tires on sale *right now*! If you will call me, I will be happy to quote you a price on the size and type you need. My phone number is 555-2971 and you can call me from 8:00 A.M. to 5:30 P.M., Monday through Saturday. Thank you.

Tony carried a supply of the printed cards in his coat pocket. Whenever he walked down the street, he kept his eyes open for cars with worn tires, and he put a card under the windshield wiper of each one he spotted. By the end of the promotion, Tony had sold twice as many tires as any other salesperson in the company.

## REMOVING BLIND SPOTS WITHOUT PAIN, RISK, OR INJURY

Bob Alexander made a sales call with the intention of selling The Zig Ziglar Corporation's Business Development Course. The president of the organization he was calling on was convinced that his salespeople were not closing sales properly, and they had an immediate need (as most companies do) for sales to be closed and cash flow to be increased. In a Need Analysis meeting with the president, the sales manager, and the comptroller, Bob was going through all the things we have learned to this point in the book.

"I'm not convinced our salespeople have a clue about what to do in the sales process," the president began, "and I know for a fact that they are not asking for the order because sales are 'in the dumper.' In other words, we ain't selling nothing!" The sales manager dropped his eyes to the floor and began studying his shoelaces. Red flag #1.

The comptroller, sensing the sales manager's discomfort, said, "Yes, but last year at this time sales were slow and statistical trends indicate . . ." He was cut off by the company's president. "We're not talking about last year! And if sales don't improve, we won't be talking about having a next year!" Red flag #2.

Bob entered the Need Awareness segment of the sales process by continuing to probe regarding the lack of sales training and closing skills the sales staff was demonstrating. He was at a crucial point in the sales presentation because his diagnosis during Need Analysis determined that one of two products was the solution for his client's needs. Secrets of Successful Selling answered the sales skills questions the president was raising. See You at the Top answered the concerns that Bob was seeing as he watched the interview unfold.

## TWO DISTINCT LIGHT BULBS TO ACTIVATE

After we complete phase one of the sales process, Need Analysis, we move into phase two, Need Awareness. There are two distinct parts to the Need Awareness segment of the process. First, the light must go on in the salesperson's head. Bob knew that the president's abrupt and insensitive attitude was at least a portion of the problem. However, the president was convinced that the fault was with sales training and closing skills. Bob probably wouldn't have been making the presentation had the company president suspected the real problem. You see, even if you have a thorough understanding of the company's problem (your light is on), UNLESS THE PROSPECT SEES, UNDERSTANDS, AND BELIEVES THERE IS A PROBLEM, THERE IS NO PROBLEM and thus no need for your solution. The light must go on for the prospect. Need Awareness applies to the salesperson AND the sales prospect.

As we analyze Bob's situation, look carefully to see if the principles he uses would work for you. I believe they will, regardless of your product or service.

## THE SPEAKER IS A CATALOG

One of the ways our company demonstrates our capacity to help an organization with training needs is with speaking engagements. Fortunately for the company Bob Alexander was working with, Bob had been invited to do a two-hour presentation. During the beginning of his presentation, he promised to talk about sales skills and particularly closing skills. He quoted a very wise sales trainer (who shall remain humbly anonymous) as having said, "The sales professional knows it is impossible to close all the sales. He or she only wants to close the next one—which is kind of like the farmer who didn't want all the land, he just wanted the land next to his." At this point, the president of the organization brightened considerably as Bob attacked his "signaled" needs.

As Bob got into the body of his presentation, he talked about the importance of "people" skills, referencing the fact that 85 percent of our success is dependent on our people skills and attitude—regardless of profession. He quoted the following story from my book *Top Performance:*

> Andrew Carnegie said, "No man can become rich without himself enriching others." He went on to live this philosophy, as evidenced by the 43 millionaires he had working for him. A reporter interviewing Mr. Carnegie asked how he was able to hire that many millionaires.

Mr. Carnegie patiently explained that the men were not millionaires when they came to work for him, but had become millionaires BY working for him. When the reporter pursued the line of questioning as to how he was able to develop these men to the point they were worth that much money, Mr. Carnegie said, "You develop people in the same way you mine for gold. . . . When you mine for gold, you must literally move tons of dirt to find a single ounce of gold. However, you don't look for the dirt—you look for the gold!"

## THE EYES HAVE IT

When Bob shared the importance of looking for the good in others, he noticed some eyes being cut toward the president. It didn't take a psychologist to discern that "good-finding" was not a basic principle upon which the company was being built. As he continued, Bob noticed the president of the organization was obviously in deep thought. Bob thought that he might be losing the prospect because he hadn't yet begun addressing the "closing skills" part of the presentation. Pressing forward, Bob continued sharing how he had personally seen companies dramatically affect bottom-line profits and productivity as well as reduce absenteeism and improve morale by adapting and adopting the positive principle of looking for the good in people and situations.

The president got the point. And Bob got the sale—for both programs! Please understand, he did not create a need. Instead he identified the *true need* (a more positive, encouraging, "good-finder's" environment) without getting caught up in the *symptom of the need* (closing sales). Was the symptom important? Obviously! Would the sale have "stuck" had Bob addressed only the symptom? Possibly. Would the product have worked completely and successfully? Probably not!

## PROBLEM DENIAL

So how does this apply to you and your situation? (Good Open Door Question—see, you're learning already!) Even when you are sure you have discovered the client's need, you must continue to probe for two basic reasons: (1) to be sure you have the true need and not a symptom of the need; and (2) to be sure the prospect understands that there really is a need.

Fact: Ninety percent of the people who have problems (including everything from alcoholism to "stinkin' thinkin'") deny those problems. Since companies, especially small ones that do not have an active, competent board of directors, are often run or dominated by one person, they often deny problems even when they are told and shown the specifics. However, when a skilled sales professional probes with the right questions, the same person who was denying the problem is permitted to "discover" the problem. Since he discovered it, he will be far more open to discovering solutions—your goods or services (which he has also discovered).

## HOMEOSTATIC BALANCE

Bryan Flanagan introduced me to the term *homeostatic balance* several years ago. The natural law of homeostasis says that an organism stays in perfect balance until acted upon by an outside force. The outside force causes the status quo to be disrupted, and the organism becomes out of balance. We rarely take ACTION until we are out of balance. Once we are out of balance, we will take the proper steps to correct or right our balance.

Now, homeostatic balance may sound "highfalutin" to some of you. I know it did to me the first time I heard the term. However, a willingness to grow and learn is the sign of a true professional—and if you and I are going to be successful in the nineties, we need to be willing to learn and grow! Homeostatic balance is helping the prospect understand there is a need (turning on the light for the prospect). And by showing where the prospect is out of balance, the sales professional upsets the homeostatic balance.

## I'LL NEVER FORGET OLD WHAT'S HIS NAME

Something as simple as seeing a person across a crowded room and not being able to remember the name can upset your balance. Remember how good you felt when you finally recalled that lost piece of information? Human beings do not make changes while in balance. From stopping destructive habits (smoking, drinking, overeating) to increasing good habits (making new friends, attending social functions, improving job skills, or joining a church), we don't make changes unless we can see we are out of balance.

I am NOT advocating that you knock the prospect off balance. You must discover where there is an imbalance and point it out in a convincing manner. In essence, this makes your prospect uncomfortable or unhappy with his condition or situation, which means you are now in position to make a sale because your prospect wants to solve his problem.

## UNBALANCED PROSPECTS

What happens when prospects become unbalanced? A good Closed Door Question! (Remember, a Closed Door Question keeps the answer in a certain area and is built upon a previous question.) There are three things that can happen when customers discover their area of imbalance. In the first place, the professional salesperson (who has helped point out the lack of balance) places the product or service in the hands of the prospects, makes the sales, and now has to worry about how to spend the commissions. Will problems never cease? (That is a fair but slightly facetious Yes or No Question.)

In the second place, the prospects discover their imbalance, and if the salesperson doesn't ask for the order, over a period of time the prospects regain balance and forget they were ever uncomfortable. This is disastrous because the prospects are not doing very well and neither is the salesperson.

In the third place, when prospects discover they are out of balance and the salesperson doesn't ask for the order, many times the competition comes in and asks for the order, rights the prospects, and makes the sales. Then everyone is happy—but you!

## BRYAN'S SONG

My buddy Bryan Flanagan told me how this happened to him when he was selling for IBM in Baton Rouge, Louisiana.

"Zig, I was a good sales rep for 'Big Blue' with the exception of dictation equipment. For some reason, I had a mental block against the stuff. I could make a call on a lawyer and prove beyond any shadow of a doubt that using my equipment was much better than writing longhand. I would teach him to use the equipment, have him read a paragraph, and show him he could read it six times faster than he could write it out. We would call in his secretary and show him he could talk into the dictation equipment three times faster than she could take shorthand. But for some 'rookie reason,' I could not (or would not) ask for the order. I would show the person that the equipment was better than what he was currently doing (upset the balance) and then drive away.

"I had a competitor in town named Jimmy. As I would pull out of a parking space, Jimmy would pull in. He walked into the office, asked for the order, and left happily. When I would return for my follow-up call a few days later, my competitor's equipment would be on the desk. Jimmy came in, righted the prospect's balance, and made the commission.

"When I changed territories two years later, Jimmy gave me a going away party. I financed it! Never have I seen a man more depressed about losing a competitor!" And Bryan was only half kidding.

## FOCUS

As we work to help the prospect understand that there is a better, more efficient, or more effective way to operate, we begin to focus on Closed Door Questions. We have used primarily (but not exclusively) Open Door Questions in Need Analysis. As we move into Need Awareness, we will use primarily (but not exclusively) Closed Door Questions. You will remember that Closed Door Questions cause the prospect to stay in a specific area and allow us to gather more information about that area. They usually build upon information gathered in an Open Door Question.

"How important would ________ be to you?" (insert the BENEFIT about which you need additional information). Benefits such as earning more money, saving time, working fewer hours, spending less on support services, cooking healthy foods, reaching more people, going on that ski trip, and living in a new home fit nicely on the blank line.

"What do you mean by ________?" (insert items about which you need additional clarification or definition). Items like net profit, G & A account, profit margin, downsizing, return on investment, and due process are terms/phrases that may have more than one interpretation. Be extremely careful when you hear an item/term/phrase that may have more than one meaning. The natural tendency is to accept it for what it means to you—which may *not* be pertinent to your prospect.

## TRAINING FOR NEED AWARENESS

If you are going to help the prospect become aware of specific needs, five areas of knowledge will benefit you. Since I cannot address every product or service, these areas are somewhat generic, but they make ideal starting points for you to work on in developing your goals.

## 1. PRODUCT KNOWLEDGE

You can never know too much about your product. Get information on the history, how it is made or manufactured, and how it does what it does and why.

Enthusiasm for the product or service comes from product knowledge. How can we develop enthusiasm for something about which we have little or no knowledge?

Confidence in our sales presentation is dramatically affected by product knowledge. Regardless of how good we feel about ourselves, if we don't thoroughly understand our product, we will face great difficulty in generating confidence.

### PROPER PRODUCT PERCEPTION

The more we know about our product, the more we believe in our product. Rick Robinson, a senior sales manager for a custom clothier in Hickory, North Carolina, proved this point vividly.

Rick did everything right in the sales process. He called on his local Cadillac dealer and discovered the needs and wants of his prospect (Need Analysis). He probed with questions until both he and the prospect were aware of the needs and wants (Need Awareness). Rick showed how his custom clothes would solve the concerns his prospect had expressed (Need Solution), and he asked for the order (Need Satisfaction).

At the point of purchase, however, the prospect balked, saying he had never paid that much for clothing. Since there were two sport coats that Rick knew the prospect was fond of, he was not surprised at the next question. "If I take both, how much can I have them for?"

Rick's company does not discount its fine line of clothing, and he carefully explained this policy to his prospect. Being a fellow salesman and an automobile dealer, the prospect went on to ask, "If you were buying a Cadillac from me, would you ask for a better price than my original quote?" Rick shocked the man by replying that he would not, to which his prospect responded, "Then you would be the first!"

At this point in the sales process, Rick lowered his voice and, with the complete sincerity that product knowledge that led to product belief had given him, said, "If you and your dealership were referred to me by a mutual friend and I came in, I would hope that you would give me the best price possible for the quality and type car I was interested in. Therefore, we are the same. You came to me from a very good client, and I am giving you the best value for the money you want to invest in clothing."

The prospect bought both sport coats and several other items. He bought because Rick believed fervently in what he was selling and the value of his products. This allowed him to overcome the objections with a genuine conviction that what he was doing was right! That conviction, reinforced with the *right* words and the proper voice inflection, combined with genuine concern for the customer, will help any and all salespeople become powerfully persuasive.

The question I have to ask is, Do you know enough about your product, and do you have the conviction, sales knowledge, integrity, and courage to do what Rick did? A "yes" answer assures you of a long, happy, and successful sales career.

## 2. INDUSTRY KNOWLEDGE

The more you know about your industry in general, the more you are able to understand the all-important "why." Your prospects have varying levels of knowledge about what you do and why you do it. The more you understand about the industry you have chosen to invest your career-life in, the more effective you may become.

Again, go back to the history of your industry. Understand how the group of products or services evolved to their current level. Then go beyond history to industry analysis. Where is your industry going over the next five to ten years? What are the future trends that would help you help more people?

### CUSTOMERS AND PUBLICATIONS

Every industry has several trade publications filled with feature articles, trend analysis charts, the latest information on legal matters, ideas on advertising, and news about people in the industry. Your effectiveness in your next sales call might well depend on your understanding of your industry.

Basic industry knowledge and in-depth customer profiles will set you apart from the vast majority of people in the sales profession. Becoming a student of your customers and letting them know in an unobtrusive way that you have gone to the trouble of learning about the persons and the businesses will be a breath of fresh air to your clients. A strong awareness of what is happening in your industry can go a long way toward establishing trust between you and your prospects.

One veteran sales manager in the publishing industry reports that over several years of dealing with a large national headquarters account, by investigating thoroughly and reading everything available, he was able to discover multiple departments and influence centers that required several days of work each sales cycle. His research allowed him to call on many clients in the same organization and same location, which obviously cut down on travel time and costs. The competition, calling on the same account, spends a half-day with one customer in one department.

Our veteran sales manager helps his client more efficiently and effectively, and he offers a great time savings by being a "one-stop shop." He also generates more than five times the sales revenues of the competition.

## 3. PRICING KNOWLEDGE

Why does your product or service require the investment that you are asking from a prospect? How can you justify asking that amount of money for that number of benefits? What are your profit margins? Do you understand the difference between cost and price?

Your pricing knowledge might be called "in-depth" product knowledge. When you understand pricing, you understand how you are helping yourself, your organization, and your prospect.

Pricing knowledge includes many different areas: maximizing profits in difficult markets, proper pricing for the market, adapting pricing strategy to the changing economy, and negotiating prices. However, most of us in sales will not deal with these areas. We need to focus on showing the prospects how and why the price of our product or service is fair to them.

### THE DETERMINING FACTOR

In today's selling climate, there are many salespeople who honestly but, I hasten to add, erroneously believe that price is the determining factor in most sales. I'm convinced that in most sales the exact opposite is true.

Bill Callaway, from Farmington, Missouri, shares my belief. Bill is a salesman for an office supply company in Flat River, Missouri, that sells typewriters, word processors, and personal computers. He called on a nursing home and was told that the owners would have to discuss his proposal. In other words, they wanted to "think about it." Despite his best efforts, he could not close the sale because they really did need time to discuss his proposal and think it through. A week later, he got the bad news that the nursing home owners had checked out a similar computer system in St. Louis, which was made by the same manufacturer and was $1,600 cheaper, so they were quite naturally interested in the less expensive model.

Bill decided he was not going to take "no" for an answer but would help them get what *they* really WANTED and NEEDED.

Bill used the following approach: "Considering your needs now and in the future, how long do you feel would be a reasonable life span for the computer you choose?" The buyer responded, "At least ten years."

"The difference," Bill continued, "between the computer I offer and the one you looked at in St. Louis is approximately $1,600.00. So let's look at what the difference means over the ten years you agreed would be an acceptable life span. Actually, that's only $160.00 a year, or about $13.00 a month, which is roughly $0.43 a day." Then Bill asked the big question: "Would it be worth an extra $0.43 per day to do business with a company that you have repeatedly agreed would offer you the proper training and service that are so important to you?"

"Yes, it would!" was the response, and Bill was ecstatic!

## BILL DIDN'T SPILL HIS POPCORN

Some folks go to the movies and spill all their popcorn in the lobby and don't get to enjoy it with their movie. Some salesfolks spill all their information in the initial stages of the presentation and don't have anything to enjoy when the time comes to ask for the order.

Bill had some additional points to use if necessary. Since the fear of loss is often greater than the desire for gain, Bill might have asked, "Is $0.43 a reasonable price to pay for peace of mind?" or "Have you ever calculated what it would cost you to be without this computer if proper service were not available for even one day, much less a week or longer?" The fear of not having the machine, which is a real fear, would be of paramount concern to the customer. In this case, the manufacturer was the same, and the physical equipment was almost the same. The BIG difference was the salesperson and the service he could offer.

Major Point: Never, never, never forget that price involves a great deal more than money!

## PRICE VS. COST

Sales training doesn't cost; it pays. And this is the thought I want to challenge you to consider: Does it really cost the prospect to buy from you, or does it pay the prospect to buy from and deal with you? Your answer to that question will help you to understand if you really know what pricing knowledge is all about—and the proper answer will go a long way toward helping you be even more successful (than you might imagine at this moment) in your chosen profession.

# 4. APPLICATION KNOWLEDGE

The use or application of your product will help you enormously in showing the prospect the need for your product. Implementation is vital to usage, and usage is vital to your "word-of-mouth" marketing that can aid you tremendously.

**Never, never, never forget that price involves a great deal more than money!**

If you understand how your product, goods, or services can be used, AND you can help others understand the process, you will help more people and make more sales.

## FAMILIARITY CAN BE DANGEROUS

Be careful! Many times our familiarity with our product or service breeds contempt regarding usage. We understand it thoroughly, so everyone else must understand, also. Once I was selling a machine that I had demonstrated for several hundred hours—and at the risk of seeming immodest, I was very good. Actually, this is more indicative of the ability each of us has when talent and attention are focused, but my point is this: When prospects would ask me if they could use the machine "that well," I would have to say, "No, absolutely not—unless you use it eight hours per day. Now you will be able to use it . . . ," and I would go on to demonstrate the benefits.

Be sure you understand all the ramifications of your product or service.

## 5. COMPETITION KNOWLEDGE

When you fail to make the sale, do you know why? You may well be your own worst enemy. In this case, lack of training is your competition. In most cases, however, you are up against an "outside" competitor.

Do you know with whom you compete? Do you know why you are beating them? Do you know why you lose sales to them? Can you demonstrate a knowledge of your competition without being critical?

Your knowledge of your competitors will help you in many ways when you are showing the prospects how you can meet their needs.

## DISCOVERING AREAS OF IMBALANCE

How do you discover the areas of imbalance? Again, questions are the answer. However, by this time in the presentation, you have gotten to know the prospect on Personal, Organizational, and Goal bases and have learned about Obstacles (P.O.G.O.). This information gives you the right to ask the tough questions. Taken out of context, these questions seem challenging, but by this point you must have earned the right to ask tough questions that are IN THE PROSPECT'S BEST INTERESTS. Once again, you are not creating the imbalance. You are helping the prospect see, understand, and believe there is an imbalance.

Consider a slightly facetious question like, "Mr. Prospect, what do you like best about losing money?" (I encourage you to smile when you ask this one.) "Just give me the top three things" will certainly get his attention. The reply will normally assure you that there is nothing he likes about losing money. You are then free to ask, "Are you willing to take action so that you can stop losing money?"

Please understand, these are "toughies" and don't work for every personality style, but remember you have earned the right to ask the hard questions. And if you truly have the prospect's best interests at heart, you may ask a question that the person NEEDS to hear instead of WANTS to hear.

When you use poor judgment in pointing out an imbalance, or your tone of voice is inappropriate, you will know it immediately because the person will hang up on you or throw you out on your ear. Be sure you have earned the right to ask a question that points out the prospect's imbalance.

## PEOPLE DON'T CARE

You have probably heard the statement: "People don't care how much you know until they know how much you care—about them." To be supersuccessful in helping others discover and cure their imbalance, we must constantly keep prospects' best interests in mind.

Lonnie Amirault of Halifax, Nova Scotia, sells encyclopedias. One evening while making calls, he was suffering from a very serious head cold. The prospects had two boys, ages eleven and seven, who had no educational material to help with their schooling. Lonnie had a deep conviction that his product was an absolute must in their home. During a part of his demonstration, the boys looked at the various pages, diagrams, and picture and became enthralled with the books.

However, the parents kept insisting they were not interested "at the moment." Lonnie was persistent, but despite his best efforts, the answer continued to be the same.

Finally, the father of the boys stood up, said, "Well, I guess we're not interested at this moment," and walked into the front room to watch a ball game. Quietly, Lonnie packed his kit and showed no disappointment. As he left, he shared one question with the boys' mother: "If you are interested in your family's education, when do you think is a good time to start?" He gave her his business card, smiled, and added most politely, "Mrs. Prospect, do this as soon as possible. You'll never regret it." Then he left.

As Lonnie walked to his "pick-up station" where his team leader was to meet him, it began to rain. He had a long walk and was sneezing about every two steps. Suddenly, a big car pulled up beside him. Since it was late at night and there were no street lights, the vehicle startled Lonnie. But when the window came down on the driver's side, he saw a familiar face and heard some of the most beautiful words ever: "Lonnie, do you have a contract with you now? We've decided to go along with the program." The people told Lonnie that his belief was so obvious and his concern for their family was so obvious, they could not say no either to him or to their children.

Selling is a transference of feeling. When you believe in what you are selling; honestly feel that the prospect is going to be the big winner in the transaction; show genuine concern and interest in the client; and terminate all sales calls politely, pleasantly, graciously, and in a friendly manner, EVERYONE wins!

When you miss the sale, it is even more important to make a cheerful, friendly, optimistic, and courteous exit than it is when you make the sale. Remember, the prospect is going to justify the decision—whether it is a yes or a no. If the decision is yes, the buyer will talk primarily about the product and secondarily about the salesperson. If the answer is no and there has been any personality conflict, you can rest assured that negative comments will be made about the salesperson.

## COMMON AREAS FOR IMBALANCE

Lonnie pointed out an imbalance to the prospects because he cared about them and knew his product met their needs and wants. Following are some questions you might use to help others discover their areas of imbalance.

### Time Commitment from Prospect

"Do you control your time?" (Yes or No Question). If yes, book an appointment. If no, then your follow-up question is, "How does that make you feel?"

### Procrastination

"There are two ways to climb an oak tree, Mr. Prospect. You can climb limb by limb, or you can just sit on an acorn. Which one do you believe is the most practical?"

"Would you agree (or Don't you believe), Ms. Prospect, that every step forward or upward begins with a decision? Would you also agree that the right decision will move you forward or upward much faster than the wrong one?"

---

**When you miss the sale, it is even more important to make a cheerful, friendly, optimistic, and courteous exit than it is when you make the sale.**

---

"Would you agree that you are where you are right now based on past decisions? Would you be willing to make what seems like a difficult decision now that could improve your future?"

### Challenge for Achievement

"Are you committed to your goals? Have you asked yourself why you haven't reached more of them? When do you feel is the right time to start working toward your goals? Are you worthy of more? How strong is your desire?"

### Too Busy

"Is it that you don't have the time, or is it that you won't *make* the time? Everyone has the same amount of time, and I'll bet you've noticed that winners control their time."

### Don't Have the Money

"Is your future worth $____? Is your problem that you don't have the money or that you are not making the money? Who is responsible? If you're not getting paid what you need or what you are worth, what steps are you taking to change the situation?"

## QUESTIONS TOO TOUGH?

If you have read this far, you may be wondering if I have gone "off the deep end." Obviously (I hope it's obvious), you will not ask those questions in exactly those words. But go back to my earlier statement: Those who know "what" and "how" will always work for those who know "why." Think this through until you understand the following: (1) What is the purpose of each question? (2) How could you ask those questions working within the framework of your personality without being too challenging? and (3) *Why* are you asking those questions?

YOU are the only one who can answer (1) and (2). The answer to (3) is, To help the prospects understand they are out of balance in some area of their lives.

## FINDING SOLUTIONS

The most important thing to remember when showing the imbalance to the prospect is to be sure that you have a solution. What could be more frustrating than discovering a serious problem with no solution? Are you in this business to help or hurt people? If you make a sale that solves a problem (corrects an imbalance) and you are rewarded, don't you AND the prospect win? Why would you want to do anything that would harm the prospect? If you don't have the prospect's best interests at heart, shouldn't you find something else to do?

# ARE ALL THE LIGHTS ON?

Once the light goes on for you (you know the prospect's need and know you have the solution) and then goes on for the prospect (the person knows that there is a need and that you have a solution), you must move to the Need Solution segment of the sales process.

## PART II OF THE SUCCESSFUL SALES PROCESS: NEED AWARENESS

1. **Need Awareness means:**
   A. The sales professional understands the prospect's wants and needs.
   B. The prospect understands the wants and needs

2. **To make the light go on for the salesperson and the prospect:**
   A. Probe for areas of imbalance.
   B. Show the imbalance to the prospect.

3. **To discover areas of imbalance, learn everything possible about:**
   A. Your product.
   B. Your industry.
   C. Your pricing.
   D. Your product's application/use.
   E. Your competition.

4. **People don't care how much you know until they know how much you care—about them.**

5. **Your most powerful weapon at proving imbalance is the "tough" question. Earn the right to ask.**

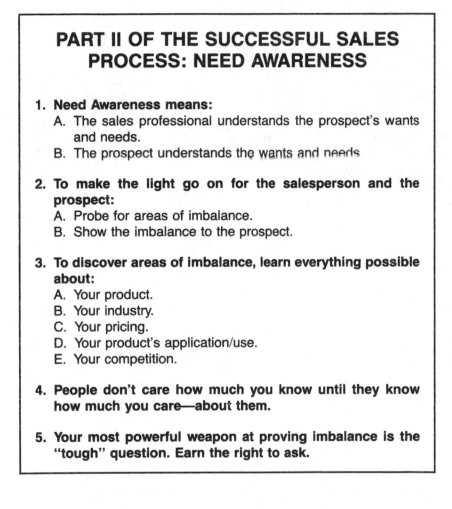

CHAPTER NINE

# SELLING SOLUTIONS TO PEOPLE'S PROBLEMS

## *Lead with Need*

My friend Walt Clayton tells the story of a young man who needed a job and specifically wanted to work at Macy's Department Store. He presented himself to the personnel director who was cordial but firmly stated that no jobs were available. In addition, many other applicants were ahead of him.

As the young man left the office, he was even more determined to work for Macy's. So instead of just taking "no" for an answer, our hero spent a couple of hours browsing through the store and made notes regarding places and situations that could be improved.

Later, he called the personnel director from a phone in the store. "I want to work for Macy's," he said. "I've just spent the past two hours in the store, and I've found at least ten places where I could make a significant contribution. May I come up and tell you where they are?" The young man was invited up for another visit, and he got his job at Macy's.

### THE OBVIOUS IS NOT ALWAYS SO OBVIOUS

Paul is a sales representative for a custom men's clothier. His specialized product line includes shoes, socks, suits, ties, belts, pants, and shirts—anything and everything to make the "professional's appearance match his level of competence." He made a very interesting call on John at a medium-sized insurance agency in Chicago last October.

During the Need Analysis segment of the sales process, Paul discovered the following:

> *Person.* John graduated from high school and college in Chicago and has lived in the Windy City all forty-two years of his life. John and his wife have two sons, ages twelve and nine. John is a weekend golfer. Other than having a chronic cold, he seems to be in good health.
>
> *Organization.* He owns the agency, has six sales representatives working for him, sells a full line of insurance, and has one support person working in the office.
>
> *Goals.* John wants to be able to double his personal production, help his six reps increase their production by 25 percent, play golf more often, and spend more time with his family.
>
> *Obstacles.* It would seem that "time" is the primary obstacle between John and his goals. Paul has convinced John that he has a problem and is out of balance. The question that must be answered: Is time the problem or a symptom of the problem?

As we join the presentation, Paul has completed the Need Analysis and is finalizing the Need Awareness segment of the sales process. He is at the point of transition to Need Solution. Now let's have a little fun AND learn an important sales lesson.

"John," Paul wondered, "how long have you had that cold?" "It seems like all my life," responded John hopelessly. "I can't remember the last time this fiscal year I was able to get out and work with my salespeople in the field. I am just convinced that they could really improve if I could only spend the time necessary."

"Well, what do you see as the reasons you can't get out with them?" Paul asked. "Too tired!" was John's immediate response. "By the time I make my sales calls and do a little paperwork, I'm bushed! This cold has me so run down that I never seem to have the energy to do anything I really want to. Haven't played golf in over six months. Had to pass on taking our younger son on a scouting retreat two weeks ago. I'm sick and tired of being sick and tired!"

"Have you been to the doctor?" Paul questioned, hoping for a clue to this chronic sickness that seemed to be the key factor cutting into John's time. "Oh, yes," said John. "But he just recommends rest and paying his bill—and if I rest, I won't be able to pay his bill!"

"You do have a dilemma," Paul added, when suddenly he was struck by the answer. As John continued to expound on just how serious the need really was, he reared back at his desk, putting his hands behind his head and his feet on the corner of his desk, revealing that he had on no socks.

"Socks!" exclaimed Paul. "You need socks!" "Whaaaat?" John asked. "What do you mean?" Paul was alive with excitement as he zeroed in on John's reason for having the chronic cold. "No socks. If you had socks, you'd have time." "No, no, no," said John, "you don't understand. My family has never worn socks. My grandfather didn't. My father didn't. Why, not wearing socks is practically a family tradition. I don't need socks."

Paul was incredulous: "Well for heaven's sake, why don't your people wear socks?" "I don't have a clue" was John's somewhat indifferent response.

"Let's ask your grandfather." "Can't." "Why not?" "He died before I was born." "From pneumonia?" "No, and I don't think that's very funny." "Well, what happened?" "Chronic bronchitis. My dad died from pneumonia."

## A SLIGHT TUG

Just in case you haven't felt the sensation yet, I am obviously pulling your leg. Incidentally, when this scenario is presented to live audiences in the form of a skit, they really get a charge out of it—and I hope you got the picture. But my desire is to make a vitally important point: When we provide solutions, we do not sell products. People do not buy products. They buy products of the products—known as BENEFITS.

In our example, John had no desire for socks. He wanted the time and energy to train his people, play golf, and participate in more activities with his family. His obstacle was poor health; his solution was socks.

If we go back to our example and pick up at the point where Paul notices John's lack of socks, we can see how the process might play out more effectively.

## ANOTHER CHANCE

"John, if I could show you a way that you could feel better, have the time and energy to train your people, play golf, and participate in more activities with your family, would you be interested?" (Yes or No Question—with an obvious answer).

"John, would it make any difference to you what I called my product if I could meet your needs and solve your problem?"

Now if Paul is as much an expert as we want him to be, even when he has the solution, he will continue to probe to be sure the light is on in the prospect's mind. He will use questions such as:

- "Why do you want to sell more insurance?"
- "What would you do if you could sell more insurance?"
- "How would you feel about having more time for your family?"
- "What would you think about being able to play more golf?"
- "What would it mean to you to be able to train your salespeople?"
- "How would your family feel about your spending more time with them?"

## WINNERS SELL BENEFITS

J. Kevin Jenkins of Lafayette, Louisiana, sells proper pelvic tilt, blood flow, relaxed muscles, peace of mind, lack of stress, and a rested and relaxed mind and body that are completely prepared to take on the daily challenges we all must face.

Kevin begins his presentation with scientific validation from chiropractors and medical doctors substantiating factual information that shows how using his product for an extended period enhances health and well-being. Next, he brings in customer testimonials and shows how using his product can save the prospect 2 hours—when comparisons are made to his competition.

He goes on to point out that 2 hours per day mean 14 hours per week, which mean 728 hours each year—or more than 30 days. Most of us could get really excited about gaining an extra month per year. Kevin ties his prospect's extra month into 30 additional family, golf, education, fishing, selling, resting, or "whatever you want" days. Everything he talks about to his prospects translates into a customer benefit, which is, after all, the only reason anybody buys anything from anybody.

By now, some of you have realized that Kevin sells waterbeds, but may I ask you a question? If you could be shown how you might receive all those benefits, would you care what the product was? By painting a compelling picture of free time and health benefits while using simple arithmetic, Kevin Jenkins is winning AND helping others to win.

## TWO VITAL QUESTIONS

Let me challenge you right now to stop and answer what should be two simple questions. There may be as many as three answers to each question, but please answer these as completely as possible.

The first question: What do you sell?

1. ______________________________

2. ______________________________

3. ______________________________

The second question: What do your prospects buy?

1. ______________________________

2. ______________________________

3. ______________________________

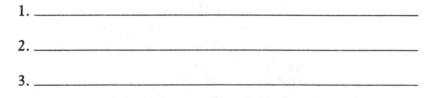

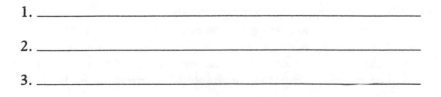

And now if you will allow me a third question, it will be this: Do those lists match? If the answer is yes, you are miles ahead of many of your competitors. If you did not stop to think about your answers, let me encourage you to take the time to give these seemingly simple questions your sincere effort. The answers will reveal a great deal about you. Those who refuse to take the time to answer these questions and minimize their importance are most often those who don't have a clue about the answers.

## BOOKS AND TAPES

On occasion I have encountered people who think I am in the business of selling speeches, books, and tapes. As a matter of fact, several years ago I received a beautiful letter from a man who was genuinely concerned about me. Here is the essence of what the letter said:

"Dear Zig: Let me encourage you to discontinue the sale of books and tapes from the platform when you make your public appearances. I believe it damages your image and perhaps affects the attitude of the audience in the process."

I am completely convinced that this man's motivation was aimed at my best interests, and for that I am most grateful. Here is my response to him:

"Dear Friend: Thank you very much for your beautiful letter of concern. Yours is the type letter I love to receive. It was not judgmental, nor did you condemn me for what I am doing. You simply offered, out of your heart, a suggestion you felt was in my best interests, and I am grateful for that. However, let me explain to you why we offer the books and tapes to our audiences.

"First is the fact that one person in seven who calls to buy tickets to a seminar asks if we are going to have the books and tapes available. If that many ask, I have reason to believe others are also interested.

"Second, if the people who come to a seminar like what they hear, they often want to carry the facts and 'feelings' home with them. Making the books and tapes available allows them to do this. Less than 4 percent of the actual presentation time is spent in explaining what products are available, so there is no teaching time lost. Actually, because of the way I do the product presentation, I teach as I am explaining the buying options.

"Third, and most important, by actual count, for every letter we receive that says, 'Your seminar changed my life,' we get two hundred letters, phone calls, and verbal accounts that say my books and tapes changed lives.

"With this in mind, I would like to emphasize that I am not in the speech business, seminar business, or book and tape business. I am in the business of changing lives. Yes, I realize that I run the risk of offending some who attend the seminar, and I regret that. I wish it were possible to accomplish all the objectives without offending even one person. However, years ago I accepted the fact that there was a certain amount of risk in anything we do, and I decided that the benefits the prospect gains from the purchase were greater and more important than any risk I took to explain the products that were available for sale."

## FOR CLARIFICATION

As you read these words, let me make this abundantly clear. When you truly believe what you have to offer is for the benefit of your prospects, you will take a certain number of calculated risks to persuade your prospects to take action in their own best interests. You will do it politely, pleasantly, and professionally, but you WILL do it.

When you want your prospects to take action, you will talk about the benefit to them and lead with need.

## MY ANSWERS

Allow me to answer the two questions I asked you to answer on page 201. The first question: What do you sell? I sell life-changing tools that empower people to overcome negative patterns of the past and make progress in the present while having hope in the future. The second question: What do your prospects buy? People purchase tools that give them power over their past, progress in the present, and hope in the future. And yes, these two match.

## FOR CONSIDERATION

The reason the benefits are so tremendous from the books and tapes is simply that when you read something or hear something a number of times, you are following one of the oldest educational principles known to man—repetition.

When you attend an inspiring seminar, read an inspirational book, or listen to a moving motivational tape, your thinking and feelings are literally moved to new heights. From these heights you will be able to see and hear things that you missed before. I am repeatedly told by people that they're still hearing things on the tenth, twentieth, and even thirtieth listening to a set of tapes. The message has been there all the time, but the listener was simply not ready to receive all of that message. Listen to the right messages on an ongoing and repetitive basis.

Repetition is the mother of learning and the father of action, which makes it the architect of accomplishment.

## A GIFT

One of my Christmas gifts this past year was Jockey underwear from The Redhead. As I started to open the package of the Jockey Classic, I looked down and read the printing. Here is what got my attention: "You spend two-thirds of your life in underwear; spend three minutes reading why it pays to buy the best."

Then they proceed to give a beautiful description of why they feel their product is the best. The major point I'm making is that the opening got my attention. In the world of sales, you lead with need—with your best shot—because sometimes that is the only one the prospect is going to hear. In this particular case, I was so impressed with the opening line I read the rest of what they had to say, and I was impressed with that as well. However, I'll confess that had the opening not grabbed my attention, there is no way I would have finished reading their "sales talk."

## FEATURE—FUNCTION—BENEFIT

In the great profession of selling, there is much talk about features, functions, and benefits, but what are these wonderful items?

In order to "lead with need" we must have an understanding of the basic definitions of these key words.

By definition, a FEATURE is a part of the product or service—or what the product or service *IS*. There may be several features per product or service. A ballpoint pen has a clip; this is a feature.

By definition, a FUNCTION is the act that particular part of the product or service performs—or what that particular part of the product or service *DOES*. There may be several functions per product or service. The clip of the ballpoint pen functions to hold the pen to your pocket.

**Repetition is the mother of learning and the father of action, which makes it the architect of accomplishment.**

By definition, a BENEFIT is the ADVANTAGE in using the feature and the function—or what the feature and function *DO FOR THE PROSPECT/CLIENT.* There may be many benefits per product or service. The clip of the ballpoint pen SAVES YOU MONEY AND FRUSTRATION because you don't keep misplacing or losing it.

## PROSPECTS LISTEN

Please remember that every prospect listens to radio station WIIFM (which stands for *W*hat's *I*n *I*t *F*or *M*e?).

To this point, I have been spending a great deal of time "pounding" the importance of benefits. However, for the successful sales presentation, you will need a thorough understanding of all three parts. I have emphasized benefits to impress upon you the importance of selling "products of the product" and not the product alone. These three elements (feature, function, and benefit) are not equal thirds. When providing a solution to a prospect's need (solving a problem), you ALWAYS lead with need. There were be times when you will need to reference features and functions.

## THE CLASSIC EXAMPLE

Those who train feature, function, and benefit often use the ballpoint pen as the classic example. However, the classic example for you is your product or service. Would you stop right now and list at least three features, three functions, and three benefits of what you are selling?

FEATURES

_______________

_______________

_______________

FUNCTIONS

_______________

_______________

_______________

BENEFITS

_______________

_______________

_______________

Let's look at a specific example:

*Ziglar on Selling*
The Ultimate Handbook for the Complete Sales Professional

FEATURES

1. Attractive cover design
2. Expanded Table of Contents
3. Well over three hundred pages
4. Summary pages with main points
5. Stories, one-liners, and analogies

FUNCTIONS

1. Gets your attention/causes you to pick up book
2. Allows a quick overview of the contents
3. Plenty of information available
4. Allows for quick review of material presented
5. Keeps your attention/enhances understanding

BENEFITS

1. Ease
2. Convenience
3. Resource tool
4. Speed
5. Evaluate what is learned as you go.
6. Application oriented
7. Improves your quality of life
8. Improves your effectiveness
9. Gives peace of mind through security and professionalism
10. Raises standard of living
11. Develops confidence
12. Improves self-image
13. Brings you closer to your family
14. Enhances your image in the community

## CONFUSION

You can probably understand why some people sell only functions (what it *does*). Beware of this trap! What your product or service (or a part of that product or service) may DO is very interesting, and it may even *convince* the prospect that you know your business and understand the value of your product. However, functions probably won't cause me to give you my money. That will happen when—and only when—you PERSUADE me to take action by clearly spelling out *W*hat's *I*n *I*t *F*or *M*e. When you show me the advantages I get from using your product or service, we are truly communicating.

Many times salespeople are told not to talk about the features of a product without talking about the benefits (advantages) as well. This is only partially true. The complete truth is, the successful sales professional talks about AND demonstrates features LEADING TO benefits. Personalize the benefits for the prospect. Paint the person into the picture driving that luxury car, receiving compliments on the beautiful dress or suit, looking at the sunset on the lake where the new home has been constructed, or sitting in the comfortable retirement environment provided by the investment being made. Paint the picture so your prospect SEES personal benefits.

Some people might not think of award-winning actor, writer, director, and producer Alan Alda as being a salesman, but in a speech he made to a medical school, he gave doctors AND salespeople some good advice. He said, "The head bone is connected to the heart bone. Don't let them come apart." From a sales perspective, he is telling professional salespeople that when we demonstrate or explain the benefits of our product in a clear and logical manner, we must also involve the prospect emotionally. We must let the prospective client know how it will *feel* to enjoy the product or service.

To avoid the confusion, and make the proper use of feature, function, and benefit, we need to add the BRIDGE. The Bridge is a phrase preparing the prospect to hear the benefit. The phrase shouts, "Look out, here comes the BENEFIT, ADVANTAGE, or REASON for you to buy." Sample Bridges might include:

"The advantage to you, Mr. Prospect, is . . ."

"You will enjoy this because . . ."
"The benefit to you, Ms. Prospect, is . . ."

## BACK TO YOUR BOOK

*Ziglar on Selling* features an attractive cover, which gets your attention and causes you to pick it up. The advantage to you is ease in locating the proper book when you want to refresh your memory on selling fundamentals.

*Ziglar on Selling* features an expanded Table of Contents, which functions to allow you to make a quick overview of the information available. The benefit to you is convenience in locating information.

*Ziglar on Selling* features well over three hundred pages of information, which functions to bring you a variety and volume of information. The benefit to you is that you have a thorough resource tool for future reference.

*Ziglar on Selling* features summary pages with the main points of each chapter capsulized. You will enjoy this because you can save time by reviewing important points just prior to sales calls.

*Ziglar on Selling* features stories, one-liners, and analogies, which keep your attention and help you understand the principles. The benefit to you is that you can then apply this information to become even more successful in your career.

## PRODUCTS OF PRODUCTS

Salespeople need to clearly understand that prospects do not buy what the product is; they buy the benefits that the use of the product will bring to them. "Antilock brakes" mean very little to the average driver until you explain that they may prevent those dangerous skids on slippery highways. "Steel-belted radial" might mean very little unless you explain that it enables the motorist to get an extra fifteen thousand safe miles out of a set of tires.

My guess is, you have seen the commercials on TV where the mother and daughter are stranded in the rain and might not have been had the husband bought the proper battery for the automobile. The cad! What could he have been thinking of to buy an inferior battery and cause his family to be stuck in the rain on a dark night in a dangerous part of town? Point: Our battery keeps your family safe.

"Guaranteed renewable" might mean little to a senior citizen until you explain that the company cannot cancel the policy at any age.

Five inches of insulation mean nothing until you translate them into lower heating and air conditioning costs. In short, always give a benefit when you describe a feature and function.

## YOUR CHALLENGE

If you are struggling with feature, function, or benefit for your product or service, imagine how your prospects must feel. If you don't CLEARLY understand and cannot clearly ARTICULATE the difference, you may be losing sales to those who can.

Since you are working to become even better today than you were yesterday; since you desire to become a true professional in every way; since sales success is vitally important to you; would you take time to answer a few questions?

What are the three most important parts/aspects of your product or service? (What IS your product or service?)

1. ______________________________

2. ______________________________

3. ______________________________

What act does that part/aspect perform? (What does your product or service do?)

1. ______________________________

2. ______________________________

3. ______________________________

What is the most effective statement for you to use with your product or service that states loudly and clearly, "Look out, here comes the benefit to you!"?

______________________________________________

What are the primary reasons that others would want to purchase your product or service? (What does your product or service do for the prospect?)

1. ______________________________________________

2. ______________________________________________

3. ______________________________________________

## LEADING WITH NEED, THEN AND NOW

Some principles should not and do not change. In the late 1950s, I was briefly in the hospitalization, health, and accident insurance field. I was living in Columbia, South Carolina, and frequently drove to Newberry, South Carolina, to work. Mostly by accident, I learned that Newberry had an extremely large number of single schoolteachers (female) in their forties and fifties who were the sole support of their mothers. As you realize, many things were different in the 1950s. There were very few nursing homes, and governmental aid was not as readily available as today.

When I gathered this information, putting two and two together was fairly easy. If something happened to the primary breadwinner, the single teachers and their mothers would be faced with dire financial circumstances. I started concentrating on this relatively small but extremely lucrative market. Lucrative because the need was so great that the sales were not difficult. I did not create the need. I just offered a solution to a particular problem faced by these people. Without exception, when I made the presentation, even for the few (and there were very few) who did not buy, the ladies were most appreciative that I had singled them out specifically and made a concerted effort to see them.

## A SIMPLE PRESENTATION

During the Need Analysis and Need Awareness segments of the presentation, I gathered information that allowed me to learn if there was any means of support for either the teacher or her mother should she suffer a career-ending illness or accident. This conversational "innerview" often revealed only small savings accounts.

Then I asked the obvious question: "Have you ever wondered what would happen to you and your mother if you suffered a career-ending accident or illness and you had exhausted your savings?"

Most had given at least some thought to the question, but since there was no clear-cut solution readily available, they were taking the "Scarlett O'Hara" approach and choosing to "think about it tomorrow."

The Need Solution question was also quite obvious. I asked, "If there was a solution to the problem, you would be interested in knowing what it was, wouldn't you?" Across the board, the answer was in the affirmative.

During this segment of the sales process, I would "lead with need" as I have been encouraging you to do in this chapter. In addition, I wanted to encourage the prospect to take action, so I would paint a vivid word picture that would allow her to see what might happen if she did not take immediate action.

"Miss Prospect (this was before the Ms. days), at age forty-nine, your life expectancy is approximately twenty to thirty years. Generally speaking, when there is an accident or illness, that life span would be substantially reduced to approximately seven years. Now $400 (the amount the insurance would pay after disability) per month for seven years—or longer—represents a considerable amount of money ($1,200 to $1,500 of today's dollars). For this reason, the underwriting procedures are pretty strict (which was a fact). As a representative of the company, I obviously cannot guarantee that your application will be approved. However, I will be glad to submit it and see what the underwriting department says." A very high percentage would say, "Well, let's do that." Yes, the fear of loss is often greater than the desire for gain.

If there was any resistance or uncertainty, the question was, "Well, you are certain that in the event of illness or accident you would want to be able to provide for your needs, aren't you?" The answer was always in the affirmative. So I would simply ask, "Then why don't we see how you look on paper and let the company make the decision?"

This was good for a closing rate of over 90 percent of the people I called upon.

## WHAT ABOUT THE NINETIES?

So what does this example mean to you in the 1990s? In the January 30, 1991, issue of *Bottom Line* magazine, an article by Harold Evensky called "Long-Term Disability Insurance, How to Buy It Right—Mistakes to Avoid" said, "Long-term care insurance is expensive . . . but worth it because owners are very likely to collect. More than 25% of people over 65 years old will eventually need long-term care, as will 50% of people over 89."

My friend Roger Peet, from Bismarck, North Dakota, presented me with an interested sales problem in this area. He was having problems with creating a sense of urgency for action on the part of the prospect. The solution I recommended (which originated in my work with the schoolteachers) has worked dramatically well for him, and Roger tells me he uses the terminology just as I am sharing it with you. The numbers may change through the years, but the principles do not.

## IMPORTANT VERBIAGE

Based on a sixty-two-year-old person buying long-term care insurance, Roger could offer $80 per day for life with a $100 monthly premium. Again, don't get caught up in the numbers because there are several details I am leaving out for the sake of simplicity and making the point. Instead of focusing on the numbers, look at the verbiage that paints the "lead with need" picture and creates the sense of urgency for action.

Roger begins this segment of the presentation by saying, "You know, Mr. and Mrs. Prospect, we go through life making lots of choices. In your life span you have made tens of thousands of them. Some have had earth-shattering consequences, but most of them really were insignificant.

"At this moment, however, you have a choice that can be extremely significant. Here is that choice: Right now, everything indicates that you can choose whether or not you want this coverage. I have no way of knowing—nor do you—whether or not you will have that same choice tomorrow, next week, next month, or next year. You probably will, but it is because of the uncertainty that insurance was created in the first place. With that in mind, let's look at what you are choosing.

"If you choose to install this coverage, you have just chosen to invest $100 each month. That probably is not a major decision for you because it does not affect where you will live, what you will eat, the car you will drive, or your basic standard of living. In short, if you say yes, the only thing that will be materially affected will be your peace of mind.

"On the other hand, if your choice is to delay, or if you say no, then as indicated earlier you might not have that choice at a later time. If that should happen and a stroke, accident, heart attack, or any other debilitating disease or catastrophe overtakes you, then your 'no' answer today would have devastating results. The amount of $100 once each month going out of your bank account won't make much difference, but $80 every DAY going out of your resources, over a period of time, would make a dramatic difference not only in your financial life but in your peace of mind as well. It would also possibly affect, in a very negative way, people you love very much, and it might even deplete your resources and theirs, too.

"With so much to gain by saying yes and so much to lose by saying no, doesn't it make sense to let the insurance company carry the risk and not you? I believe you will sleep better tonight, knowing that for very little—if any—sacrifice, you have eliminated the possibility of a financial tragedy. We can have this contract in full force by . . . !"

## A.A.F.T.O.

Now that you thoroughly understand the importance of leading with need, and the difference in features, functions, and benefits, you are ready to Always Ask For The Order, and A.A.F.T.O. is what chapter 10 is all about!

## PART III OF THE SUCCESSFUL SALES PROCESS: NEED SOLUTION

1. **Need Solution means:**
   A. The sales professional sells BENEFITS, not products.
   B. The sales professional will "Lead with Need."

2. **Features, Functions, and Benefits help solve prospect's problems:**
   A. Features are parts of the product or service—what the product or service IS.
   B. Functions are the acts that particular parts of the product or service perform—what that particular part of the product or service DOES.
   C. Benefits are the advantages gained by using the features and functions of the product or service—what the features and functions DO FOR THE PROSPECT/CLIENT.

CHAPTER TEN

# THE ABC'S OF CLOSING SALES

## *A.A.F.T.O. = Always Ask For The Order*

Many years ago, the Detroit newspapers carried a feature story about a monstrous insurance policy purchased by Henry Ford. A close friend of Mr. Ford who was in the insurance business was considerably upset and asked him why on earth he had not bought the policy from him. Mr. Ford's answer is a lesson to everybody who sells anything to anybody at any time under any circumstances—and that's all of us! He said, "You didn't ask me."

## THE "TIMID" SALESMAN

If ever there was a classic example of what hard work, courage, and perseverance can accomplish, Horace "Judge" Ziglar was that example. Judge was not spectacularly successful when he entered the world of sales, but he went on to set many records that stood for many years. My younger brother loved to sell! Later in life, when others pressed him to share his selling secrets, he became one of the finest platform speakers in the country. Before his premature death in October of 1990, Judge had helped literally thousands of people become more successful in sales and in life.

When I think of closing the sale, I can think of no more effective closer than my brother. He had the strongest "closing attitude" of anyone I have ever known in the great profession of selling. As I said earlier, Judge's basic philosophy was that you had *his* money in your pocket. That was O.K. since he had *your* product on his shelf.

Now before you rush to judgment, let me quickly add that my brother was one salesman who ALWAYS had his prospect's best interests in mind. He ALWAYS believed in the product he sold, and he ALWAYS knew that people were better off after he made the trade (his money for your product).

Judge wrote a book called *Timid Salesmen Have Skinny Kids*, and he was exactly right. The year he set the world's record for cookware sales, he overcame more adversity than most salesmen face in a career, including a child with an extended hospital stay (Judge sold to the nurses); an automobile accident that totaled his car (he sold to the insurance adjuster); the deaths of two close relatives; and the loss of his voice (the doctor told him he couldn't speak for six weeks, so he did the only thing he could do—he got another doctor).

## A CLOSER REALLY CARES

Visualize this scene with me, please. The date is December 31, New Year's Eve. Everybody knows you just do not make sales on New Year's Eve. The time is 10:15 P.M., and Judge has a sales appointment. He has already broken the world's record by over $2,000, but he is $140 short of his goal. What would you have done?

The young couple Judge Ziglar called on lived in a small one-room apartment. They had no stove and no refrigerator. By 11:30 that evening, they *did* own a set of heavy-duty stainless steel cookware.

There were many reasons for Judge's working so hard to make the sale. He had set a goal to sell a specific amount of merchandise, and being that close without achieving his goal (especially after what he had gone through) was unacceptable to him. But more important, Judge knew that the couple with so little NEEDED a set of cookware that would work on the hot plate they were using to cook. He knew they NEEDED vacuum-sealed, precision-made, heat-conducting, heavy-duty stainless steel cookware that would provide nutritious meals and grocery savings that would allow them to recoup in a relatively short time the money they invested that evening.

In short, Judge KNEW he was doing the RIGHT THING FOR THE PROSPECTS, so he had no reservations about asking for the order.

Your closing style or attitude may be entirely different from my brother's. I know mine is. The point here is not so much "how" you go about asking for the order. The point is that you DO ask for the order—*go for it*!

## NEED SATISFACTION

Everything we have done so far in the first nine chapters of this book has been designed to bring us to this point in the sales process. The fourth step in our successful sales formula is Need Satisfaction. When we do the proper Need Analysis, we understand the prospect's needs and desires. We follow this with Need Awareness; we make sure that we understand the needs and desires AND that the prospect understands the needs and desires. After the sales professional and the prospect are both aware, we offer the Need Solution in the form of our product or service. And now, at long last, we have reached the moment of truth—Need Satisfaction.

**Timid salesmen have skinny kids.**

When you reach this point in the sales process and the prospect says, "You're not trying to sell me something are you?" and you reply, "Noooooo, no, of course not!" then I have to ask, "Well, what are you? A professional visitor?!?!" Closing sales doesn't have to be painful for you or the prospect. On the contrary, if you are the "right" kind of person selling the "right" kind of product at a fair price with the "right" intentions, you are in a win-win situation. And a win-win situation means that closing the sale is a positive and pleasant experience for both you and the prospect.

## DO YOU *ALWAYS* HAVE TO ASK?

Some "wit" once said that we miss 100 percent of the sales we don't ask for. That's not quite true because despite all our ineptness, and despite whether or not we ask for the order, there will be those rare occasions when we encounter individuals so determined to buy that they will, in fact, say, "Well, go ahead and write it up. I'll take it." How do I know this? Very simple.

One evening in an unnamed city in an unnamed shopping center, I saw the most gorgeous sweater display I've ever seen. I was instantly attracted to the bright red sweater in the center of the display, despite the high price. I walked in, searched desperately for somebody to acknowledge my existence and, finding no one, left feeling somewhat discouraged. After shopping for another ten minutes or so, I returned to take one more look at that beautiful sweater. If they wouldn't let me buy it, at least they were kind enough to let me look at it in the display.

To my surprise, I was approached by what appeared to be a salesperson. I was mistaken. The woman worked for the store, but she was so wrapped up in thought that though she was there as evidenced by her physical presence, I have no idea where her mind was. She spoke in the abstract, displayed zero interest in dealing with me (or anyone else), reluctantly showed the sweater, and had a "take it or leave it" attitude. I was so provoked I left, went back to my hotel (which was a part of the shopping center), and read a few minutes. Who would have thought it was so hard to buy a sweater?

By now I had a serious problem because I couldn't get that magnificent red sweater off my mind. After a few more moments of reflection, I decided I wasn't going to let one indifferent and nonprofessional clerk cost me the enjoyment of wearing that sweater. I went back to the store.

After some little time and effort, I managed (because of years of experience and the desire to persevere in the face of resistance) to overcome all of their objections as to why they should not sell it to me, demanded my right to purchase, and triumphantly walked out with my new red sweater.

P.S. Just in case you couldn't tell. I love that sweater! But let me encourage you not to make it that difficult on your prospects. You MIGHT make some sales, but you WILL NOT make a living.

## THINK ALONG

If (and I realize this may be another BIG "IF") you have taken the first three steps in our successful sales formula, asking for the order is the natural progression that must occur.

What is the worst thing that can happen? Is the following scene the one you have been imaging in your mind?

"Do you want to take action?" you ask with some fear and trepidation. "Absolutely not!" the prospect loudly and rudely responds. "Well, why not?" you counter with your own voice rising in pitch and volume. "Because your inferior, no-good product is exceeded only by your own ineptitude and incompetency!" is the reply. And your only possible reaction is, "Oh, I see," as you leave the room, dragging your self-esteem along behind you.

## PEOPLE WANT TO SAY YES

Remember, as a persuader, whether you are a doctor, dentist, or computer salesperson, in most cases the prospect really does want to say yes, particularly if you are pleasant, professional, and at least reasonably friendly. We all really do not like to say no because that could possibly end the relationship. Even though you might have been involved in the sales process for only a brief time, if you are a pleasant person and have genuine interest in the prospect, he or she instinctively knows that a "no" would mean it was all over between the two of you. The prospect might not be able to verbalize the feeling, but it is there, so the odds are in the professional salesperson's favor. So ask for the order, my selling friend. Do it pleasantly and professionally, but ASK!

## THE COURAGE TO ASK THE QUESTION

David A. Mezey sells medical equipment in North Olmsted, Ohio. When his territory was expanded to cover some areas previously covered by the Pittsburgh territory manager, he had a number of phone conversations with his friend from Pittsburgh who updated him on the status of some accounts. He told David that one particular account had two key radiologists, and one of them was a very receptive man who would usually buy any new product for evaluation. The other would listen closely to the presentation but would never be willing to make a decision.

On his first call on the client, David presented the features, functions, and benefits of several new products to the technical supervisor of the radiology department who suggested that one of the doctors would be interested in seeing David. David comments, "This was just fine with me because I knew he would buy something. After my presentation, the doctor did agree to buy several products. The following evening I again spoke to the Pittsburgh representative to thank him for the lead because Dr. Lazeroni did buy. To my surprise, he informed me that Dr. Lazeroni had never purchased anything from him in the past, regardless of the offer! Clearly, I had called on the 'wrong' man. Since then, Dr. Lazeroni has become a steady customer and has helped himself and his patients by ordering other products."

As I have said before, and will say countless times again, in selling, as in life, we are all BORN TO WIN. But to be the WINNER we were all meant to be, we must PLAN to win, we must PREPARE to win, and THEN we can EXPECT to win. In David's case, he planned his presentation, prepared his presentation, and fully expected to make the sale. And this is the sales attitude that all successful sales professionals work to develop—the sales attitude that YOU must work to develop. If you PREPARE and PLAN, then you have every reason to EXPECT to sell!

## WE MUST "ASK" TO "HAVE"

Earlier, I mentioned my friend Gerhard Gschwandtner, the publisher of *Personal Selling Power* magazine. I sincerely believe his publication is the finest pure sales magazine on the market. Gerhard says that over the past seventy-five years more than three thousand books were published on the art and science of professional selling. However, less than 1 percent of these books deals exclusively with the closing process. This is one of the reasons my book *Secrets of Closing the Sale* has been so popular and is still the only pure sales technique book to ever make the *New York Times* "Best-Seller" list.

Although *Secrets* includes over one hundred specific closes, seven hundred sales questions, and dozens of tips, techniques, and secrets for the successful sales professional, I did not present a specific chronological process that would help us close more sales more often. That is what this chapter is all about. This is important because sales technician Chris Hegarty reports that 63 percent of all sales interviews end with the salesperson not specifically asking for the order.

## ANOTHER "SHOCKER"

Research from Dr. Herb True of Notre Dame reveals that 46 percent of the salespeople he interviewed ask for the order once and then quit; 24 percent ask for the order twice before giving up; 14 percent ask the third time; and 12 percent "hang in there" to make four attempts before throwing in the proverbial towel. That's a total of 96 percent who quit after *four* closing attempts, and yet the same research shows that a full 60 percent of all sales are made after the fifth closing attempt. Since the percentage of salespeople not asking for the sale the necessary five times equals 96 percent, it's obvious that 4 percent are making 60 percent of the sales (and 60 percent of the commissions).

**We miss 100 percent of the sales we don't ask for.**

For those of you who are reluctant to ask for the order more than once or twice for fear of coming across as "high pressure" salespeople, think about this: When baseball pitchers reject a ball, the ball is returned to the umpire who puts it in his pouch with other baseballs. Later that same ball will be given to the pitcher. Seldom, if ever, is the same ball rejected twice. The prospect will look at your offer in a different light the second, third, fourth, and even fifth time. Just as the professional baseball umpire offers the same baseball to the pitcher, so must the professional salesperson offer the same product to the prospect several times.

## PERSISTENCE AND PERSUASION

John Cummings of Mundelein, Illinois, is the general manager at an automobile dealership. One of John's trainees tried unsuccessfully to get a client to purchase an "experienced" vehicle.

The manager for the area was also unsuccessful in closing the sale. Since between the two of them they had asked the closing question at least four times, the outlook for closing the sale seemed dismal. And then the trainee, Jim Borgman, had an idea. About an hour after the prospect had gotten home, Jim called him and greeted him quite cordially, saying, "Mr. Prospect, Jim Borgman from Bernard Chevrolet. Did I take you away from anything important?" After finding out he was calling at a convenient time (which was a wise move), he continued, "I wanted to ask you a couple of questions, may I?" Upon receiving permission to continue, Jim asked, "Did you visit our competition?" The prospect responded, "Why, yes, I did." Jim got directly to the point (or as some folks say, "cut to the chase") and asked, "Did you purchase?" "No" was the prospect's one-word reply. "Pretty expensive over there, aren't they?" said Jim. "Yes, they are."

"Mr. Prospect, do you mind if I ask you just one more question?" "No," the prospect responded. "Super!" Jim said enthusiastically. "Mr. Prospect, where are you going to take your first trip in your Suburban from Bernard Chevrolet?" After a slight pause the prospect replied, "Kentucky!" And with a huge smile on his face (that says a prospect and a salesman just experienced the "double win") Jim continued, "Fine, fine, Mr. Prospect. Come on back. I'm sure we can arrive at a fair trading difference." "I'm on my way, Jim."

Initially, Jim and the prospect were $1,500 away from making a deal, but due to the sales rookie's enthusiastic, creative, courteous, and persistent approach—combined with his understanding of the prospect, getting the prospect emotionally involved, and ASKING FOR THE ORDER ONE MORE TIME—Jim Borgman made the sale. It's worth repeating because it's true: A growing "green" salesperson will sell more than an experienced "blue" one.

Asking for the order five times or more can be extremely difficult if you (a) don't have a deep belief in the value of your product or service; (b) haven't done the proper job with the first three steps (Need Analysis, Need Awareness, and Need Solution) in our four-step selling formula; or (c) don't expect to make the sale.

Not so incidentally, let me point out that between each closing effort you must give additional reasons, features, functions, and BENEFITS for the prospect to make the "yes" decision TODAY. When you offer added information, you allow the prospect to make a "new" decision based on additional information. At the risk of overemphasizing the importance of expectancy in making the sale, let me share another example.

Positively expecting to make the sale can make a dramatic difference in your career as shown in the following example.

## THE NEW MAN WATCHES AND LEARNS

When I was in the insurance business, I made a call with my general agent to an overweight fifty-five-year-old client. I had sold a $100,000 policy to this man who did not have any insurance coverage. I was really a neophyte then, and when we delivered the insurance policy, the general agent did such a marvelous job explaining the benefits of this particular policy that the client had no hesitation about buying a second policy on the spot. To my surprise, the general agent pulled a second $100,000 policy from his briefcase (which he had asked the company to issue in advance) and handed it to our client. I really learned a great deal about positive expectancy that day—AND how to serve my client because with his family and his health (due to his weight and age, the policy was rated) the original $100,000 policy simply was not an adequate amount of coverage.

## FEED YOUR FAMILY OR FEED YOUR EGO

We talked about feeding your family or feeding your ego in an earlier chapter from a different perspective, but the lesson applies here, too. Many times we don't ask the question because we don't want to hear the "no." This is where you will want to give yourself a "gut-check."

I have already recommended that you "debrief" each sales call immediately after the presentation—that is, get alone and relive the experience. This is most effective when you keep a written journal, which we will talk more about in chapter 15, "Organization and Discipline." But regardless of how you coach yourself, you MUST answer at least one question about each presentation that ends WITHOUT your asking for the order. The question is, Why?

Was it: "The timing just wasn't right"; "The prospect was distracted"; "There were too many people around"; or "She needed time to think it through"? These are often EXCUSES used for not asking for the order. Don't misunderstand. There are occasions when it is wise to back away and return another day, especially if the amount of investment you are asking the prospect to make is significant. However, in the overwhelming majority of cases, you need to muster what Louise Padgett identified earlier as old-fashioned "guts and gumption" and in the modern vernacular, "Just Do It!"

For every sale you miss because you try to close at the wrong time, you will miss a dozen because you don't try to close at all.

## CONFIDENCE VS. OVERCONFIDENCE

Unfortunately, salespeople also miss sales because they "assume" everything is "all set." The sale is not a *sure* thing until the order is signed, the goods or services are delivered and paid for, AND the customer is satisfied.

Confidence in yourself as a person and then as a salesperson is essential; however, overconfidence leads to arrogance, and that's when Buster Douglas knocks out Mike Tyson and becomes a "one fight" heavyweight champion. It's also when salespeople lose those "sure" sales.

David Ray, the admissions counselor from Malone College in Canton, Ohio, tells of taking an idea, adapting it to fit the college's situation, and increasing enrollment there. David mailed a postselling letter, modeled after a letter created by sales trainer Thom Norman. Three days later David bumped into one of his students in the hallway as he was leaving for the day. He was a student that David had been working with since October of the preceding year and "was what I considered one of my 'certain' students, someone I could count on being here in the fall." However, when David questioned the student, he soon learned that the young man had been sitting at home, scared about college, and had decided not to come, despite his original commitment. Then David heard words that were "music to his ears." David said, "He had been scared until he received my letter in the mail. After reading the postselling reassurance letter, the student said he knew he had made the right decision to go to college and had rushed down after work to pay his bill."

Here is a copy of the letter David sent:

> As I write this letter to you, I am reminded that it is now less than one month before you will finally be a student at Malone. If memory serves, I too felt excited, scared, thrilled, nervous, positive, confused, and worried before going to college. Are you relating? If so, you are not alone. Many of your future classmates feel the same way. If I could offer one word of encouragement, it would be *congratulations*.
>
> I am proud to know that you have decided to be a part of Malone College history as we celebrate 100 years of quality Christian education in 1992. You are about to personally experience the benefits that have made Malone a first-choice Christian college for the nineties.
>
> Thank you for the trust and confidence you have placed in me as your admissions counselor. I hope our relationship will continue once you begin your studies; my door is always open.
>
> I have enjoyed meeting and visiting with your family. I hope they are as excited for their new "Pioneer" as I am. Welcome to the class of '94.
>
> I look forward to seeing you on August 25.

## LESSONS FOR ALL OF US

We can learn a couple of critical lessons here. Number one, there's no such thing as a sure sale until the order is signed, the merchandise or service is paid for, and the customer is happy with the transaction.

Number two, the "sure sale" wasn't sure until the prospect was *re*assured. I might point out that this letter demonstrates considerable empathy and understanding. It also reassures the student that others are having the same feelings he's having. David's letter indicates that he is proud of the young man and gives the added value of thanking the "future student" for his display of trust and confidence. David also personalizes the letter by saying, "I have enjoyed meeting and visiting with your family. I hope they are as excited for their new 'Pioneer' as I am. Welcome to the class of '94." Interestingly enough, the day the student got this letter he rushed down after work to complete his admissions requirements.

## COMPLICATED CLOSING

Howard Donnelly of Aurora, Colorado, uses his lunch hour as a physical AND mental feeding time. He reads some inspirational and educational material or listens to cassette recordings to "remotivate" himself. During one of his "luncheon learning labs," he was listening to some particularly good cassette recordings that addressed the importance of asking for the order. (These same cassettes are available by writing or calling our company.)

Howard sells for a consumer electronics wholesaler, and that same afternoon a customer called in and wanted information on one of his company's more expensive products. Howard gave him the information, the availability, and the investment (price). The customer was appreciative and closed the conversation by saying, "Well, thank you very much." Fortunately, Howard remembered what he had just heard on tape, and before the prospect could hang up, he asked, "Would you like to order one?" That was all he said.

There was a brief pause, and the customer responded, "Yeah, I guess I might as well get the thing and be done with it." As simple as that, the sale was made. The worst that might possibly have happened would have been for the prospect to say no. The reality is, as Howard put it, "If I did not ask for the order, that fellow probably would never have called again."

## DON'T MAKE IT HARDER THAN IT HAS TO BE

Donald Henry of Glenview, Illinois, used ingenuity and creativity, mixed with a sense of humor, to help the customer take action. Donald was offering a prospect the opportunity to make an investment in an entertainment stock company. It so happened that Donald had known the gentleman for quite a while, so he decided to take a calculated risk right in the middle of the conversation. He took his telephone and banged it on the desk three times, then he renewed the conversation by asking, "Mr. Prospect, did you hear that?" His prospect had obviously heard the loud sounds and said, "Yes."

Donald asked if he knew what that sound was, and when the prospect said, "No," Donald explained, "That was opportunity knocking, and you shouldn't miss out on it!" The prospect started laughing quite hard and said that was a great approach and he just couldn't believe a salesman would do something like that. So Donald asked for the order again. The prospect said, "It must be good if you would do something like that. I'll take it." Corny? Yes! Creative? You bet! And this time a little "creative corn" enabled Donald to make some hay.

Now remember, Donald knew his prospect. He had learned much about him in dealing with him over the years. Donald was also willing to try something a little different, particularly since it involved humor. And most important, it led to asking for the order—and getting the sale.

## ASKING AND RECEIVING

Although there are literally hundreds of ways to ask for the order, I am going to encourage you to focus on only three. K.I.S.S.—*K*eep *I*t *S*imple *S*alesman—has been the battle cry since the cave dwellers sold each other "fire sticks." Yes, you may well know over one hundred closes, but do you know them well enough to use them at a moment's notice in the proper sales environment?

If you will use one or all of these three ways of asking for the order for ninety days, you will close more sales more often—AND you will be prepared to develop three closes of your own based on your experience. The key is this: Don't reinvent the wheel. Go to school on other people's experience. Let these three methods be the foundation upon which you build your successful sales career.

Please remember that you may be selling why a teenager would want to behave and pay attention to the lecture in your classroom; why your patient would want to continue the particular treatments; why an employee would want to come to work on time; or why your spouse would want to stay married to you. The persuasion process is always the same, and with sensitivity, love, and concern, you can ask for the order regardless of product or service using these ideas.

## THREE QUESTIONS REVISITED

Earlier we talked about the three questions successful sales professionals utilize in asking for the order. I hope you have put these in your own words. As a reminder, let's review them.

- "Can you see where this would ______?" Your primary benefit (save you money, increase time with your family, etc.) that would cause the prospect to buy goes on the line.
- "Are you interested in ______?"
- "If you were ever going to start ______, when do you think would be the best time to start?"

There are more details on these three questions on page 139, but remember that you may use any buying motive in the space as long as it is the dominant buying motive that you have analyzed and made the prospect aware of in the earlier segments of the sales process.

## THE PROBABILITY CLOSE

Once your prospect is at the moment of truth, you may ask the following questions to obtain the order or the information you need to get the order.

"Mrs. Prospect, on a scale of 1 to 10 with 10 meaning you are ready to place your order, where would you stand right now?" Notice the subtleties of the question, and choose your words carefully.

I did not say that 1 meant "not interested" or "where do you *fall*" on the scale. You do not want to plant seeds of disinterest or falling for anything.

Wait patiently for the response, and when it comes, follow with this question: "If you are at __ (the number given you) right now, what would it take to move you to a 10?"

If you are consistently getting numbers from the first question that are less than 7, the first parts of your selling process are the problem. This close is best used when you are very close to getting the order but feel there is some resistance you need to get into the open. Handling this resistance (objections) is so important that I have spent an entire chapter on the process (chapter 11), but you cannot deal with an unknown objection. This close gets the problems into the open and enables you to deal with each one properly.

## THE SUMMARY CLOSE

The Summary Close may seem very basic to some of you, but don't minimize the significance of what may seem obvious. In the Summary Close, you recap the areas of the presentation that caused your prospect's eyes to light up—that turned the light bulb on—and then ask for the order. For example, "Mr. Prospect, you said that you needed to be a more effective closer. You said that if you could teach your salespeople more specific closing techniques, they could close more sales more often, and your company's business would increase substantially. You also said that *Ziglar on Selling* provided you with just what you are looking for. Is that correct?" Receiving an affirmative answer, you step forward confidently and say, "Mr. Prospect, since you obviously want to increase your business, may I have your order for 250 copies of 'The Ultimate Handbook for the Complete Sales Professional'?"

During the selling process, the prospects light a fire for themselves based on your providing the starter fluid and the matches. During the selling process, the fire will sometimes die down due to any number of circumstances or distractions. By summarizing what caused the fire to burn brightly, you rekindle the flame at the moment you are asking the prospects to make their investment. The more "feeling" they have at this moment, the more sales you will close.

## THE NAIL DOWN

After the prospect has given you the order, one of the most effective "nail down" comments (making sure the sale is "nailed down") I have come across is this: "Ms. Prospect, it would be a big help to me and I would consider it a personal favor if you would tell me one more time why you are so excited about ______ (owning this product)!"

At this point, you don't need to feel hesitant to ask for a favor. They just bought from you, and one reason is that they like you. The prospects will be willing and even anxious to do you the favor of granting your wish. The relationship will be strengthened, and the sale will be even more securely "nailed down."

Don't be afraid of their not knowing specifically why they bought. If people bought entirely because of a "feeling" and can't give you any logical reasons for buying, you stand a good chance of losing the sale or having dissatisfied clients. If you have to remind them why they are excited, that is O.K., too. You have the perfect opportunity to enumerate the logical and exciting benefits the clients will enjoy by owning the product. The "nail down" allows you to finish the sales process on a really high note!

## EVERY CALL RESULTS IN A SALE

Even though the most insensitive sales manager does not expect you to close 100 percent of the prospects you call on (though you should ask for the order on 99.9 percent of those calls), every call does result in a sale. Just because the order was not signed does NOT mean a sale was missed.

A sale is made on every interview. You persuade the prospects that they need your goods or services and they need them now—so the transaction is completed—or the prospects sell you that they do not want your goods or services or they do not want them now.

Theoretically, the odds are in your favor because very few consumers read books, attend classes, or listen to recordings on how not to buy. You, by the very fact you are reading this book, are making a serious effort to learn how to get the prospect to say yes. However, the reality is that for the sale to be made, there must be two "yes" decisions: The prospect must say, "Yes, I want it," and you, the salesperson, must be willing to say, "Yes, I want to sell it." On the surface the latter one seems slightly ridiculous, but the conduct, lack of professionalism, negativism, shortage of integrity, and a host of other things lead me to believe many salespeople really don't want to sell or don't expect to sell, and in both cases, the results will be the same.

Now I clearly understand that the sale should not be made on some calls. From time to time, I talk with salespeople selling products that do not meet my needs or desires. The real professional recognizes and acknowledges this fact. Under these conditions, it is infinitely better to miss that sale than to make the wrong kind of sale (one where neither prospect nor salesperson benefits long term). The one thing worse than missing a sale where the need and the capacity to buy are present is making the sale where the need did not exist or the product did not fill the need to the prospect's best advantage. Under those circumstances, future references and sales possibilities are virtually nonexistent for the salesperson. In our business, the only way we are going to survive—much less prosper—is to have customers who become assistant salespeople and feed us prospects and references.

## THE REAL SECRET OF CLOSING THE SALE

At the end of the sales presentation—whether it results in a yes, no, or maybe—the successful sales professional always asks the prospect for the names of people who might benefit from using the product or service just described. You really have to ask yourself about your level of belief in what you are selling if you are not willing to ask this question. With leads costing anywhere from $20 to $2,000 to generate, the referral goes a long way in reducing costs to the company. And even more important, referrals keep the sales professional in business. Remember, no matter how good your product may be or regardless of the quality of your presentation, you are bankrupt and out of business if you don't have someone to tell your story to. Early in my career, I was fortunate to have an outstanding sales manager, Bill Cranford (to whom I dedicated *Secrets of Closing the Sale*). Bill really helped me to understand this most important point.

One of the best compliments I have ever received occurred while asking a brand-new customer for referrals. In an effort to help this new client understand that no pressure to buy would be put on her friends and acquaintances, I explained that when I called on people who were referred to me, I simply made the presentation and if they chose to buy that was fine, but if they chose not to buy that was O.K., too, because I certainly wouldn't put any pressure on them.

With that the prospect interrupted and said, "Yes, I'm sure that's true. You're just about the sorriest salesman I think I've ever seen." Interestingly enough, that prospect had just bought everything our company had for sale. But the key words were these: "That prospect had just BOUGHT." She did not feel she had been SOLD, which in my judgment is the key. Your role is to become an assistant buyer and help the prospects make the purchase—not to make them feel you have just sold them.

## BACK TO THE JUDGE

Since I started this chapter talking about my brother, it only seems fair to close in the same way. In addition to being the strongest closer I have ever watched work, my brother was something of a showman. He had a closing instinct (knowing when to ask for the order) that accompanied the conviction that what he was selling was the greatest product any prospect could ever buy.

When it came to closing, he and I were at completely different ends of the spectrum, despite similar results. Even though the last year I was in direct sales on a full-time basis, I closed over 90 percent of the people to whom I made presentations, he still had the audacity to accuse me of being one of the poorest closers he had ever seen! The difference was style, not results. Judge "went for the jugular" and was convinced that if he didn't ask—and ask often—he was doing a disservice to the prospects. My conviction was that if I built enough logic and emotion into the presentation, the prospects' desire for ownership would be so great that when I asked them to buy and believed they were going to buy, the close was almost automatic. The lesson for you is to work within the framework of your own personality and don't give up your backbone—ALWAYS ASK FOR THE ORDER!

## THE JUDGE AND THE ATTORNEY

One night my brother Judge (his name, not his title) called on an attorney and his wife. The attorney's mind was somewhat like concrete—meaning that it was all mixed up and appeared to be permanently set. He told my brother he wasn't going to buy and gave him the reason. Judge dealt with the objection and asked for the order. The attorney gave him another objection, and again, my brother answered the objection and asked for the order. This went on for a dozen objections. I sat there watching, waiting, and wondering why my brother was wasting his time. It was obvious to me that this man had no intentions of buying.

**Work within the framework of your own personality and don't give up your backbone—ALWAYS ASK FOR THE ORDER!**

When the attorney brought up yet another objection, my brother loudly slapped his leg, jumped straight up, and said to the attorney, "You rascal you! I ought to have you shot!" The expression on the attorney's face was one of total astonishment, shock, and disbelief. His face started to get a little red, and he said, "What are you talking about?"

My brother responded, "I finally figured out what you are doing. You just want to see how far I will go. You want to learn every answer to every objection in the book, and you're going to use it in your law practice and the courtroom." Then Judge laughed and continued, "Man, I appreciate a guy like you who knows exactly what he wants, but the sales class is now over. Go get your checkbook. Give me the check for the order, and then I will continue the sales class—but not until then."

To this day I could not tell you why the attorney bought. He never pleaded guilty to what my brother had accused him of, though they did chat pleasantly for a few more minutes after he wrote the check. We left with a happy couple and a smiling attorney who was still shaking his head in disbelief.

Confession: That's one sale I would have missed. I also believe that 99 percent of all salespeople would have missed it. The story has one message to you: Regardless of circumstances, technical knowledge, type of prospect, experience, investment, or anything else, ALWAYS ASK FOR THE ORDER!

## WHAT IF THEY SAY NO?

When your prospects say no, the reason is most often that they do not "know" enough to say yes. There is a method that will allow you to discover what additional information is needed to close the sale. I call this concept the Q.U.I.E.T. Method for overcoming objections and closing more sales more often. Chapter 11 is designed to help you overcome "no" by placing prospects in the "know."

## PART IV OF THE SUCCESSFUL SALES PROCESS: NEEDS SATISFACTION

1. **A.A.F.T.O. = Always Ask For The Order; Salespeople miss 100 percent of the sales not asked for.**

2. **The Three-Question Close helps ask for the order:**
   A. "Can you see where my product or service would ______?" (The primary benefit that would cause the prospect to buy goes on the line.)
   B. "Are you interested in ______?"
   C. "If you were ever going to start ______, when do you think would be the best time to start?"

3. **The Probability Close helps the prospect understand how close he is to making the purchase:**
   A. "On a scale of 1 to 10, with 10 meaning you are ready to place your order, where would you stand right now?"
   B. "What would it take to move you to a 10?"

4. **The Summary Close may seem basic, but don't be fooled by simplicity:**
   A. Summarize all the reasons the prospect has given you for buying and ASK FOR THE ORDER! Relight the fire through summarization.

5. **Ask the prospect to tell you why he decided to make the purchase to "nail down" the sale.**

CHAPTER ELEVEN

# CLOSING MORE SALES MORE OFTEN

## *A Q.U.I.E.T. Method for Overcoming Objections*

In my early days of selling, prospects would occasionally ask why a deposit was required. The usually acceptable explanation was that making a deposit was an act of good faith. I would go on to explain that since the company had to make an investment in packing and shipping the merchandise, the managers needed to know for certain that the customer was serious about ordering.

From time to time, a prospect would say, "That deposit is really yours, isn't it?" The implication was that I was pushing for the sale because the down payment would be mine. Over the years I developed a response that allowed me to break the ice, make a friend, and get the sale all at the same time. While looking the prospect right in the eyes, I would respond with an absolutely straight face, "No, the deposit is not mine, but I know that many companies work that way." Then keeping the straight face I would say, "I send the deposit to the company, and then I get all the rest!" The customer would invariably laugh, and then we were in business.

I have had a prospect say to me, "You just want me to buy so you can make money." Since the statement was always said in a serious manner, my response was, "Mr. Prospect, if 100 percent of your investment came directly to me, it still would provide only a small fraction of my monthly needs. If that was my reason for selling, I would not be in this business for very long. In a matter of days—or even hours—my profit from this transaction will be gone, but your benefit from using my product will last the rest of your life. Here's my question: In all fairness, if we complete the transaction, who do you think is going to be the bigger winner?"

## THE PROFESSIONAL SALESPERSON'S BEST FRIENDS

The person selling elephants gets three basic objections: Where does that thing sleep? What does that thing eat? Who cleans up after it?

You may not be in the business of selling elephants, but all sales professionals deal with questions and objections. Some fear that these questions and objections lead the prospect toward the dreaded "no" response when attempting to close the sale. Actually, OBJECTIONS ARE OUR BEST FRIENDS.

Asking a question or raising an objection indicates interest or feeling. Think of an area that holds little or no interest to you. Whether you thought of basketball, opera, fishing, golf, television, ballet, or race-car driving, you have no questions (objections) if you have no interest. For me, it's fishing. Regardless of the quality, brand, resort, or basically anything in this area, I just don't care about fishing, so I am a poor prospect. The fishing gear salesperson could waste a considerable amount of time with me because my tendency would be to respond kindly and courteously, but the chances of my buying are remote at best.

Now the golf enthusiast is an entirely different story. If an equipment salesperson wants to discuss the merits of rubber versus leather grips, I will be there expressing an opinion and asking questions. Steel shafts versus graphite? Let's talk! Because I love the game of golf, your opportunity for "hooking" me emotionally is much greater than in discussing fishing.

Do you ask questions about things or ideas about which you have no interest? If there is a discussion concerning something you feel passionately about, are you prone to give your opinion? True selling professionals look forward to questions and objections because they realize that few sales are made without the prospects having enough interest to ask questions and raise objections.

## CHANGING "NO" TO "KNOW"

O.K., now that you're convinced that it is good for the prospects to ask questions and raise objections, what happens when the answers are not satisfactory and the prospects say no?

This may surprise some of you, but once your prospects say no, they are not going to change their minds and buy from you. Sales veterans will often tell you that the majority of their sales are made after prospects say no, and earlier, I shared some statistics about 60 percent of the sales occurring after the prospect has said no five times. However, I stand by my statement that your prospects are not going to "change their minds" and buy from you.

Your prospects, however, will make a NEW DECISION BASED ON ADDITIONAL INFORMATION. You see, when prospects say no, the successful sales professional understands that the "no" must mean the prospects don't "know" enough to make the right decision. Never argue with them. Just understand that you haven't finished your job, and accept the responsibility for going back and providing the information needed. With additional information, they will "know" enough to make a new (and favorable) decision.

## TO REPEAT MYSELF

The great life insurance salesman Ben Feldman said the same thing in many different ways: "The sale begins when the customers say no. In many cases, the 'no' just means the customers or the prospects are saying no because they do not 'KNOW' enough to say yes. They're really saying, 'I've got to say no because I value my big stack of money more than I value your little stack of benefits.' "

## THE Q.U.I.E.T. METHOD

Let's look at a concept that will allow you to handle real objections in an efficient and effective way so you can close more sales more often.

When objections occur, the professional salesperson will get Q.U.I.E.T. Each letter in the formula stands for a word that will allow you to help your prospects gather enough information to overcome their objections. When you get an objection, you pause and think Q.U.I.E.T.

*Q.* Begin with a QUESTION.

*U.* You must ask *Q*uestions so that you can UNDERSTAND the objection.

*I.* Once you *U*nderstand the objection, you must IDENTIFY the objection.

*E.* To *I*dentify the proper objection (and not be fooled by a false objection), you must EMPATHIZE with the prospect.

*T.* If you *E*mpathize instead of sympathize with the prospect, you are ready to TEST the objection. When you *T*est the objection and prove it real, you can eliminate the prospect's concerns and dramatically improve your chance of making the sale.

## QUESTIONS

*Ziglar on Selling* has emphasized asking questions, and the questions you ask here are very similar to the ones you have been learning about throughout the book. You are going to ask Closed Door Questions because you want to confine the prospect to a certain area with the response. There may even be occasion for the Yes or No Question.

Our three-day seminar, Born To Win, is taught six times per year here in Dallas, Texas. I lecture each day and then visit with the participants during the breaks and lunchtime. Our staff "coaches" the participants on how to personalize the principles in their lives. This is done through small group interaction. The tuition investment is just $595, and as you might guess, that amount is incredibly low (especially considering the comprehensive personality evaluation, special leadership training session, and the large amount of support materials) for most businesses accustomed to paying $1,500 to over $3,000 for three-day seminars. However, some individuals and families who aren't involved in training on a regular basis are surprised by the amount. What does surprised mean? That is precisely what we must find out by asking questions.

When our ZZC sales professional invites people to spend three days with us here in Dallas and informs them that doing so will require an investment of only $595, the salesperson hears many different kinds of responses. When the prospect responds, "Wow, $595, wow!" with full enthusiasm, what does that mean to the salesperson? Until the sales professional asks a question, the response means nothing.

"How do you feel about that investment?" would be an excellent Closed Door Question. "This is a wonderfully low investment for a three-day seminar, isn't it?" would be a possible Yes or No Question. Until you know whether the "wow" is for unbelievably high or incredibly low, you don't have anywhere to go in the sales process.

## Most of the Time You Know!

Yes, I admit that in the majority of situations, you know if you will face price sensitivity or not. I use the example above to make a point. What is the purpose of the *Q*uestion in the Q.U.I.E.T. formula? The successful sales professional asks the question to *U*nderstand and *I*dentify the objection.

As I mentioned earlier, one of the most effective ways you can ask a question about the price objection is by turning the prospect's statement into a question. When the prospect adamantly states, "That price is too high!" You simply pause, lower your voice, and respond, "The price (pause) is too high?" In reality you don't know what the "price is too high" means. The price objection can mean: "I don't have the money today; accessing the money from accounts is too much trouble; we did not budget for an expenditure like this; your "little" stack of benefits does not outweigh my "big" stack of money; or I just don't understand why you value the product that highly." Each reason for a price objection must be handled differently, and if you just launch into a prepared response to price objections in general, you will not be as successful as is possible.

## *U*NDERSTANDING AND *I*DENTIFYING OBJECTIONS

The questions asked will lead to *U*nderstanding and *I*dentifying the objection. Let me give you a specific example. Don Jarrell of

Garden Grove, California, sells enrollments in a fine accredited vocational college in Long Beach, California. He is completely sold on the school and everything it represents. Several years ago, a man and his three daughters came to his office to discuss enrolling in the college. The total cost was more than $16,000. The prospect was understandably hesitant.

Since Don had done the Need Analysis, Need Awareness, and Need Solution portions of the sales process, he had the information he needed to ask for the order (Need Satisfaction). Don had discovered that the man was quite capable of affording the investment. When the prospect showed some hesitancy (there was an unidentified objection), Don got Q.U.I.E.T. He began *Q*uestioning the prospect by asking, "Do you invest in the stock market?" After the man responded in the affirmative, Don continued by asking, "Do you consider the funds needed to put your daughters through school an investment or an expenditure?" When the man responded that the tuition would be an investment, Don continued his questions by asking, "And just how much are your daughters worth as an investment?"

With this question, Don asked the prospect to think about how much he valued and loved his daughters; how important their futures were; and how an investment in the stock market paled in comparison to an investment in his daughters' futures. An investment in the stock market may or may not bring a profit, but an investment in the education of his children would bring a guaranteed result that would continue to produce dividends as the years went by.

This simple, yet profound approach produced results that made Don Jarrell a winner, the father a winner, and all three daughters winners! Don's Q.U.I.E.T. approach was truly a win-win-win situation because the man's response was to enroll all three daughters in the college. I am pleased to be able to report that all three graduated and are competing successfully in the work force today!

Don was successful because he asked *Q*uestions that helped him to *U*nderstand and *I*dentify the man's objection, which was a lack of knowledge about return on investment. Using the principles of the Q.U.I.E.T. formula, Don led the prospect to clearly understand that he wasn't "spending" money to send his daughters to college; he was "investing" money in their futures.

Would the man have made the investment had Don not asked the right question? The answer is that we will never know. But this I do know: Many people take positive action that is right for them because a skilled professional salesperson (selling worthwhile goods and services) persuaded them to act in their own best interests. Unfortunately, I also know that many people neglect to take positive action in worthwhile ventures because they do not have a professional dealing with them—one who asks the right questions and leads them to make the right decisions. As professionals, we have a responsibility to continue to grow and improve so we can render even more service.

## *E*MPATHY VS. SYMPATHY

Don could have sympathized with the man by saying, "Yes, I understand your hesitancy because I feel the same way. I have children, and when I think about them going to college, I just don't know what I am going to do. College tuitions are outrageous today, aren't they?" However, instead of feeling like the prospect felt (sympathy), Don understood how the prospect felt without having the same feeling (empathy), which allowed him to make the sale.

**The successful sales professional asks the question to *U*nderstand and *I*dentify the objection.**

If you are sailing with friends and one gets seasick and begins to throw up, you may well understand how he feels. The chances are good that you have thrown up at some point in your life. When you understand how that person feels because you "have been there," you can have great empathy for another human being. However, if you are sailing with friends and one gets seasick and begins to throw up, and you rush to the rail and begin to throw up, too, this is sympathy. And I might add that this won't help your seasick friend a bit. If you have empathy, you will join your friend at the rail with a cool cloth to bathe his face and some medicine to quiet that upset stomach.

## Empathy Overseas

Empathy is required to build a successful sales career. Along with empathy, you will develop intuition and psychological insights into people, which can make a substantial difference in your results. Many times experience is required, but as you work to develop genuine sensitivity—by listening to what your prospect is really saying and not just the words used—you develop empathetic sales skills.

K. J. Hartley of Cheshire, England, called on a young couple to sell the wife an insurance policy. The husband had adequate coverage, but the wife had no insurance. K. J. knew that the couple had one small child and one on the way, so the need was obvious. The objection the couple kept using was, "We can't afford it," although the monthly premium was only £12 (less than $21 at today's exchange rate). By asking *Q*uestions so he could *U*nderstand and *I*dentify the problem, K. J. discovered that the couple had determined that £10 per month was their limit. Since so many of their other expenses were covered in £10 increments, they had a mental block against paying more than that amount per month.

As K. J. began to close his folder in preparation for leaving, he realized that he might be sympathizing with the prospects, and he stopped for a Q.U.I.E.T. moment. He had been listening to their words, but had he been listening to what they were saying? "Do you think that £3 or less *per week* would cause you a problem?" was K. J.'s question. They both agreed that this amount would be easy. The answer showed that they did not have a financial problem. Their problem was the perception of the monthly £10 barrier.

At that point K. J. multiplied the £12 by twelve months, which equals £144. He divided £144 by fifty-two weeks and came up with the perfectly acceptable premium of £2.76 per week. The objection of £12 per month reduced to acceptable figures made the sale.

Obviously, £2.76 per week and £12 per month are the same thing. But please notice K. J. wasn't "tricking" the people; he was filling their need in a manner that was psychologically acceptable. The couple needed the protection. They had the money. They needed an empathetic salesman who could understand how they felt and show them a way to take action that would be comfortable for them, their children, and their future. K. J. Hartley took the Q.U.I.E.T. approach and broke a psychological barrier (they couldn't take a *big* £12 per month step, but they could easily take a *little* £2.76 per week step) for a couple with a problem who needed the solution he had to offer.

## *T*ESTING THE OBJECTION

Some prospects will not *tell* you the true objection, and some prospects will not *know* the true objection. In both cases, they are often operating on a "feeling" level. The prospect who is embarrassed to admit he doesn't have the money or doesn't understand the offer may not admit the true objection. He feels poor or uneducated, and his pride or ego demands that he say he is not interested.

### Gorilla Dust

The sales professional recognizes false objections as "gorilla dust." You may have seen the PBS television series showing the behaviors and habits of wild gorillas. When two males engage in battle, there is quite a show. They circle each other several times and in the process rake their hands in the dirt, scooping up handfuls that when thrown in the air make quite a dust storm or smoke screen. This is "gorilla dust," and many prospects will often go through a similar process.

Most of you have heard the old joke about the fellow who refused to loan his lawn mower to the next-door neighbor. When pressed for a reason, he replied, "Because all planes are leaving late today."

"What kind of reason is that?" was his neighbor's indignant response. "Not much of one, but when you don't want to do something, and you're not gonna do something, one reason is about as good as another," said the fellow.

For the professional sales representative, one reason is NOT as good as another, so to discover true objections, you will want to *T*est.

## The "Suppose" Test

Two kinds of tests for prospects will help you identify the difference between "gorilla dust" and true objections. These tests also help the prospect who really doesn't know what her objection is but knows she can't get comfortable with the decision to buy.

**Some prospects will not *tell* you the true objection, and some prospects will not *know* the true objection.**

The first test is the "Suppose" Test. "Ms. Prospect, just suppose that condition didn't exist. Would you then buy my product or service?"

- "Suppose ______ were not a consideration, then would you buy?"
- "Suppose you felt good about ______, then would you buy?"
- "Suppose ______, then would you make a 'yes' decision?"

If you can identify the proper objection, then you can take steps to overcome it or move on to the next prospect instead of wasting time eliminating "gorilla dust" or trying to close a sale that will never be closed.

## The "Isolate and Validate" Test

The second test is the "Isolate and Validate" Test. This two-step process proves whether or not you have discovered the true objection. The first step comes when you ask, "Is there any *other* reason that would prevent you from taking advantage of my offer today?" Your objective here is to draw out any and all objections. One of the most frustrating things that can happen to a salesperson is to deal with an objection competently and professionally and then have another one spring up. After you have answered two objections, you need to specifically ask on the third one, "Is this the only thing standing between you and ownership of our product, or is there something else?" You don't want to give the impression that you are going to be with the prospect all day until he finally comes up with an objection you can't answer.

Once you get the "no, that is the only thing" response, you will summarize to validate. "So, Mr. Prospect, you're telling me that if ______ and ______ were not issues, you would buy today?" At this point, you are prepared to close the sale.

## The Classic Story

One of my favorite stories concerning the "Isolate and Validate" Test was included in *Secrets of Closing the Sale.* I paraphrase it here because it is such a strong example of the Q.U.I.E.T. method of closing sales.

Jay Martin, a good friend of mine from Memphis, Tennessee, is the president of National Safety Associates, a company that sells smoke-and-fire detectors. One evening he was working with one of his young dealers who made a solid presentation and finished by asking for the order. Then Jay described the scene: "Zig, this old boy, who probably didn't finish the first grade, reared back on the hind legs of his chair, folded his arms, and said, 'Well, son, of course you've heard about my wreck!' The young man hadn't, so the prospect proceeded to give him all the details."

The prospect began the Q.U.I.E.T. formula for Jay's associate without even being asked the *Q*uestion. Fortunately, Jay and the young salesman listened for *U*nderstanding and *I*dentification. They listened to the words the prospect was sharing AND what he was saying as he explained, "Me and my wife were driving down the highway a couple of months ago, and this dude who was passing on the wrong side of the road hit us head-on, tore our car all to pieces, and put us both in the hospital. As a matter of fact, I was in there nearly two weeks, and the accident left my ankle kind of stiff. Since I work on a piece-good basis, I haven't been able to get around as well, and my income's down. Man, that sure hurts!

"My wife was in the hospital over six weeks, and she was gone so long her company phased out her job, so she's not even working. When you've been used to two incomes and all of a sudden you've only got one, man, that sure creates a problem! The hospital bill for both of us was over $20,000. Now I know the insurance company's eventually going to pay it, but they sure have us nervous in the meantime!

"On top of all of that, just last week our boy came home from the navy and the first night at home he rounded a curve too fast, went over an embankment and down into a service station, tore up our other car, and destroyed a $6,000 oil company sign. Now, I know the insurance is going to pay for the car, but I don't know about that sign. I'll tell you right now, if we have to come up with $6,000, we're really going to be up a creek, and I don't know what we'll do!

"If all of that isn't enough, just last night we checked my mother-in-law into the most expensive nursing home in the county. The only other living relative is a brother, and I know he won't do anything. He hasn't even been heard from in over a year, and he's not worth shooting even if we did know where he was. I know I'm going to have to carry the whole load."

## Would You Sympathize or Empathize?

If you were the salesperson on this call and you had a lot of sympathy, you would probably say, "Oh, that's just terrible, and I'll bet it's even worse than that! You just don't want to make me feel bad, and that's the reason you're not telling me the rest of it! But let me ask you a question. Won't the government do something? What about the Red Cross? What about your neighbors? Won't the church make a contribution? Can't you at least get food stamps?" Now that's sympathy, but according to Jay Martin, this salesman did not have sympathy. He had empathy.

With empathy you are emotionally detached from the problem, so you can offer solutions. You move from your side of the table to the prospect's side. Realistically, that is where the sale is going to be made, and the chance of that happening is greatly increased because from the prospect's side of the table you can make your presentation from his point of view.

## Sales Professionals Isolate and Validate

Our young hero looked the prospect in the eye and said, "Tell me, sir, in addition to those things, would there be any other reason you could not go ahead and protect the lives of your family by installing these smoke-and-fire detectors in your home?"

What courage! Can you imagine having the audacity to ask a prospect with all those problems if there was anything else that would prevent him from buying? Well, Jay's associate did exactly that, and the prospect was about as shocked as I was when I first heard the story. He literally roared with laughter, slapped his leg, and said, "No, son, those are the only reasons we couldn't go ahead and buy the alarms today. Ha, ha, ha!" (At that point I believe it would be safe to say that he did not consider himself a prospect.)

## This Is Why You Are in Business—to Make Sales

Strategically, the salesman had done his job very well. The pro will bring out all the objections as early as possible so each objection can be dealt with effectively. As a matter of fact, sales professionals often take the objection—the reason for not buying—and use it as the major reason the prospect should buy. Notice how that happens in this situation.

When the salesman learned there were no other reasons for not buying, he never hesitated. He reached down into his sample case and removed one of the detectors. He held the detector up against the wall to let the prospect see how it looked and said, "Sir, as nearly as I can tell, you now owe nearly $30,000 (pause) and $300 more just won't make any difference at all." He lowered his voice, looked the man in the eye, and quietly said, "Sir, fire—under any circumstances—is devastating. But in your case, it would wipe you out!" The technique was professional; the logic was sound. He got the sale by being Q.U.I.E.T.

# OBJECTIONS WE ALL SEE

The objective of the sales presentation is to provide service to the prospects because you *can* have everything in life you want if you will just help enough other people get what they want. The objections give you insight into the prospects that can help you meet their needs and wants.

Objections, of course, are part of every sales professional's life. Our attitude toward them makes a tremendous amount of difference in how effective we are going to be in handling objections. Dennis Landrum of Bryan, Texas, heads a company that provides many business services, including microcomputer consultation. Two objections he frequently encounters are the two virtually every salesperson encounters hundreds—even thousands—of times in a career. I think you will like the little twist he gives to his answers.

For the standard, "We have a friend (nephew, college professor, uncle, etc.) who helps us when we have a need for this kind of service," Dennis has a great response. Pay close attention to his wording.

"You are fortunate to have someone you can call on. However, we're here right now, offering you ways to improve your business. More important, we will be here in the future to help you as your business grows, and we won't wait for you to call us when there's a need. Whenever we learn of something that will help you, because it is our business and in your best interests, we will contact you. Helping successful businesspeople like you is all we do, so we can devote the time and effort to your business that it deserves, and that really is the kind of service you want and need, isn't it, Mr. Prospect?"

## THE CEREBRAL STALL

For the famous, "I want to think it over" or "Let me think it over for a few days," Dennis has an equally appealing response.

"In running my business, I have often found myself on the opposite side of the table from a salesman and have made that very same statement. Over a period of time I came to realize that whenever I asked for time to 'think it over,' I was really saying one of three things.

"In the first place, I might really want to think it over because I had some questions that had not been answered. If this is what you are saying, I will be glad to answer those for you right now.

"Or I might really be saying, 'I'm not interested in any way,' but

I just didn't want to hurt the salesperson's feelings, though I had no intentions of considering the proposal any further. I can respect your decision and would only ask that if this is the case, please tell me now and save us both time.

"Or I might ask for time to 'think it over' when I really had another objection. Again, I would only ask that you be honest with me, as I have been with you, and allow me the opportunity to answer whatever questions or objections you may have."

I might point out that these responses to common objections draw out the issues so that each can be dealt with in the most efficient, effective, and professional manner possible so you can get a decision at that time. After all, if the decision is yes, then you, your company, AND the client can start enjoying the benefits NOW! If the answer is no, then you can direct your energy and attention to the next prospect with the comforting knowledge that you did not leave an order lying on the table.

## I'LL BE RIGHT BACK

Tim Jones, from Campbellsville, Kentucky, discovered a very interesting way of dealing with the "think it over" objection. After going through extensive paperwork and data for the prospect, he would ask the obligating question. If the prospect would ask for time to "think it over," Tim's friend would smile, stand up, and say, "Fine, I'm going to run down to the corner and get a cup of coffee. I'll be back in fifteen to twenty minutes, so you folks go ahead and talk it over." Before the prospect had time for a response he was out the door, leaving the paperwork behind.

Upon returning, Tim would resume where he left off, saying, "Which way did you decide would be best for us to provide this savings to you—monthly, automatic check, or annualized premiums?" More often than not, he gets the sale.

## THE GUNFIGHTER

Some salespeople learn to enjoy dealing with objections a little too much. They let their ego enter the picture and may actually encourage objections so that they can demonstrate their intelligence and skill. These salespeople become like gunfighters, hungry for the fight: "Make your move, you dirty prospect. Anything you ask, I have an answer for!"

## IS PRICE THE PROBLEM?

Before we leave the area of objections, let me share a classic example of how to handle the "Is this your best price" or "Come on, get your pencil out, you can do better than that!"

Larry Spevak of Maplewood, Minnesota, responds this way: "No, it is not my best price." In most cases the eyes of the prospect will pop open, and his mouth will follow suit. Larry follows up with this logical explanation: "I can give you a lower price than what I just quoted, but it will have to come out of my pocket, and I can't work for nothing anymore than you can. I'm sure you wouldn't want that for me, anymore than I would want that for you."

Larry said that on one occasion a prospect "stared straight into my eyes, apparently overwhelmed by my very candid explanation, and with a look of relief written across his face, he stuck out his hand and very solemnly declared, 'Larry, you're an honest man, and I appreciate that. Write up the order!' " Obviously, Larry had just cashed a credibility deposit he had built over a period of time.

## AND FINALLY...

Larry also has a great way of handling another common objection: The prospect who "forewarns" the salesperson that he WILL NOT be buying today. The excuses vary from "I always think it over" to "I always talk over every decision with my brother-in-law."

On one specific call, Larry says that after the initial "how are you's," the prospect said, "Now, look, Larry, I want you to know right up front that we're not buying tonight because we never buy the first time. If you don't want to give us an estimate and let us think about it, then you're wasting your time and ours." (Larry sells home improvements.)

"He was expecting me to pick up my bag and leave," Larry explains, "but I surprised him. I looked him squarely in the eye and in a very serious and deliberate tone of voice replied, 'Mr. Prospect, you're absolutely right. I agree with you. Like you, I never like to buy the first time, but (and I emphasized the BUT) when I see something I really like and I know it will solve my problem and the price is right, I give some very serious consideration to making an exception. Now, let me show you and your wife what our product can do for you.' "

This actually formed a Bridge from presentation to the close. Larry took the man off the defensive and opened his mind so that he would listen to the presentation. As Larry said, "Because I agreed with him, my image as a nice guy rose at least ten points, and it wasn't very difficult to convince them both, because I was their friend, that my product was going to solve their problems as of now."

Larry gave a convincing demonstration, which left no room for objections. With a little finesse, he managed to convert this husband and wife from frustrated shoppers to happy buyers. As Larry says, "If you permit a prospect's declaration of 'not buying tonight' to intimidate you, your presentation becomes dull and routine and lacks the power to stay in control, so you end up letting your competition get the job."

## DANGER

Remember, your objective is not to prove how many objections you can answer but to prove how much your goods and services can benefit the prospect.

## IMPORTANT

The sale does not end when you have overcome objections and the customer says yes. Actually, the sale is just beginning. The next chapter is designed to help you understand how to deal with the happy AND the unhappy prospects and clients.

A great danger in dealing with objections (and in many other parts of the sales process) is crossing the line from "caring/aggressive" to "irritating/abrasive." Remaining aggressively concerned about the prospects and maintaining confidence without alienating customers are what chapter 12 is all about!

CHAPTER TWELVE

# BEYOND CUSTOMER "SERVICE" TO CUSTOMER "SATISFACTION"

## *Do You Give Up, Clean Up, or Follow Up?*

In the "yesteryear" days of selling, an older salesman and a younger salesman were riding the train back home at the end of the week and were involved in a serious conversation. The younger salesman was "singing the blues" about how badly he had been treated all week. Business was bad, people were rude, and he had been insulted time after time. The older salesman grew thoughtful for a moment and then remarked, "Well, you know, I've had doors slammed in my face, I've been invited to leave and encouraged not to come back, I've been fussed at, cussed at, and even spit at, but INSULTED?!?! Never!"

### PREVENTIVE MEDICINE

The days of "customer service" as the standard of excellence are long gone! Today, EVERYBODY talks about the importance of customer "service." In today's competitive market, the only way to get ahead (and sometimes, the only way to survive) is to go beyond customer service to customer satisfaction.

The best way to prevent the customer or prospect from becoming unhappy is to provide excellent service BEFORE the problems are allowed to arise. As I said earlier, the Norwegian word for *sell* is *selje*, which literally means "to serve." The question is simple: Is that good sales strategy? Carl Sewell is convinced that service is the key. In his book *Customers for Life*, he offers profound insights into the concept. It seems to work for him because he has a $250 million-a-year automobile dealership network in Dallas, Texas.

Mr. Sewell has figured that each customer is worth $332,000 over a car-buying lifetime, and he obviously wants that money spent at one of his five dealerships. What does his company do to ensure the second, third, fourth, and fifth sales? Well, let's start with a fleet of over 250 loaner cars made available to his customers when they have a car serviced. Incidentally, the service rep will drop the loaner off at the customer's home and pick up the car to be repaired. Trouble on the road? If you bought your car from the company, just call the emergency number and a service technician will do everything from making you a new key to bringing you gasoline or repairing a flat tire.

Does this sort of pampering the customer pay off? Answer: An average salesperson at an average dealership will sell six or eight cars a month, but Carl Sewell expects his professional sales staff to sell fifteen luxury automobiles. After all, they have an awful lot of help in the public relations department and, more important, in the service department. If the service people do a less-than-perfect job, they do it again—do it on their own time. Do his people resent that? On the contrary. They feel like they are partners in the business, and his service manager is probably the best-paid service manager in the area, if not in the industry. He gets 10 percent of the department's profit increases each year, and a $150,000 income is not uncommon.

There are some who would say that Sewell has gone the extra ten miles, not just the extra mile. But he is not satisfied to be only as good today as he was yesterday, so he studies from experts to learn how to be even better. From the Disney people he learned to be conscientious about the little things. The floors are spotlessly clean. If there's a piece of litter on the grounds, he is inclined to pick it up himself. Stanley Marcus of Neiman-Marcus taught him the importance of saying yes to customers. The Japanese and the greatest management consultant of this century, W. Edwards Deming, taught him the value of measuring everything. In short, here's a salesman who believes that keeping a customer is only one-fifth as expensive as advertising for a new one.

## I SELL CARS

For years, Tom Armstrong was the best Cadillac salesman in Texas. Working for Sewell Village Cadillac, Tom sold in excess of $7 million in cars in a single year, and that's when cars sold for about 40 percent less than in today's market. Roughly 80 percent of his sales were to previous customers. Tom really has a handle on what his business and his life are all about. He's a man who works the high-rent district, earns a six-figure income each year, and won't even talk about getting his own dealership because he wouldn't want to take a cut in pay.

He runs in the elite social circles, and when he's asked what line of work he's in (much to the chagrin of some of his friends), he simply responds, "I'm a car salesman." He doesn't include the prestigious qualifier—"Cadillac." He points out that car salesmen are supposed to be not highly regarded, but he says, "I'm proud of my success. I work at it, and I love it. That's why I call myself a car salesman—period." In one year alone he sold 326 Cadillacs. That's a lot of automobiles! He sponsors his own Little League baseball team who wear "Armstrong Cadillacs" on their jerseys.

What does he really sell? Tom says, "I sell the American dream. The Cadillac is still most people's idea of success." He's a hard worker, and he gets particularly revved up when he makes a sale to those people who have worked and scrimped for years to make the purchase of their dream car come true. He makes a big deal out of delivering a brightly polished new automobile to the proud owners. New Cadillac owners are made to feel like the king and queen Tom believes they really are. He is perhaps the most service-oriented salesman you'll ever meet, working for the most service-oriented dealership you can imagine.

Tom recently moved to Carl Sewell's Lexus dealership and is now selling the luxurious Lexus automobile with the same attitude toward service.

## SELLING DOES NOT END WITH CLOSING THE SALE

Within twenty-four hours after the "red-carpet" delivery of the car, Tom makes a call on the new owners just to make certain all things are working properly and they're very happy. He also knows that at that particular moment he has the best chance of getting new prospects (which he generally does). He makes it crystal clear that if there are ever any problems, he is the one to call. Tom emphasizes the fact that he and the service manager work together with one primary objective in mind: to serve the customer!

Tom is one of the hardest workers you will ever meet. He works hard not because he has to, but because he absolutely loves to. He begins the workday at 6:00 A.M., arriving at the dealership to begin what will be about a three-hour review process of service reports on cars purchased from him. By 10:00 A.M., he turns his attention to his prospects list made up of previous buyers, people who have visited the showroom but didn't buy, and referrals from other customers. He makes at least ten calls every day. He also keeps his previous buyers apprised of the current trade-in value of their automobiles. He doesn't work the floor in the dealership; he works from his office. He does most of his business by appointment, and it generally takes him about an hour to make a sale.

Needless to say, he deals with some very wealthy people, and here's where he gives us some tremendous advice. He says, "Wealthy customers are not that much different from most people. But you definitely don't give them the hard sell. The thing that makes an impression is the air of confidence—they have it, and they want you to have it, too, if they're going to buy from you." He also is aware that people don't buy what the automobile is but what it does and what it represents. He doesn't get hung up on the technical details of the cars, and he never opens the hood. "They're far more interested," he says, "in what a first-class form of transportation means to them."

## "UPSELLING" AND SERVICE

A farmer went into an automobile dealership to buy one of the "low-priced three." By the time he'd finished purchasing all the options, the price was considerably higher than the original quote. He pondered the matter for a number of days, and then one day the automobile salesman came calling on him to buy a cow. The farmer told him the cow was $275, and the salesman said, "That's fine. I'll take 'er." The farmer said, "Excuse me for a moment, and I will make out the bill of sale." A few minutes later he returned and said, "Here it is. The total is $805 plus $64 in tax, for a total of $869." The automobile salesman was astonished and said, "But I thought you told me the price was $275!" The farmer responded that that was the price for the "standard" cow, but this one came with some "special attachments." "For example," he said, "this beauty comes packed in a genuine two-tone, hand-brushed leather cowhide at $175. She has one built-in fertilizer plant, $95. Two custom-built horns at $30 for a total of $60. Four milk dispensers, $10 each, $40. One extra stomach, $95, and one customized flyswatter at $65 for a total of $805 plus sales tax of $64 for a grand total of $869."

I'm certain many of us have experienced a degree of frustration as we've purchased vacuum cleaners, computers, insurance coverage, automobiles, house cleaning services, yard and garden work, and a host of other things only to discover that when all the "extras" were added, the price was considerably higher than we had anticipated. Please don't misunderstand. Many times those "extras" make the difference between pure enjoyment and efficiency and certainly are worthwhile additions in most cases. The prime reason I include this example is to alert you to the fact that we need to always remember that as salespeople we have a responsibility to offer clients the things that will make their lives easier and make them more productive and profitable, but we must keep in mind that the overriding question is always, "Do I recommend this for the prospect's benefit or for my benefit?" I recognize this is a fairly thin line to walk. We're certainly in no position to make a prospect's decision. In many cases offering the option is adequate to make the sale, but it's an offer about which we should feel good. At the same time, we have a responsibility to that prospect.

A classic case of a salesperson not acting in the best interests of his client took place early in my life insurance days. I had worked awfully hard to sell a young postmaster in a small town one of our life insurance contracts. The man had zero insurance, a wife, and a small baby. It was one of the toughest sales I ever made, and it was for a grand total of $5,000. This happened many years ago, but $5,000—even in those days—was woefully inadequate. The additional premium for double indemnity, in the event of accidental death, involved just a few more dollars; however, I was afraid that if I pressed the issue, even for a moment, I would lose the sale. I'll confess that at that moment I was thinking about my losing the sale and not my client's best interests. I never offered him double indemnity. Less than a year later, it was my sad duty to deliver to a young widow a totally inadequate check that could have been twice as large had I only had the courage and concern to look after my client's best interests. I never forgot the lesson I learned that day. The real tragedy is that the young widow paid for my education.

Message: If your "extras" are in the best interests of your client, you certainly have a professional responsibility to offer them and encourage your prospect to act upon them.

## THIS IS SELLING

Your interest in your customers after the sale plays a major role in whether they will help you make additional sales. In 1985 we built our dream home overlooking the fifteenth tee at Glen Eagles Country Club in Plano, Texas. We were tremendously excited about the home and are enjoying it enormously today. Unfortunately, we built it as the real estate market started deteriorating dramatically. The rates of interest were high, and the market was difficult for selling existing homes.

Penny Magid, a highly skilled professional real estate salesperson, was involved in helping sell our home (which we had occupied with considerable delight and enjoyment for seventeen years). Penny and her associates really had only one legitimate prospect and sold that prospect. But that's not the reason the story is appearing in this book.

Two years after the purchase of our dream home, the rate of interest had declined. Out of the blue, Penny called one day and with considerable excitement shared the fact that she had located better rates for a mortgage. She put us in touch with a lender; we were able to get a new loan at a much better rate than the one we had originally acquired. Since then The Redhead and I have enabled Penny to sell at least one other home and possibly two or three more. Why did we do it? Very simple. We did not think of Penny as a salesperson, although she certainly is a superb one. We thought of her as a friend. She demonstrated that she was the kind of person we would want to recommend to others by demonstrating an ongoing interest in us.

The professional who is interested in building a career will not forget the customer when the sale is made. The pro will, through meticulous record keeping, follow up when something of interest or benefit comes along that will benefit that customer. Penny Magid is a primary example of the professional salesperson's credo we have mentioned throughout this book—YOU CAN HAVE EVERYTHING IN LIFE YOU WANT IF YOU WILL JUST HELP ENOUGH OTHER PEOPLE GET WHAT THEY WANT.

## THE STORY CONTINUES

The Penny Magid story has yet another chapter. Again in 1991, interest rates declined, and Penny worked out the details on a home loan that was even better than the great deal she discovered for us in 1987! At closing time, Penny suffered a serious heart attack and was pronounced clinically dead. Fortunately, after major surgery, she is recuperating rapidly and headed for a full recovery.

Even as I write these words, however, Penny is having one of the best months of her career. How can this happen when she is recuperating in the hospital? The answer is very simple: Penny is not only a special friend to The Redhead and me; she is also a special friend to all of her other clients and associates. All of the business she had working at the time of her surgery (including that of my son and his wife) is being credited to Penny. Her clients are asking for this, and Forester-Clements, the real estate broker with whom she works, and all the people affiliated with the company are delighted to handle the details and paperwork until Penny gets back on her feet. Yes, it is absolutely true. When you are the right kind of person, you become the right kind of salesperson!

## SMALL COURTESIES

On February 15, 1991, I was scheduled to leave Orange County, California, on flight #538 for Dallas. I much prefer to have an aisle seat, but they were all taken when the reservation was made. I explained to the gate agent that, if it was possible and one came open, I would like to have that seat. She enthusiastically wrote my name down and said that she would carefully note that fact. If one became available, she would see to it that I got it.

**YOU CAN HAVE EVERYTHING IN LIFE YOU WANT IF YOU WILL JUST HELP ENOUGH OTHER PEOPLE GET WHAT THEY WANT.**

I boarded the aircraft, took my seat, and was comfortably working away when a pleasant male voice leaned over and said, "Mr. Ziglar?" I looked up to see the friendly outstretched hand of Geoffrey M. Gregor. He introduced himself as the special service manager of American Airlines and said he had found someone who would be delighted to exchange seats with me. At that point, Don Wilhelm, who had an aisle seat, entered the picture. I thanked him for his courtesy, and we made the exchange.

During the flight Don passed by my seat, and I asked him if he was an employee of the airline. He assured me that he was not, so I asked him how the conversation came about when Geoffrey asked him to make the exchange. He said that he and Geoffrey had been friends for a long time and that it was typical of Geoffrey to go out of his way to do favors for people and render service.

Many of you might not think this is a big deal—and it really isn't. But the difference between those people who build successful careers and those who don't is the fact that the winners always take that extra, "simple" little step. That's professional selling at its finest. Now, obviously, the fact that Geoffrey took this step is not going to dramatically affect the bottom line for American Airlines, nor will this one gesture dramatically enhance his career, but I've an idea that he already has the excellent job he has because this is the way he treats so many other people.

## SELLING SERVICE

Bob Dunsmuir in Victoria, British Columbia, runs one of the largest service stations in the world. He has some unique ideas that are enormously effective in the world of sales, service, and persuasion. The instant a car pulls next to a gas pump, four service personnel converge on that car. One fills the gas tank, one checks under the hood, a third starts cleaning the windshield and windows all around, and a fourth starts vacuuming the interior of the car and cleaning the ashtrays. Even when the station is "flooded" with cars and every pump is full, you will always have a minimum of one additional service person there who swings into action and works even faster and more effectively to give the kind of service that Bob's customers have come to expect.

Dunsmuir Shell has one of the highest rates of personnel turnover of any business in all of Canada. Don't misunderstand. It's not because the young men and women don't like their jobs and are not appreciative of what Dunsmuir has done for them. For most of these conscientious, service-oriented winners, a career servicing automobiles is not their primary goal. So, Bob Dunsmuir trains them and inspires them to treat every single person who comes in with genuine respect and courtesy; to go above and beyond the call of duty as far as service is concerned; and to be enthusiastic, cheerful, and polite. Bob teaches them exactly what to say and how to say it so that they can reach those objectives. He then points out that the very next motorist who pulls in might be the one who is going to be their next boss. Many of the local employers searching for extraordinary personnel simply shop at Dunsmuir's and find the enthusiastic, highly motivated people they are seeking.

This actually represents an interesting twist: Dunsmuir's has become a training ground for many of the companies around the city. Bob's relationship with these companies is excellent. There is absolutely no resentment on his part when others employ one of his people. As a matter of fact, he's enthusiastic because he can continually point out to the young men and women who seek employment in his service station that when they go "above and beyond the call of duty," giving the job their best effort, in turn they will have an opportunity for a much better job.

## THE *ONLY* SALES AND SERVICE PHILOSOPHY

What about that for a philosophy? Doesn't it again prove that "you can have everything in life you want if you will just help enough other people get what they want"? Isn't providing extraordinary service truly a win-win situation? Isn't working in a service station "pumping gas" a classic example of how an individual can take an apparently negative situation and turn it into one of the most positive situations imaginable? Bob Dunsmuir has proven that those with the proper sales attitude can take life's lemons and make lemonade.

Another vital lesson to be learned from Dunsmuir's Shell Service Station is to do your best, regardless of how mundane or hopeless the situation may seem. In the first place, doing your best is your responsibility. You took the job. Now do the job and do it well. In the second place, every job is an opportunity. In over sixty-five years of living, I can tell you from experience and firsthand observation that those who do the job and do it well do not have to seek employment—they are found! Not always as quickly as they would like, but they ARE found. If you really want a better job than the one you currently have, then do the job you have as well as possible. Either your job will become the best job there is, or the job you are seeking will come to you!

Note to ambitious people: If you are not effectively and enthusiastically handling a "menial" or entry level job, why on earth should your current or possible future employer believe you can or will handle a more demanding job?

## CATCH THEM DOING SOMETHING RIGHT

When Ken Blanchard published *The One Minute Manager,* he was absolutely right when he encouraged each of us to "catch the people in our lives doing something right." That same philosophy applies beautifully in the world of sales, regardless of whether we are helping the anxious, unhappy, upset, irate customer or prospect or we are helping prevent customers and prospects from experiencing this discomfort.

Too many times those involved in a difficult sale or a confrontational situation have a tendency to "prove" their side of the issue and point out where the customer is wrong. I do not necessarily subscribe to the theory that "the customer is always right," but I do strongly subscribe to the philosophy that our job as professional salespeople—and especially as service-oriented sales professionals—is to work extremely hard at CATCHING THE CUSTOMER DOING SOMETHING RIGHT.

**Ken Blanchard: "Catch the people in our lives doing something right."**

Let's quickly move to the prospect's side of the table, hear his side of the case, find out why he feels as he does, and listen attentively to what the prospect is saying. Throughout the conversation you need to ask yourself the question, "What difference does it make?" For example, let's say you "win" and reject the customer's request for an adjustment or a refund. How much would it cost you? If the customer's problem or concern can be measured in pennies or a few dollars, you might want to consider what the ongoing goodwill of that customer would mean to you. Why not evaluate (unemotionally) what the future business could be worth? Do you really want to win this battle and take a chance of losing the war, or can you find some area of agreement? Can you legitimately, without compromising your standards, acknowledge that the customer has some points that merit serious consideration? Are you wise to ask the customer the "magic" question: "What do you think would be fair?"

## EGO VS. CARE, COMPASSION, AND CONCERN

In many, many cases the customer simply wants to be heard. Everyone wants to be right, but with even more certainty we can say that everyone wants to be understood. When the customers know they're understood, often they will make an adjustment that would be to your advantage. When this happens, it would be wise for you to allow the clients to gain as much as possible. Increase that adjustment; win your customers' hearts and minds to your way of thinking. Make concessions smilingly and gladly, reiterating how much you appreciate the business and how pleased you are that they have trusted you and your company with the account.

## CAN WE "AFFORD" UNHAPPY CUSTOMERS?

When you encounter a rude, belligerent, unhappy individual, do you in turn react by being rude and belligerent, or do you remember that you have the power of choice? You can choose to respond in a friendly and courteous manner, or you can choose to react in a rude and belligerent manner.

---

**CATCH THE CUSTOMER DOING SOMETHING RIGHT.**

---

I'll be the first one to admit this is often easier said than done, but stay with me because I want to share ways that will help you make the proper choice more often than not.

Specifically, how do you feel when you or someone in your company has dropped the ball, fouled up, or committed some horrible sin (like not getting the shipment out on time, sending the wrong color, improperly billing, etc), which created some humongous problems for the customer? What do you think when though you might have had nothing to do with the problem because you were "only the salesperson," the client is still holding you responsible for everything and is enormously upset? The way you deal with that person now will determine to a tremendous degree your success in the profession of selling.

Research indicates that roughly 90 percent of our unhappy customers simply stop doing business with us without saying anything at all about it to us. Unfortunately, they do tell friends, relatives, neighbors, and complete strangers. Question: Can we afford unhappy customers?

All of us can be kind, gentle, courteous, friendly, enthusiastic, and optimistic to the people who give us the order, treat us in a friendly manner, and are easy to deal with. My friend, if that's all you're capable of doing, just remember—your company could hire anybody to deal with those people (and pay considerably less than you're capable of earning). Your value to your company comes basically from the skills you develop in dealing with everybody, including those disgruntled customers and prospects, in an effective and professional manner.

## BASIC "PEOPLE" SKILLS

How can you make sure you are treating people properly? If you will just begin by remembering that everyone wants to be right and everyone wants to be understood, you will have moved in the proper direction. Everyone obviously can't always be right, but when you treat people right (professionally, courteously, and with dignity), making everything right with them is much easier. Try to remember that if you were in their position, you, too, would probably be unhappy with the events that led to the situation.

## TAKE CONTROL PHYSICALLY—OF *YOU*!

Instead of wringing someone's neck, which is often the first response to the angry person, just relax, force yourself to let your hands hang limply by your sides, and HEAR THE PERSON OUT—

don't interrupt! I cannot overemphasize this portion of dealing with the irate person.

Regardless of how angry someone may be, it is difficult to EXPRESS that anger through speech or actions for more than two minutes. If you don't believe me, try it. Get as angry as you want to and shout, scream, rant, rave, whoop, holler, and do anything you like to express your anger/aggravation/irritation. If you will listen until the anger is released, you will have taken much of the steam out of the person with whom you are dealing. *When you interrupt, you allow the person to regain momentum, and the two minutes start over!*

## HEAR THE PERSON OUT.

You've seen this happen time and time again when discussions deteriorate into "Yes, you did!" versus "No, I didn't!" as the comments fly back and forth. Instead, LISTEN! How can you address or solve a problem you don't completely understand? When you listen, you show the prospect or customer a courtesy, and you allow yourself the great advantage of getting information about the problem or situation.

## VOICE AND DICTION

When the steam is released, your next strategy is to lower your voice and articulate each word clearly and deliberately. Remember, the person you are dealing with is in a highly charged emotional state. Too many people go *to* the level of the upset person. The mistake is to get animated, loud, and "nonsensical" like the angry customer or prospect. If you relax physically, hear the person out, and then respond in a lower voice, articulating each word clearly, you can bring the individual to your level of calmness.

You may not agree with that person, and not agreeing is perfectly permissible—if you express yourself properly. Begin the content of your response by thanking the person if it is at all possible. I know that some of you are wondering how you can stay calm enough to thank someone for chewing you out. Well, it "ain't" easy. The best way to stay calm is to remove yourself emotionally from the situation. None of this is personal. And if it becomes personal, you need to remove yourself from the situation physically. When you calmly respond, "You know, Mr. Prospect, I want to thank you for sharing your honest feelings with me," you haven't compromised yourself or your company. Nor have you agreed that the irate person is correct in thinking and actions. You have let the person know you are going to handle the matter professionally and courteously.

Continue to assure and reassure the person that you are going to help. As a matter of fact, state that you want to help. If you will memorize the following little script, you can use it in most situations where you are faced with an angry person.

"Mr. Prospect, thank you for sharing your honest feelings with me. It is important for you to know that I really want to help you. I understand how you feel. You have every right to feel that way. Would you be willing to work with me to find a solution to this uncomfortable situation?"

With this little "sales presentation" you have shown good faith without giving up your base of experience or authority. You did not agree; you allowed the prospect to express personal feelings—after all, each of us has that right.

Remember as you seek a solution to the problem (and not someone to blame) that very few people can get really mad and even fewer can stay that way with an individual who is sincerely trying to solve the problem and resolve the situation.

## ADMIT YOUR MISTAKES

When a mistake has been made, don't get on the defensive. Acknowledging that the mistake was made is a major step in making things right and getting the customer cooled down. Interestingly enough, when no mistake has been made on the company's part, it is even more important that you go through the steps we have been sharing. Many times the complaint, the anger, and the irritation come as a result of a series of other events in that individual's life, such as abuse, neglect, poor treatment by other people, or any number of personal "challenges." However, by displaying a helpful attitude you can frequently defuse that anger and not only keep a customer, but make a friend in the process.

What happens when the customers or prospects cool down and collect their thoughts? At this point you have a chance to retain them as customers and actually to increase your business with them. Here's a vital step in providing excellent service to your customers and prospects while helping yourself as well. After the confrontation and the resolution, if the customers are completely in the wrong, they will often realize their mistake and become embarrassed. It's critical that you get back to them in a friendly, cheerful, optimistic, upbeat manner and reiterate how much you appreciate their openness and their willingness to share. Tell them how much you value their business.

**LISTEN!**

This approach will solidify customers. Otherwise, because they've been in the wrong, they might be so embarrassed about their conduct that they would not continue to do business with you. It's the old "extra mile" principle applied again in life and in selling. As sales trainers have said for many years, you must bring the "and then some" principle to life. When you have done everything expected of you as a professional "and then some," you are building an extraordinary sales career.

## A CLASS ACT

One of the clear marks of a sales professional, and one that will lead to greater sales success, is class. The dictionary says that *class* is "a high rank in society, grade, or quality." A *class act* is "a person or thing of very high quality or excellence." A sales professional has class, and the best way to tell this is to observe the way that "pro" deals with a person who has no class. What do you do when you deal with those less fortunate or with less class than you? Do you stoop to their level and deal with them as they deal with you, perhaps in a rude, loud, thoughtless, inconsiderate manner? Or do you demonstrate your class by making every effort to maintain your poise and dignity and raise their conduct to your level?

## "I CAN'T BELIEVE YOU SAID THAT!"

One of the least classy acts of any individual is to resort to foul or profane language. The primary reason for cursing is a language deficit, which is often revealed by immaturity and lack of emotional control. Individuals who use improper language are in essence saying they do not have enough intelligence or control to speak properly at that given moment.

The professional salesperson must ask, "How can I most effectively deal with someone who chooses to use abusive language?" Since eight out of ten times the sales professional is cursed over the telephone, these guidelines are written from this perspective, but the same principles work in person.

Begin by remembering that in almost every case, the words should not be considered a personal attack. In most situations, the prospect or client will not know you well enough to launch a personal attack. You are experiencing the venting of frustrations.

The second step in dealing with the angry person who curses and uses foul language is doing NOTHING. Remain silent. Say nothing. Absolute silence will surprise AND, more important, calm the angry person. Cursers are often "provokers" who are looking for a word fight. Why play their game? Pause until the person asks, "Are you still there?" At that point, if you want to have a little fun and "win the client over" instead of "winning over the client," pick out a portion of the tirade that was the most ridiculous and exaggerated. Say, "As I understand it, your major problem is ______." And then you repeat in a clear, concise manner what was just said. Odds are long the client will, with some embarrassment, "confess" that maybe it wasn't quite "that bad."

At that point, you are on your way to a solution. You will have "won the client over," and isn't that what real selling is all about? Question: How much business have you ever generated by "winning" a confrontation and telling someone off? BUT in no way does this mean you must accept abusive or demeaning treatment. Read on.

## YOUR RESPONSE AFTER LISTENING

Here is another sales presentation that you can memorize or write on an index card to use on those special occasions when someone swears at you:

"Mr. Prospect, when you talk to me like that, I feel I can no longer be helpful to you. If you will work with me and focus on the problem, I believe we can come up with a solution. However, if you continue to use profane and abusive language, my integrity demands that I terminate this conversation."

**"Mr. Prospect, thank you for sharing your honest feelings with me. It is important for you to know that I really want to help you. I understand how you feel. You have every right to feel that way. Would you be willing to work with me to find a solution to this uncomfortable situation?"**

If the cursing continues, do as you have promised. If you are dealing with someone on the phone, allow for a "cooling-off" time and then call back. Chances are excellent that he will be embarrassed by his behavior and will be much easier to work with. Actually, if your spirit is right and you show no anger or vindictiveness, you are in an excellent position to make a sale or solidify the account. Here's why: The prospect or customer feels he did something *to* you; now, he should do something *for* you. That "something" could include an apology, a willingness to listen, and even a desire to "make it right" by buying or continuing to buy from you.

## KEY PRINCIPLES

To deal effectively with irate persons, remember the following information.

NO ONE CAN GET "UNDER YOUR SKIN" AND UPSET YOU WITHOUT YOUR PERMISSION, SO:

- HEAR THEM OUT—LET THE ANGER ERUPT.
- BE PATIENT.
- BE TACTFUL.
- EMPATHIZE.
- ACKNOWLEDGE THEIR IMPORTANCE.
- ARTICULATE YOUR RESPONSE SLOWLY, QUIETLY, AND CAREFULLY.
- NEVER GRANT THEM PERMISSION TO CONTROL YOU!

## A "SERVICE" FACT OF LIFE

It's a fact of life that if you're going to be in the world of selling very long, there are going to be disagreements and complaints. That's inevitable. The way you handle those disagreements is going to determine to a very large degree the length and success of your career. At the same time, just remember the Arabian proverb, "All sunshine makes a desert"—meaning that unless you have some difficulties along the way, you will never develop all of your skills and techniques that move you from the depths of mediocrity to the heights of enormous success. Look at those disgruntled clients and unhappy prospects as opportunities to grow and become even more successful in your career.

CHAPTER THIRTEEN

# THE GLAMOUR OF THE ROAD

## *A Myth of the Selling Profession*

As you undoubtedly know by now, I do believe everything is selling. Pastor Rex Hensley of the Addyston Baptist Church in Addyston, Ohio, tells of a young man who had his résumé printed on twenty-five T-shirts and then delivered them personally to twenty-five different companies. At the bottom of the T-shirts he'd printed these words:

"I believe I am a perfect fit for your company."

He got twenty interviews. Some who had no job openings interviewed him just to meet him. More important, he had his choice of several job offers!

## THE TROUBLE WITH TRAVEL

The concept of travel has been idealized since the invention of the wheel. Many want to know what's "over the horizon" and are willing to spend enormous amounts of time and money to find out. If we had the opportunity to view most people's "wish" list, travel would hold a special priority.

However, like many parts of life, travel must be viewed from two different perspectives.

## THE PROPER PERSPECTIVE

The couple had not received a letter from their daughter for several weeks so they were delighted when they saw the letter they had long awaited. As they read, however, their delight turned to dismay.

"Dear Mom and Dad, I apologize for the lengthy gap since our last correspondence. I want to say in the beginning that things are O.K. I am recovering from the accident beautifully.

"There was a fire in the dorm and in climbing from my second-story window I slipped and fell and suffered a concussion. Fortunately, a young man in the neighborhood was passing by and saw my difficulties, so he took me to his home and has cared for me in a loving way. The doctors say I suffered no permanent damage.

"My benefactor turned out to be one of the most kind and loving people I have ever known. He's from a marvelous family, and you'll be delighted to know we plan to be married in the very near future. You've always wanted grandchildren, so you'll be pleased to know that in a matter of months the arrival will be announced. The sonogram reveals it's going to be a little boy, and everything is coming along as expected. I'll keep you posted as time moves along.

"Your loving daughter, Sally.

"P.S. There really wasn't a fire in the dorm; I did not suffer a concussion; I am not living with a young man; and there is not going to be a grandchild. But I did make two *F*'s and a *D* on my last report card, and I wanted you to see them in the proper perspective."

## TWO SIDES OF THE SAME COIN

Being away from the mundane activities of routine daily life; eating in restaurants where meals are prepared and dishes are picked up for you; sleeping in hotels where beds are made FOR you instead of BY you; seeing historic landmarks and walking the same steps that men and women who have shaped our world have walked; flying in jet airliners, riding in superfast luxury railroad cars, or driving through scenic panoramas with views that have only been seen on postcards—yes, the exciting benefits of the life of a traveler are vivid in the imaginations of so many.

Unfortunately, the life of the business traveler is viewed from an entirely different perspective. Taking the mundane activities of our routine daily lives with us on the road; eating "chicken fingers" in one restaurant is very similar to eating "chicken fingers" in another—regardless of who picks up the dishes; sleeping in hotels and reading books with the light from lamps bolted down to bedside tables while wondering IF the bed has been made up since the last visitor; seeing landmarks on the "fast forward" video screen of your mind as you are whisked from airport to meeting site or office; looking into the face of one more flight attendant, conductor, or rental car agent in anticipation of missing directions or misreading street signs designed for confusion—yes, the eyes of the business traveler look upon a different scene from those of the recreational traveler.

The irony is that it seems that those who get to travel often loathe the reality of the road while those who cannot travel love the illusion of the idea. Our attitude is often controlled by our perspective or outlook, and that is where we begin to learn to tolerate traveling and to enjoy the opportunities presented.

## OUR "BREADWINNER" HITS THE ROAD

Since the earliest days of recorded time, there have been confusion and misconception about what happens when the "provider" leaves home for an extended period. The person "left behind" often feels "left out" of all the fun and excitement. And although there are those who thrive on the rigors of the road, the overwhelming majority of sales travelers feel like our hero in the following scenario.

### ONE TRAVELER, MANY PERSPECTIVES

As Chris approached the counter, the shop owner recognized his favorite traveling salesperson. "Chris, how in the world are you?" he called loudly. "Just great, Mr. O'Connor, and how about you?" Chris replied.

"Good, just good. I'd probably be great, too, if I was just getting back from Las Vegas."

"Now, Mr. O'Connor, you know there was a sales conference

there, and besides that I had to leave a day early to go to Chicago to meet with one of our major accounts."

"Chris," O'Connor continued, ignoring Chris's effort to downplay the trips to Las Vegas and Chicago, "I hear Las Vegas is quite a place. Maybe someday I'll be able to go see the 'bright lights.'"

"Well, I'll have to admit that in all my traveling I've never seen anything quite like it. The gambling continues all night long, and the shows are really extravagant. The costumes, the music, the excitement—I tell you, it's easy to understand why they say Las Vegas is the city that never sleeps!"

Mr. O'Connor chuckled in agreement, "Yeah, and I hear the Windy City isn't too shabby a place either. Who were you calling on in Chicago?"

"The Sears buyer. She was a little harder to get to than you, Mr. O'Connor. I had to take a pressurized elevator up ninety-eight floors in the Sears Tower."

"Ninety-eight floors!" exclaimed Mr. O'Connor. "That must be the tallest building in the world!" "Actually," Chris responded, "The Sears Tower has 110 floors, the same number as the taller of the two towers at the World Trade Center in New York City. The last time I was there, the client told me that more than twelve thousand people work in that one building." Mr. O'Connor got that "faraway, wistful" look in his eyes as he said, "Chris, you are really lucky to get to be in all those great places. Me? I'm married to this store twelve to fourteen hours every day of the year. Even the days we're not open there's paperwork and shelf-stocking to be done. Sometimes I think I'll never get away."

Chris didn't want to burst Mr. O'Connor's bubble by telling him the "whole truth and nothing but the truth," so rather than taking any more time away from the sales call, our selling professional began the presentation. "Yes, those cities are wonderful! Never a dull moment. Hey, I have got a great new product to tell you about, but before I do, tell me about how your sales are going on the supply we delivered after my last trip."

## NOT ONLY CLIENTS

This wasn't the first time Chris dealt with misconceptions regarding the "glamour of the road." When he arrived home, Chris's spouse, though obviously pleased to see him, had some questions. "Welcome home, honey! How was your week?"

"Pat," Chris responded, "you just wouldn't believe it! You should see Caesar's Palace! The lights at night are incredible! And the tour of Wayne Newton's Arabian Horse Farm—what beautiful animals! The speaker from The Zig Ziglar Corporation was the highlight of the sales conference. The best news of all is that I finalized the Sears sale on Friday, and unless the company makes them a house account, we are going to see some serious commission dollars!" And almost as an afterthought, Chris added, "How was your week?"

"Well, let's see. I decided to cut the grass and do all the yard work we normally do together because it just wouldn't wait for you to get back. Kelly's preschool teacher had to call me at work three times due to an ear infection. I finally got in to see the doctor on Wednesday, but the medicine hasn't helped much and Kelly has cried and been fussy all week.

"Your mother called," Pat continued, "and she sounded depressed. She must have asked me three times when we were coming to visit. Everyone asked about you at church on Wednesday night, but we had to leave early because Kelly was so fidgety. Chris, do you think we might go to Las Vegas together if you get the commission check on the Sears sale? A long weekend might be great for both of us."

"Of course, Pat," Chris replied, looking through the week's mail. "By the way, did your brother call about going to the movies tomorrow night?"

## TRAVELING TOGETHER

The next trip is made in tandem. Upon the couple's return, the neighbors want to know all about the great trip.

"Chris, Pat, good to see the two of you back! How was the vacation? Denver, wasn't it? Man, I love those mountains!"

"Well," Pat began, "it really wasn't a vacation. Chris's sales meeting was done in conjunction with a national trade show and convention, and since I helped, we ended up working eighteen-hour days."

"Right, all work and no play, ha!"

"If you count one canoe trip and cookout in eleven days as playing," Chris interjected, "then we sure did play. Oh, we had a good time, but frankly, we didn't see much of Colorado. The trip was a change of pace, but I'm exhausted! I'm gonna need a vacation to recover from this vacation!"

## THE TRUTH ABOUT TRAVEL

Today's selling professional realizes that the glamour of travel wears off (if not out) after a very few trips, and what remains is plain old-fashioned hard work! But I don't want to paint an entirely negative picture for the traveling sales professional. With the proper perspective, we can take this potentially negative situation and turn it into a positive winner!

As a matter of fact, why not go to school on some of our own "medicine" and use the Ben Franklin Close (the Great Statesman Close) we discussed earlier to help us examine the subject of traveling. You will remember that we make a "T" bar on our paper, and list the negatives on the right of the vertical bar and the positives on the left side.

### VARIETY

The new salespeople and the veterans we interviewed for *Ziglar on Selling* reported that one of the things they love best about the selling profession is the variety of experiences. "No two days are the same." "Every day is a new challenge with something new to learn." "Definitely not boring!" This variety is simply not possible in many jobs (and even in some sales positions that don't require traveling). Let's list "variety" in the plus column.

### COMPETITIVE EDGE

The sales professional who learns to travel successfully on a regular basis, represent the company properly, and keep family life well balanced has a competitive edge in the job market. The person who functions well in these areas is creating value within the organization and will also gain a positive reputation in the industry specifically and the sales profession generally. This competitive edge allows your company to pay you more (or the competition will). Since you are often the only person from the company the prospect or client meets, you ARE the company! The management of stable companies recognizes your importance, which increases compensation and job security.

Let's place "competitive edge" on the plus side.

## EDUCATIONAL OPPORTUNITIES

Travel time in the car or plane can allow you great quantities of listening or reading time that you just cannot get in an office setting. Traveling salespeople have written me to say they have earned undergraduate degrees and advanced degrees, learned financial planning skills, foreign languages, vocabulary skills, and just about every conceivable concept. Some become experts in their industry. Others become experts in apparently unrelated areas that broaden their base and make them better people, better mates, better parents, and ultimately better employees. When you seize educational opportunities, the time spent away from home becomes a true win-win-win situation where company, employee, and family enjoy the benefits and rewards!

Another plus on the Great Statesman Chart.

## CULTURAL ENRICHMENT

When company travel takes you to areas of cultural interest, you can broaden your cultural base and enrich your personal and family life. In addition, cultural enrichment will make you even more valuable to your company. Expenses are minimized because your travel and hotel are accounted for, and with just a little planning, you can seize opportunities that might otherwise never present themselves.

Who would have imagined that a little boy from Yazoo City, Mississippi, would grow up to stand on a hill and see where the green of the Indian Ocean and the blue of the Pacific Ocean meet; share the platform and confer with the current president, former presidents, and future presidents; give the keynote address to the International Jaycees Convention in Sweden (they let only the king of Sweden welcome them the night before); ride on the back of an ostrich in the outlands of South Africa; jog in the park across the street from

Buckingham Palace and jog "down under" in Australia, land of koala bears and kangaroos; and share many of these exciting cultural opportunities with family members? The "plus" list grows.

## SOCIAL SKILLS

Travel invariably forces you into daily use of social skills that might lay dormant in the office environment. Making introductions, abiding by formal mealtime etiquette, remembering names, choosing gifts, sending thank-you's and follow-up notes of gratitude, conducting appropriate social conversations, and relying on many other skills are "musts" for the traveling professional.

The social skills you learn and practice become a way of life, allowing you to operate at a comfort level beyond what most people experience.

## PHYSICAL FITNESS

Too many of our friends in selling use the road as an excuse for poor physical fitness instead of a reason for success in this primary area. For years, I have scheduled time to jog prior to my speaking engagements. Not only does this invigorate me and stimulate my thinking, but it allows me time to focus on the presentation and the people who will be attending. In addition, my system is infused with endorphins, the body's natural chemical that increases energy and creativity while relieving pain and anxiety. Frankly, your exercise *schedule* on the road is less likely to be interrupted by distractions than when you're at home. The problem is, most people don't schedule exercise on the road.

Some travelers think that it is difficult, if not impossible, to control weight on the road. This is a lie told to the mind and accepted by the body. The truth is that you are less likely to go to the refrigerator for a snack on the road than at home. Ordering carefully from the menu (most have "heart healthy" meals or low-cholesterol/fat/calorie meals marked) is easier today than ever before. A cafeteria allows you to load up on vegetables and the "good stuff" you need to keep going. Special meals are available at no extra cost on most airlines. The road can even offer you chances to break poor eating habits developed at home. Another "plus" listing.

This area is so important that I have devoted more space in chapter 16 to the topic of physical fitness for the selling professional. Some of our selling brothers and sisters who do not travel may not be reading this chapter as carefully as you are, and we all need the fitness message.

Let me mention two exceptional sources of additional information in this area. Shirley Billigmeier has written a book called *Inner Eating: How to Free Yourself Forever from the Tyranny of Food,* which is one of the best I have seen on helping understand why we overeat and what we can do about it. [Dr. Ken Cooper's book, *The Aerobic Program for Total Well-Being,* is another excellent source.] Buy these books before your next trip and read from either one for ten minutes BEFORE your evening meal, and you will be incredibly pleased with what you learn—guaranteed!

## SOLITUDE

The great performers in sales (as well as other successful people in all areas of life) have long touted the virtues of solitude. Travel affords you the opportunity to control your "quiet time" and spend time in solitude and contemplation.

Fifteen minutes of solitude taken twice a day can help you deal with issues and people in a manner that will surprise you. Solitude leads to peace of mind, which leads to an improved quality of sleep, and with the proper rest, sales will soar.

## CREATIVE TIME

Think time or creative time is different from solitude. In your quiet time, there will most often be no agenda; in creative time, you will focus on a specific client, customer, situation, scenario, or concern.

Creative time will be spent alone and also with clients and prospective clients. When creative people interact about a business or product or marketing idea, sparks fly! These creative sparks can generate a forest fire of innovative ideas. One of the major benefits to a traveling salesperson is this creative exchange.

Don't be afraid to share ideas that can help your customers be more successful. Having a positive attitude and a sense of expectancy will draw good ideas to you. Alert sale professionals will find that many of the best solutions to their selling situational problems come to them from others as a result of interaction. This is "good news" and means you don't have to come up with all the answers yourself.

## BEING THE SAME PERSON

To this point, we have focused on items that will go on the plus side of the diagram. However, there are some danger areas. The first danger area is being the same person on the road as you are at home. Having multiple personalities can be very dangerous. Obviously I'm not talking about Dr. Jekyll and Mr. Hyde, but simply leading a different life away from home.

Several years ago, a popular television series was called "I Lead Three Lives." The central character was an FBI agent, a spy for the KGB (Soviet Intelligence Agency and the Communist party), and an average middle-class American citizen. The show gained its dramatic edge from scripts that constantly caused the star to live on the edge of being discovered by one or more of those he was trying to fool. The truth is, no one can live very comfortably or successfully this way in real life!

Traveling salespeople often fall into the trap of playing multiple roles in an ongoing stage play each week: the straitlaced family man on the weekends—the pillar of the community; the "back-slapping, hail-fellow-well-met party animal" on the road; and the distinguished, articulate, creative good soldier in the company army in headquarters for sales meetings.

Being in a strange town, where few people know you, allows a certain freedom, but YOU know you—and YOU must be able to live with yourself. William Shakespeare said, "To thine own self be true." And to that I might add, playing a bit part in a *B* movie the rest of your life would be like having a prison sentence. Obviously (I hope), I'm talking about any conduct that would jeopardize your relationship with your company or your family if it were discovered.

My mentor, retired executive Fred Smith, says that all great failures are *character* failures. I agree.

Stop before you start. If you've started, stop now. Remember, you will be successful when you are doing the things you love to do, the things you feel comfortable doing that allow you to grow personally and professionally.

Over a period of time, people grow in all facets of their lives. This is a wonderful phenomenon because you can be more today than you were yesterday but not all you can be tomorrow. My point is this: Be the best version of YOU that you can possibly be but make sure it is YOU. After two years of serious counseling, a close friend of mine said that the best thing she had learned was to trust her own instincts. Go out and do the same!

## A SPECIAL CHALLENGE

Easily the most challenging portion of the day for the traveling salesperson is the evening when the necessary forces of your activities have been handled and you are confronted with a series of choices about how you're going to invest your time. Many hotels and motels feature happy hour, and an ever-increasing number of them make free drinks a part of the price of the room. Here's where many marriages are destroyed and careers are seriously hampered and in many cases wrecked.

I am going to strongly suggest that you make a decision in advance so you will handle this particular challenge in the proper way. If you are married, you obviously have a strong moral involvement you will want to uphold. Going into a bar with singles to get a drink is pushing the limits of temptation to a degree that many men and women simply cannot handle. This is where discipline, commitment, and responsibility do battle with imagination and emotion. The only way to win the battle is to have decided well in advance exactly what you're going to do with your evening.

In this "enlightened" society where "anything goes" seems to be a way of life, there are many who smile and wink at infidelity with the age-old "everybody does it" attitude—as if that makes it a proper approach to life. In the first place, everybody doesn't push temptation to the point of falling victim to imagination and emotion.

Many travelers show courage and determination by PLANNING AHEAD. They can tell you exactly how they will be spending their time on the road, and since everything is so carefully planned, there just isn't time for putting themselves in a situation they might look back upon with regret.

In the second place, the price for stupidity is enormous. Yes, I know that sounds harsh, but when you consider the impact on the family and career for poor judgment when traveling, indiscretion is stupid.

## Couch Potato Syndrome

I checked into a hotel recently in Houston, Texas, for a speaking engagement, and much to my shock and chagrin the desk clerk handed me a note with my key. The note said: "Beware of friendly people in the lobby and on the elevators. A criminal has been circulating in the hotels in the Houston area posing as a nice person to take advantage of guests. He will get on the elevator with you and ask, 'Don't I know you from somewhere?' He will wait for you to push your floor button and pretend to be going to the same floor. While making conversation and following you to your room, he robs the guests.

"If someone knocks on your door asking for change for the vending machine or a phone book because theirs is missing, do not answer your door."

Con artists and criminals have been around for years, and the traveling salesperson must be extremely cautious on the road. But the biggest thief is not the con artist or the person with a pistol; the biggest thief is the television.

Please don't get me wrong. I believe the television can be a great tool for education and for relaxation. But I also recognize the strong hypnotic quality that this powerful medium generates. We have all passed the set and gotten enthralled with something "mindless" and come to our senses thirty to ninety minutes later, wondering "where did the time go?" And with the strong emphasis the advertisers are placing on movies (particularly adult movies) that are available for viewing in the room, more than time is being stolen. Several business associates have told me it's difficult for them to pass up the late night adult movies. One man actually feared he was addicted to pornography and felt his compulsion had developed from movies he watched while traveling.

## Happiness Comes from Within

My friend Cavett Robert says, "Character is the ability to carry out a resolution long after the mood of the moment has passed." Let me challenge you not to turn the set on until you have consulted the guide/preview book and determined in advance what you want to watch. If you allocate a certain amount of time for a specific program—turning the set on and off at the proper time—you will be making the television work for you instead of you working for it. Will you resolve to do that now? Will you be a person of character and keep your commitment to yourself? I believe you will, and you will be tremendously pleased with your results!

## The Traveler's Evening Checklist

So, how do you spend those evenings? The answer is reasonably simple. You can do a number of extremely productive things. First, and foremost, you take care of your physical needs. That might mean a quiet dinner followed by a brisk walk, jog, or workout. The rest of the evening is free for continuing the courtship process with your mate back home. A telephone call is always in order, and certainly your mate would be delighted to receive a nice chatty letter about your activities of the day. This focuses your mind on the person you love, the commitment you've made, and will help the time pass far more quickly.

Second, you can handle all of the necessary paperwork from your sales activities of the day so that when you arrive home for the weekend you will have no job responsibilities and will be able to commit your time, energy, and attention to your family.

Third, there's the area of personal growth. You can read good books or magazines or listen to cassette recordings. Perhaps if an associate of the same sex is in town, you can visit and in essence conduct a training session, brainstorming session, or sales session with each other so that you're better prepared for tomorrow.

Next, you can get to bed early for a good night's sleep, which is excellent preparation for the activities of the day to come.

### Happiness vs. Pleasure

There is a considerable difference between pleasure and happiness. Pleasure is very temporary, whereas happiness is of long-range duration. By following the procedures I suggest, you will ensure the stability of your marriage, the happiness of your home, and the progression of your career. When you arrive home for the weekend, your family will be elated to see you, and the loneliness of the week on the road will bring into clear focus your delight and happiness at being with your mate. You'll feel much better about yourself after having had a productive week on the road. You'll be able to look your children and your mate in the eye, and you'll be prepared to give your undivided time, energy, and attention to the ones you love. The benefits are enormous.

## BITING AND CHEWING

Another danger for hard-charging sales professionals is the tendency to want to "do it all." They place unrealistic expectations on themselves related to number of calls, closing ratios, and dollars earned, biting off more than it is possible for anyone to chew. Although I truly believe in setting goals that cause you to stretch, some people set themselves up for failure.

The salesperson whose presentation averages forty-five minutes in duration and who sets a goal to make ten presentations per day from 8:00 A.M. to 6:00 P.M. is not thinking clearly. Travel time, lunch, breaks, and paperwork have not been taken into consideration. On paper, it looks like there may be time to make the calls, but a goal of six to eight calls is far more realistic.

Getting the most out of your hours is a topic that deserves consideration. In chapter 15 we will take a closer look at the difference between efficiency and effectiveness. For our purposes here, just let me say that you will want to stretch yourself because like a rubber band that stretches and never returns to its original shape and size, you, too, can become even more by stretching. However, some rubber bands break. To prevent this in yourself, start with realistic goals that can be achieved and gradually increase them on a regular basis. Don't set out to break the world record on the first day; instead, set a personal record. If you set enough personal records, you can eventually challenge the world record.

## COMMUNICATION

We live in an age of fax machines, cellular telephones, voice mail, and many other forms of instant communication. Dick Tracy's two-way wrist radio is soon to be a reality, with the only difference being that it will be a cellular telephone instead of a shortwave radio. Prototypes are already being tested. Regardless of technology, the product is only as good as the user.

My experience is that traveling can actually enhance communications. The communication opportunities people take for granted in the office are not taken for granted on the road. Traveltime lends itself to writing and reading notes, voice mail, and cellular communication.

With the family, communication is particularly important. When I am on the road, I phone home EVERY night. Yes, this can get expensive. Yes, I call to talk to The Redhead. And yes, I talk to other family members who may be visiting. Yes, the conversations can get redundant, but they can still be informative and exciting. No, I don't stay on the phone for extended periods of time. No, I don't call during the peak expense times.

The key is this: For fifteen minutes or more, every night that I am on the road, I give my family my undivided attention. Distractions are completely eliminated. As a professional word merchant and picture painter, you shouldn't let your skills go unused on those you most love. Sell them on YOU and YOUR love for them—and then place "communication" on the plus side of our Great Statesman Chart.

## WITHDRAWAL

One of the most difficult parts of traveling is the actual leaving. If you have ever been involved in a tearful "Daddy, please don't go" or "Mommy, can't you please stay home with me today" scene, you know the agony of withdrawal. And why is it that major discussions with your spouse seem to begin during the last fifteen minutes before your departure? From time to time all of us have suffered from the pains associated with "withdrawal" or leaving home for the road.

As in so many areas of our lives, the key to success in departing for the road is PREPARATION. Leave a complete itinerary with addresses and phone numbers with each family member. Predetermine how emergencies are to be handled. Let the children know the essentials: when, where, for how long, with whom, why. My friend, associate, and fellow speaker Mamie McCullough (The "I Can" Lady) keeps a "traveling calendar" on her refrigerator. She marks the days she will be at home with a certain color and her traveling days in another. Her children had a visual picture of their mother's schedule even when they could not read.

Another friend plays a geography game with his children. He has a huge map of the United States in his office at home, and before a trip he sits with the children and they "map out" his itinerary in colored stick pins. When he calls home during the week, they talk where the children can see the map and know where Dad is located. (This has the added advantages of teaching them communication skills and geography.)

Half an hour spent with the family several days before departure will be time well spent. Go through your itinerary, the people you will be seeing, some of the nice things that will happen while you are gone, some of the questions you will be asking when you call home. ("Now, I'm gonna want to know the very best thing that happens to you each day that I am away, so be thinking about it before I call.")

For those of you who travel and have small children, let me encourage you to record stories, expressions of your love, and reminders to your children of things they do that make you proud of them. Let me caution you, however. Don't try to set their schedules while you're out of town. These messages should be warm, loving, encouraging, and supportive. You would do well to buy children's books or pick them up from the library and record a story for each day you're gone. Then each night your mate can play the stories, and your children will benefit from them as well as the sound of your voice—knowing you were thinking of them.

## DECOMPRESSION

There are times when coming home can be more difficult than leaving. The "road" has a rhythm and pace of its own and rarely is it similar to the "flow" of activity in the home.

Like a meteor hurtling toward earth, our traveling salesperson is on more of a collision course than anyone might expect. Does the traveler begin by inquiring about how the week of the nontraveler has gone or sharing information about the trip? Do you initiate conversation or respond to conversation?

One couple who recognized that the first one to two hours after the traveling spouse returned home were a danger period came up with a solution. After very BRIEF, COURTEOUS, and AFFECTIONATE greetings, the traveler went to the couple's room and, regardless of the time of day or night, took a long, refreshing shower. During this time of relaxation, the traveler would purposefully fill the mind with positive thoughts about the spouse and house while considering the parts of the trip to review with the spouse who was patient enough to allow this time.

The nontraveling spouse would sit quietly listening to some soft instrumental music and focusing on the same topics—positive thoughts about spouse, house, and week's review. They alternated roles in who would begin the sharing, and after six months, the "worst" argument (and it wasn't really an argument) they got into was about who would go first!

Another traveling salesperson I know uses the trip from the airport as her "decompression" chamber. She has developed a route from the airport that takes her from a city setting through a more rural environment with trees, streams, and ducks. During this time she listens to tapes of ocean waves or rainfall. The trip takes less than ten minutes more than a direct route to her home, and due to her relaxed spirit when she arrives, she believes it would be worthwhile if it took thirty minutes longer.

The obvious key is relaxation and understanding of potential danger. If you and your nontraveling spouse and children will discuss this danger BEFORE YOU LEAVE and brainstorm suitable ideas for the "decompression" time, you will find that your return home can be a significant and positive event instead of a painful ordeal.

All of this is to say that when you return home, you should have an agreement with your mate that you will *FIRST* talk about and deal with the positive and pleasant aspects of what happened to you and the family during your absence. This approach, over a period of time, will establish in every family member's mind that it will be exciting to have the traveler home again. CRITICAL NOTE: Once the pleasant reentry has been established and things have regained some sense of normalcy (no sooner than after dinner), the "challenges" of the time away need to be quietly and calmly addressed.

It is my conviction that planning and following through on these procedures will enrich your personal and family life, improve and lengthen your career, and enhance your marriage and life itself.

## THE PLEASURE OF TRAVELING

With the proper perspective, we can make our business traveling a true pleasure. So much of the way we feel depends on the way we view our circumstances. By looking at the chart, you can see that the positives far outweigh the negatives for the business traveler. Variety, competitive edge, educational opportunities, cultural enrichment, social skills, physical fitness, solitude, and creative time are all very good reasons to consider business travel a positive part of your life.

## BEWARE

By being aware of the potential dangers we face, we can PLAN, PREPARE, and EXPECT to WIN in our travels. Being consistent to our home personalities by asking, "Would I do this at home?" will help us in being the same person on the road we are at home.

Almost everyone has heard that "Proper Prior Planning Prevents Poor Performance," and by planning, we can learn to not bite off more than we can chew AND to communicate with the proper people at the proper time.

Planning also helps us with "withdrawal" and "decompression" (going out into the world and returning home) so that these difficult times can be handled in a way that will create harmony instead of havoc.

## A FINAL—AND IMPORTANT—THOUGHT ON TRAVELING

For many years in my presentations, I shared a story of the traveling salesman who was constantly thinking of his family when he was on the road, and when he was at home, he was thinking about his job. I would demonstrate this concept by saying, "When he was in the field, his mind was at home (race across the stage). When he was at home, his mind was in the field (race back across the stage). And he told friends, neighbors, clients, family, and anyone who would listen that he never had time to do the things he really wanted to do. Well, no wonder, he was always traveling!"

Due to my running back and forth across the stage, and due to the fact that we have all felt that way, the audience would laugh heartily—and more important, learn the lesson. And at the risk of sounding like a pseudotherapist, let me encourage you to "be in the moment." When you are at home, BE THERE! When you are on the road, do a great job, using every spare moment to do whatever is necessary so that when you get home, you can BE THERE. Focus on the task at hand. Give your undivided attention to your spouse, children, and friends when you are at home. You would never think about making a sales call without planning what is going to happen. Why would you think about spending a special day with your family with no planning? I'm not saying that every day has to be filled with trips, major events, or extraordinary happenings. You can plan something as simple as a conversation. You can set a goal to spend a certain period of time alone with each family member. You might plan to be available at their convenience (be careful here that this is not an excuse for not planning).

Here is my point. A poet said, "Life is what happens to you when you're busy making other plans." Life is too fragile and short to waste even one single moment. Sure, you must stop and smell the roses, and I'm not talking about a rigid plan that you force upon others to the point of their discomfort. Seize the moment! Live each hour of every single day as if it were your last because someday your last hour will come. Was your last hour a good one? Did you seize each precious moment? What about this hour, the one you are currently in?

**When you are at home, BE THERE!**

Live each day to the fullest wherever you may be and live with purpose, passion, and persistence!

CHAPTER FOURTEEN

# THE SUCCESSFUL SALES SUPPORT SYSTEM

## *How the Office and Family Can Empower Your Career*

In the customs entrance in Toronto, Ontario, a little sign identifies "Canada's Three Official Languages." Underneath it says, "The choice is yours. The pleasure to serve you is ours!" Now that's selling.

## BUILDING A CAREER

To build a career in the world of sales, you will need the support and cooperation of many people. Let's begin with the members of the company team: the accounting department, the billing department, the shipping department, the service department, and perhaps the public relations department. While in most cases the order is received, processed, shipped, and handled without any problems, delays, or defects, there are those occasions when everything seems to go wrong. This is particularly true if any degree of customization is required in the process.

When something goes wrong, it might have nothing whatever to do with you, the salesperson, but human nature being what it is, since you are the person who persuaded the prospect to take action and place the order, you can rest assured the person will hold you responsible. Whether blame is affixed to you or not, if something happens and the sale is lost, your commission, bonus, salary, job, or career will be affected by that transaction. For that reason the career-minded salesperson is going to pay special attention to the glitches in the operation. One dissatisfied customer will tell many more people about the problem than a satisfied customer will tell about the marvelous way in which you handle the account. This is especially true if a customer is treated rudely by anyone in the process.

## THE REAL WORLD

When I had the privilege of visiting the customer support center of Hewlett-Packard in Atlanta, Georgia, I WAS IMPRESSED! From the moment Tom Walsh picked me up at the hotel until he dropped me off at the airport, I was tremendously excited by the obvious team spirit and unity.

Customer support managers Joe Lingle and David Halford took me in hand and with considerable enthusiasm and pride shared the H-P customer satisfaction success story. As Joe and David proudly explained the many systems and procedures, I was able to understand why Data Pro Survey, an independent organization, rated H-P the number one team in overall support satisfaction in the computer industry. As I listened to conversations between customers who had needs and engineers and service personnel who are there to meet those needs, I was also able to see why Hewlett-Packard is a multibillion dollar organization that is still growing.

Julie Huntington was most impressive in handling her customer's needs. As I watched, it became obvious that the customer would not give Julie a chance to answer the question or to give her advice and suggestions. Julie would patiently listen and attempt to respond, but almost immediately there was an interruption. During more than six interruptions in one phone call, Julie's expression of interest, concern, and concentration never changed. Never was there the slightest hint of annoyance, irritation, frustration, or anger. The few words she did manage to utter were always caring, controlled, and well-modulated.

## ARE THEY ALL THAT WAY?

But lest you think that Julie Huntington is the exception (though I suspect she's a star), let me point out another factor in Hewlett-Packard's commitment to serving the customer. In an effort to promote customer satisfaction over customer irritation, H-P maintains a working model of every computer the company has ever built. While most customer calls are handled with apparent ease in just a few moments, the more complicated questions and problems are handled by professionals working from the identical model the customer is using. They re-create the problem and then highly skilled engineers go to work on the solution. In most cases only minutes pass before the customer receives a return call with the solution. However, regardless of how tough the problem may be, the people I watched showed the same patience and concern mentioned earlier—and ALWAYS got back to the customer with a solution.

To give you a specific example, on March 21, 1991, at 4:15 P.M., customer John V. called. The customer was experiencing a problem with a "plotter." The engineer summary was assigned to Fred Cardinal in Atlanta. Two minutes after the customer placed the call, he had an answer to his problem. Sixteen minutes and fourteen seconds later, the customer called back with this report: "Everything is fine. Thanks a lot for all your help. If Hewlett-Packard has a hall of fame, you should be in it!" That's the way to build a business!

## ENTHUSIASTIC ENGINEERS

The engineers displayed enthusiasm about their jobs and their profession. Many engineers are introverts—quiet, dignified, and not prone to excitement. Well, this group apparently has not gotten the word because the work area was almost like a sales acquisition room instead of a sales service room! As the problems were solved, everyone got the smiling equivalent of a "high five" that said, "We did it again—a job well done!"

Here's the message: When all parts of every company display the same gung ho attitude about serving the customer and keeping that customer happy, we won't have to worry about imports, balance of trade, or any other economic problems in our society.

How can you help in this all-important area? By understanding just who your customers really are.

## INTERNAL CUSTOMERS

Have you ever stopped to realize that you have two sets of customers? The obvious clients and prospects to whom you make presentations are your external customers—those outside your organization. The second group includes the INTERNAL clients and prospects who work *for* your organization. Obviously, you are not selling the same products and services to both groups, but you are selling!

Just because the same person who signs your paycheck signs the paycheck for the receptionist doesn't mean that she or he is not your customer. The accountant, the shipping clerk, secretarial support team, and service managers are due (and deserve) the same courtesy (if not more) given suspects and prospects. Think! Would you treat a prospect the same way you treat the people in your own office? How can you use outstanding "people skills" outside your office and forget them when you walk through the doors of your building? When you fail to treat coworkers with the same courtesy and respect shown to customers, you will pay the price all unsuccessful salespeople pay for forgetting who your customers really are.

## APPLYING "CUSTOMER SERVICE" PRINCIPLES TO *ALL* CUSTOMERS

We have discovered that one disgruntled customer who is treated rudely will tell eleven other people about the incident, but she will not—generally speaking—tell anybody who can do anything about the problem, namely, the supervisor of the individual with whom she was dealing. The sad thing is that those eleven people who have been told about the problem will, on average, tell five other people. Put your pencil to it. That means there are fifty-five people who have heard your name and your company's name in a negative way.

It doesn't take an awful lot of unhappy customers to put a company out of business and derail a salesperson's career.

When you treat a coworker rudely or thoughtlessly, the same principle is in effect. Generally speaking, he will tell eleven other coworkers who will turn around and tell five more. Even in large organizations, it doesn't take long for you to establish a negative reputation.

The procedure for coping with these problems is very similar to that used for handling other customer service problems. The minute a problem arises and you become aware of it, deal with it with all possible haste. Typical customers (internal and external) are not interested in excuses; they're interested in a solution to the problem. They don't want you making excuses or blaming someone else. They're not interested in fixing the blame—they're interested in fixing the problem! If you will quickly apologize for the inconvenience and/or delay and get busy working on the solution, you will take giant strides toward building a solid "internal" reputation.

Find out what it will take to make your valued peer happy and bring the solution to the problem. Once the problem is "fixed," check back in a day or two to make absolutely certain the "fix" was permanent and the coworker is happy. A week later, a handwritten note will score lots of points. The reality is, the aggressive, professional salesperson will capitalize on those opportunities to "win friends and influence people." And speaking of this Dale Carnegie principle. . . .

## A NECESSARY APOLOGY

Many years ago when I was working with Dale Carnegie in New York, I learned a truism that has come in handy on many occasions. The Carnegie people taught me that when you lay an egg, you should step back and admire it. More important, you should acknowledge that you have just laid that egg.

Gerry Clonaris of Charlotte, North Carolina, gives this advice new significance in a story he shared. As Gerry put it, the number one fear of anybody working for a retail company is overspending the "open to buy" account. Once the "open to buy" account is spent in any well-run company, the buyer is finished until the account is replenished, which might not be until the next buying season. Gerry said that one day he had finished developing an outstanding collection of fashion handbags with one of the largest vendors from Japan only to realize that his "open to buy" was gone. He had invested every dime available. Gerry also courageously stepped up to the fact that sloppy planning on his part had caused the problem (no blame, just problem *recognition* to aid in problem *solution*).

Gerry had a problem. How could he approach the company controller who was not known for his compassionate and understanding attitude toward people like Gerry who had not planned carefully? Gerry used a technique I would recommend to you in solving his problem. He began by writing one statement that summarized his predicament. After he narrowed the situation to one statement, it no longer seemed insurmountable and allowed him to focus on finding a solution rather than being overcome by a problem.

Here is the statement as Gerry wrote it: "Problem: How do I approach the controller with my situation and explain that I need additional 'open to buy' money when I know this gentleman has an ingrained fixation to devour buyers for lunch when they ask for additional 'OTB' dollars?"

Please don't minimize the importance of writing out what you might feel is obvious. Putting things on paper allows us to look at information in the cold light of reality, while holding ideas in our minds can maximize (or minimize) necessary information. In our minds, a predicament is measured in emotion and imagination. On paper, logic can take over.

## A NECESSARY SOLUTION

After examining the situation carefully and taking time to look over the problem written out, Gerry came up with the following solution:

"I walked into our controller's office allowing all the frustration and dejection I felt to show and said, 'Ray, I'm in trouble. I really blew it!' "

"Well, what's the matter?" Ray replied. Gerry then proceeded to tell Ray, his company's controller, the story. Gerry explained how he had developed the new product line, only to squander the opportunity because he had blown the "open to buy" with some poor planning on his part.

"Listen," said Ray, "you aren't the first one to be overly zealous with your buying dollars. At least you admit it. Now, let's take a look at your plan and see what we can do." Ray found a way to get some additional money for the new line that, incidentally, was a success.

As Gerry put it, he quickly learned that when he had made a mistake, he needed to use the humble approach or "Can you help me?" approach. In this process Gerry learned a great deal about human nature. By and large, when we approach people known to be the toughest—and we approach them properly—we discover that they are not only willing to help but actually are softies who probably have developed a "crust" as a means of survival.

Do *you* need to ask someone for help? Is there an internal customer who needs (and possibly deserves) an apology from you? Do you have the courage to step back and admire that egg you laid and point it out to others? If you will treat your coworkers, employees, and employers with the same compassion you would show a paying customer, you will be able to overcome 99.9 percent of all problems while building a "super support system" for your sales success!

## BUT I DON'T LIKE SOME OF THOSE PEOPLE

Anybody can love the lovable. There is no talent involved in caring for the person who cares for you. A basic of success in life—as well as in sales—is learning to love the unlovable. And frankly, it's O.K. that you don't like everyone. You are not required to be best friends with or to seek approval from every person in your life. However, you will find that when you treat each person in your life courteously and appropriately, you will be treated "in kind."

That doesn't mean allowing people to treat you unkindly and "walk on you." I am not talking about allowing people to abuse you verbally or physically. You can walk away from a situation with courtesy and dignity (and feel much better) and get great results without losing control. When you envision people in your life as being real "flesh and blood'" and you treat them with respect, even if they don't notice, you will—and you will respect yourself, which in the long run is much more important than their respect for you.

You may have heard this comment: "Every obnoxious act is a cry for help!" If you can give others the benefit of the doubt and allow them to keep their dignity, you can help them to win while you win. And this is truly the "double win" you've heard so much about.

## GET THEM INVOLVED

A primary method you can utilize to bring your support team together and be sure you are pulling on the same end of the rope (as opposed to pulling against one another) is to work toward "shared ownership."

Gerry Clonaris, whom I mentioned earlier, also shared the following example: "At one point in my career, I shared the buying responsibility for a major line at Sears with two other bright, intelligent buyers. The three of us bought virtually the identical line with slight modifications in style and clientele. However, there was one major difference. My sales always exceeded the other two buyers', especially when a new product was introduced.

"As I look back, I have often felt that the product the other two buyers developed was at times superior in style to mine. But the sales of my new products always seemed to excel. The secret was that whenever I developed a new product I made sure to always involve the retail sales manager, the catalog sales manager, the district managers, the advertising managers, and so on. I would involve anyone in that office who walked past my door. The result was that I had the entire home office and field office personnel sold on the line BEFORE IT EVEN HIT THE STORE.

"With all the planned exposure that was ensured because the advertising manager 'helped' develop the lines (not to mention the help of the retail and catalog managers), success of my new line was virtually guaranteed. With all this guaranteed exposure, I was able to get a lower cost on the goods because of the huge volume I could guarantee the vendor. The customers in our stores couldn't help but buy this line because everywhere they turned it was staring them in the face. This was a great way to build sales."

One of the things Gerry teaches us is that when we share ownership in a project, others buy into the ideas more enthusiastically and support whatever the project may be with their very best effort.

Incidentally, that's also excellent advice for all of us to use, regardless of what our job might be, with any company or, for that matter, when we're at home with the family. Get everyone involved in the project, and the chances of success will be greatly increased.

## THE FAMILY

In 1990, we made a major decision that had a great bearing on our business and my sales career. We decided that the Zig Ziglar Corporation was going to return to being a "family business." At one point we had changed our board of directors from my immediate family (The Redhead, our three daughters, one son, an accountant, and our attorney) to a board consisting of The Redhead and me with all other members coming from outside the family. And though there were some good reasons for doing so, this board never functioned quite as effectively as before, so in 1990 we went back to the family board and far more involvement from each member of the family. Results have been even better than expected, and the future for ZZC as a training company looks brighter than ever!

My eldest daughter, Suzan Witmeyer, is a constant reader and researcher, so she represents a wealth of practical knowledge. Since she also inherited her mother's intuition, her advice and insight on company matters are extremely helpful. She made the decision to dedicate her "career time" to raising two precious children and being a household executive. Her husband, Chad, is our vice president and director of operations and holds one of the most responsible and important positions in our company.

Our second daughter, Cindy Oates, lives with her husband, Richard, in California. We are in regular contact with the two of them by phone and letter, and in 1991 we started a weekly habit of making a conference call on Sunday afternoon, when other family members were at our home, to hear their thoughts on business and family matters. Cindy is also blessed with excellent insight, and her professional sales and business experience in her work outside the home makes her a valuable board member and business partner. Our prayer is that God will allow Cindy and Richard, who is with a major national homebuilder, to move back to Dallas soon so both of them can be even more involved in our company.

Our youngest daughter, Julie Norman, a competent and humbly confident brand-new employee, is also closely involved. Like *all* our children (not bragging, just facing facts), Julie has a keen mind and rare insights into people and behavior. She is a real "people person" with a servant's heart and a willingness to do whatever it takes to get the job done. In addition, her husband, Jim, is the CEO and president of The Zig Ziglar Corporation as of June of 1990. Jim Norman brought a wealth of business experience, a "commonsense" and fundamentally sound business approach to our company, which is invaluable in the corporate world.

Our son, Tom, started his career at The Zig Ziglar Corporation by working in the warehouse and shipping area. Later, to get a "feel" for all phases of the business, he moved into the sales area and today does a great job as our sales administrator. Tom is cool and "laid back," but he, too, has a great feel for people. His keen mind and instinctive touch in the world of sales and management both inside and outside our company make him a valuable employee and board member. Tom's wife, Chachis, also works with us in the accounting department as supervisor of order processing. She is a beautiful and very bright young woman from Campeche, Mexico, and a true joy to our family. She, like the other members of the family, is warm and affectionate, so when we get together as a family it takes us five minutes to "hug in" and five minutes to "hug out."

I would like to credit heredity and environment for our children's success, but every time I do, I think of an incident that one of the girls used to keep me humble. When confronted with the fact that she had not performed well on a math examination (despite the fact that she has a near genius IQ), she asked me if I thought the reason for her poor performance was hereditary or environmental?!?!

## SAVING THE BEST

And certainly the most important member of our management team and board of directors is The Redhead. She is and has been my friend, companion, confidante, partner, helpmate, and special gift from God for over forty-five years. She encompasses every positive quality mentioned in our children. Most important, as a wife, she is my "everything" lady. She inspires, delights, and encourages me. Regardless of what happens to me "out there," I know that when I get home, I will be Number One with her, and she is going to be on my side. No, that doesn't mean she always agrees with everything I say and do, but it does mean that "when the chips are down," I know I can absolutely and positively count on her. I would never consider making a significant business decision without her counsel. How I wish I had listened to her insights and judgment from the beginning! How grateful I am that she is playing a bigger and bigger role in the company today! And I do listen very carefully not only to her intellect but to how she feels as well.

## GET THEM INVOLVED

Now if you are wondering why I mention my family's involvement in our company, let me make it perfectly clear. You, as a successful sales professional, must remember that you are the owner of your own business. As I said in the first chapter of this book, "You are in business for yourself but not by yourself." The people in your home are going to have a great bearing on your success, so GET THEM INVOLVED! I cannot overstress the importance of this statement, but I can repeat it: GET YOUR FAMILY INVOLVED IN YOUR BUSINESS!

## LET THEM KNOW

The inherent optimism of most salespeople is such that they often present a picture to the family that is completely unrealistic. For example, one of the things I learned "after the fact" was that our children seldom knew of any of the difficulties we faced, whether our concerns included making a decision or having financial worries. Since we did not keep them "in the know," they assumed that everything was always O.K., whether it was or not. By shielding them from everything, we did not teach them how to contend with some of life's difficulties. In short, we did not prepare them for some of the problems they were going to encounter later in life as well as we could have.

One very surprising thing was brought to light in the process of writing this book. I engaged the aid of the entire family—The Redhead, my three daughters, and my son. As we were discussing the book and looking at the contributions that daughter Julie Norman and Suzan Witmeyer had made, Julie and I were alone for about thirty minutes. Much to my surprise, Julie started sharing with me some of the fears she had experienced as a small child. She was afraid that one day my plane might go down or that something would happen to me and I would not come home. She was especially concerned, therefore, that before I left for a trip she always had a chance to hug me and kiss me good-bye and tell me she loved me. If, for whatever reason, that had not taken place, she was particularly fearful until I returned home. This really was a shocker to me because I always left home with the confidence that I would return. I never worried about my own safety, and it did not occur to me that any member of my family would give a thought to such a possibility.

Here's the message, parents. If your job takes you out of town or if you leave in the morning and come back in the evening, it takes only a few seconds to hug and kiss your mate and your children and tell them how much you love them. Certainly no harm can come of it, and much good—including a closer relationship—can be the specific result. This simple act can eliminate or at least reduce the fears of the family.

## EXPLAIN AND COMMUNICATE

Since the entire family is involved in the salesperson's career, the wise salesperson not only confers with the family but also shares the results of efforts. For example, there are frequently contests involving trips and prizes. These might necessitate a heavier workload and more absence from the home. The salesperson should call a sales meeting, share with the family the details of the contest, solicit their help, get their involvement, listen to their input, and then let them share in the rewards.

The contest winners might receive a trip to some luxury resort area for a few days. The prize generally includes only husband and wife. The challenge is to get the kids excited about helping Mom and Dad win a prize they will not share. In fact, they will lose their parents for a few days. Question: What can you do to encourage their support? Answer: Communicate that you, the salesperson, win the trip and also secure your job and stake out a bigger claim on the future, which means they will benefit. That's the first priority. Second, you can initiate little contests so the kids see some "now" benefits. For example, when you communicate with the family, include the kids in the details. Set up a racetrack broken into the number of weeks in the contest and get two small model cars for the track. One can show where you should be in the contest; the other car shows where you are. Every week you beat your quota, reward the kids with a small prize or treat, and if you win the big prize, get them a bigger award. The size of the prize is not nearly as important as the concept of involvement and reward.

You can also get the kids involved in reading and research. Encourage them to look for positive quotes and slogans, which they place in strategic spots all over the house. These procedures will guarantee that your kids will be pulling for you and pushing you on to win the contest. They will act as "motivators" and sales managers.

## TRAVELING AND YOUR SUCCESSFUL SUPPORT SYSTEM

In the last chapter, I focused on how to handle travel. Because the following principles apply whether you travel extensively, rarely, or not at all, I have included them here.

There are exceptions to this rule, of course, but in the overwhelming majority of cases when traveling is involved and there are small children, the man does the traveling. I especially urge the mate who stays at home to be extremely careful not to make Dad the punisher, avenger, disciplinarian, or "bad guy" when he comes home. Frequently, the stay-at-home mate will make a list of sins and wrongdoings committed by the children during the week with the promised threat to them that when Daddy gets home he will deal with them.

I have personally known of a number of households where Dad was given a list of all the things the child had done "wrong"—or not done at all—with no mention of what was done "right." As a result Dad comes home wearing the black hat, acting the part of the "heavy."

Many times without knowing all the facts, he deals with the "bad" child instead of a child who might have done a bad thing. Now, throw in the fact that Dad might be very tired and stressed, and you can understand why the kids actually dread Dad's return because of the fear he will deal with them harshly. You can well imagine the impact on the children, on Dad, and on the relationship between the father and the children. And please know this—the impact on the family and on the sales career can be disastrous.

There will be exceptions, but in most cases Mom should deal with the issue as it arises. If the situation is serious, life-threatening, or a breach of the law, a phone call to discuss the appropriate steps to take would be in order. Mom could then say, "Your dad and I have talked about this on the phone, and frankly, we've not come to a conclusion about what we're going to do. When he returns, we will discuss it more thoroughly and decide on the appropriate action."

## PUNISHMENT VS. DISCIPLINE

At this point, I need to encourage the parents to remember there is a vast difference between punishment and discipline. Punishment is something you do TO a child; discipline is something you do FOR a child. Oftentimes punishment is dished out while the parent is angry. Bad timing.

Let me encourage you to "cool off" before you decide on the appropriate discipline. If the infraction is a minor one, no anger should be involved. To head off future trouble, you can deal with the issue calmly, coolly, and quickly. In my book *Raising Positive Kids in a Negative World*, I discuss the difference between discipline and punishment at great length.

## POSTPONE PUNISHMENT

When Dad returns after a trip out of town, if there have been serious problems I encourage Dad to postpone that punishment or discipline until the next morning. Let the return home be one the kids can look forward to. Dad needs to get back into the normal activities of the house and the routine of family life. There needs to be a considerable amount of hugging and affection.

With this approach the child clearly understands that though Dad and Mom might have to deal with him the next day, they're going to deal with him out of love and concern for him. In short, give him the feeling of love and security that will make him know that whatever is done is done out of love and concern for him. If during the course of the evening the child raises the issue, in most cases it is advisable to say, "We're going to deal with that tomorrow when I've had a chance to further talk with your mom and we can decide what's appropriate. In the meantime, let's have fun together because regardless of what you might have done, you're still my child, and we need to have some fun together tonight."

## FINANCIAL PLANNING

The successful selling professional heads off one of the greatest dangers to the family and the career by developing a financial plan. PLEASE DO NOT SKIP OVER WHAT YOU ARE READING RIGHT NOW! For many years, if I had read the first sentence in this paragraph, I would have looked for the next line in bold print to indicate a change in topic. Consequently for parts of my career, I rode the financial roller coaster of highs and lows. Go to school on my experience, and refuse to repeat the mistakes of the past.

Financial problems are THE greatest cause of strain on relationships and careers. Your personal success is in many ways directly dependent on how you handle your financial affairs. I'm not talking about making the effort to become a multimillionaire; I'm talking about properly handling the money that is coming in.

Allow me to give you a "minilesson" on finances, which is going to seem terribly simple to many of you. Yet, less than 10 percent of the people in our society will be taking all of these steps. As a matter of fact, I will make you a guarantee. If you will take each of these steps for two years, the majority of your financial worries will be gone; and if you will take these steps throughout your career, you can have the joy of financial freedom.

### PLANNING FOR SUCCESS

To become free of financial worries and concerns:

1. BEGIN TODAY. The "tomorrow is soon enough" theory of

economics causes financial woes to many, many intelligent people. Begin today to read books, listen to tapes, and attend seminars concerning your finances. Start with the basics, establish a foundation, and build whatever type financial "housing" you desire for you and your family.

Read *The Richest Man in Babylon* by George S. Clason. This classic book will give you new insights on money and peace of mind in the area of finance.

Lynn Robbins and Dennis Webb have an excellent audio seminar called "Personal Money Management," which I highly recommend. It is available from the Franklin International Institute, Inc. (the address is in the Bibliography of this book). Lynn Robbins also wrote *Uncommon Cents: Benjamin Franklin's Secrets to Achieving Personal Financial Success*, which is available from the same address.

Ron Blue is an excellent financial advisor who has great wisdom and insight. His address is also in the Bibliography.

Periodicals you might consider are *Consumer Reports*, *Money* magazine, *Changing Times*, and *Sylvia Porter's Personal Finance Magazine*.

Don't get caught up in who to go to or where to go. Get started TODAY!

2. PLAN WITH YOUR SPOUSE. Family finances must be family business. You and your spouse will determine who is responsible for all aspects of family bookkeeping, but do the work TOGETHER. Even if one of you is only an observer, do the work together.

Beware of two common traps. First, do not fall into the trap of saying you will "look over" the checkbook, bank statement, or bills later. More often than not, you won't! Lack of knowledge leads to frustration and fear. Second, do not "protect" your spouse from bad information. Share all information at all times.

3. USE A RECORD-KEEPING SYSTEM. Keep all financial records in one place. A three-ring binder notebook makes an excellent "file" for financial records. Manila folders are great for record storage. WHAT you use is not nearly as important as making a DECISION on what to use and to begin using it immediately. All records must be kept together in an organized manner so that in case of an emergency, those who need access to bank account numbers, credit card information, investments, "receivables" (money

owed to), and "payables" (debts) will have the necessary information available.

And speaking of emergencies, let me encourage you to get your will made immediately if you do not have one. A dear friend of our family lost her husband suddenly, and for three years her children were officially wards of the state; her financial records were not available to her; and she experienced many hardships. Her children lived with her, and because of her personal influence, she was able to pay her bills, but her circumstances were negatively affected to an incredible extent by lack of planning. You have heard all the horror stories. If your loved ones are truly loved, get your will done. Questions about life-support systems and organ donation need to be determined in the most logical manner and time possible, not in a time of grief and despair.

4. ESTABLISH SPENDING PRIORITIES. Discuss the most important expenditures with your spouse. Look at what you HAVE to spend and what you WANT to spend. This step will help you control "emotional/impulse" spending to some extent. If you will write down your spending priorities and keep this written record with your other financial records to be reviewed each time you sit down to pay the bills, you will be incredibly well pleased with the impact on your financial planning AND the impact on your relationship with your spouse. Financial planning will NOT push you apart. Poor financial decisions are a leading contributor to divorce. Planning, scheming, and dreaming TOGETHER will help overcome financial problems and lead you toward financial control.

5. REMEMBER THESE KEY CONCEPTS. More money will not solve your problems. The American credit system encourages us to spend at least 10 percent more than we earn, regardless of income level.

Financial planning is perceived as restrictive when in actuality freedom is available only with planning.

Your finances are not out of your control. Your financial situation is based on historic choices (made by YOU!)

However, some people have gotten to the point where they need professional help and expertise. If this is your situation, the National Foundation for Consumer Credit and Debtors Anonymous are good resources. See the Bibliography for more information.

## THE SELLING FAMILY

Because this book on selling is concerned with the entire sales process and salesperson, including personal, family, and business life, I'd like to share another example of how selling is effectively used in dealing with the family. Angie Logan from Lubbock, Texas, points out that she and her husband are not in the sales business, but they've found sales principles help them get along in life and especially with their family.

Angie tells of an experience with their three-year-old daughter, Danielle, who is very intelligent and has a mind of her own. (Sound familiar, parents?) Previously, requests made of Danielle resulted in a "tug-of-war" and, on occasion, punishment that left everyone unhappy. Yet Angie and Danny felt they could not permit their three-year-old child to manipulate or control them, so they decided to "take the high road" and utilize some good old-fashioned common-sense sales procedures.

They point out that no one likes to be commanded to do something, so they started letting Danielle make her own decisions. No, they didn't abdicate responsibility to a three-year-old; they simply gave her a choice. Instead of saying, "Danielle, pick up your truck," they would say, "Do you want to carry your truck to your room or roll it?" She would jump up and holler, "Roll it!" and off she'd go. They used this approach in many different situations to encourage good behavior, and it worked wonderfully well. The family saved mountains of guilt, grief, and frustration while introducing Danielle to the process of learning to make "choices." The difference in family harmony was noticeable almost immediately.

Both parents say Danielle is outgrowing her spells of stubbornness and is becoming a happy, bubbly, well-disciplined child. Their crowning moment arrived when they heard Danielle ask her little brother, "Michael, do you want to give me my Barbie doll or lay her on the bed?" He laid it on the bed.

## CAUSING OTHERS TO WANT YOUR LEADERSHIP

The significant lesson to be learned from Angie and Danny is that *leadership* and *salesmanship* in many cases are synonymous. In this situation, Danielle ended up doing what her parents wanted her to do and actually enjoyed it in the process. Dwight Eisenhower, supreme commander of the Allied Expeditionary Force in World War II and, after that, president of the United States, defined *leadership* as "the art of getting someone else to do something that you want done because he wants to do it." Gentle persuasion is effective in all areas of life because it preserves the dignity of the individual. That's the way to raise a family, make a friend, and build a sales career.

## SUMMARY

To build a successful sales support system, we begin by understanding that *internal* customers (our coworkers) are as important as *external* customers (our clients and prospects). Once we understand the importance of internal customers, we realize that our family is more important than either internal or external customers.

When we deal with internal customers and family, we can be most effective when we use five basic principles on a regular and recurring basis.

1. *Never take internal customers and family for granted.* Familiarity must not be allowed to breed contempt. Remind yourself on a daily basis how important these people are in your life.

2. *Admit when you are wrong.* Everyone makes mistakes. Take credit for being human, and admit your errors.

3. *Love the unlovable.* There is no special talent to love the lovable; the real key to successful living is to love those who make it difficult for us to respect and appreciate them. Remember: Every obnoxious act is a cry for help.

4. *Get them involved.* There is wisdom in the counsel of many. Find out what others think. One of our basic human needs is to feel important. When you involve others, you can help them meet this important need.

5. *Explain and communicate.* Seize every opportunity to share, explain, show, confer, and ask. Everyone has a strong desire to be "in the know." Share information!

6. *Work to eliminate financial pressures.* Your coworkers and family have financial concerns. All of us can be more effective in dealing with financial pressures by following a few simple guidelines: (a)

Begin financial planning today; (b) Plan with your spouse; (c) Use a record keeping system; (d) Establish spending priorities; and (e) Break away from financial myths.

THE KEY TO BUILDING A SUCCESSFUL SALES SUPPORT SYSTEM IS TO ACCEPT PERSONAL RESPONSIBILITY FOR MAKING CHOICES.

CHAPTER FIFTEEN

# ORGANIZATION AND DISCIPLINE

## *Gaining Control of Your Time and Your Life*

Discipline yourself to do the things you need to do when you need to do them, and the day will come when you will be able to do the things you want to do when you want to do them!

### BECOMING A "CAN'T MISS" SALES PROFESSIONAL

One hundred and seventy-five of the Fortune 500 CEO's are former United States Marines. I don't need to tell you that the United States Marines teach organization, discipline, and commitment. They also teach loyalty, personal responsibility, and mental and physical toughness. In the sales world those qualities will take you a long way. As a matter of fact, combine those with sales knowledge, a caring attitude, and some reasonable social skills, and I would label you a "can't miss" salesperson.

### BELIEF AND COMPATIBILITY

Now take those qualities and tie them to a product you believe in and with which you're compatible, and you are on your way! We have already talked about the importance of believing in what you sell. By now, this factor should be obvious. The compatibility factor might not be quite as clear. By way of example, I would have to work harder to achieve success in selling a highly technical product or one of a mechanical nature. As a very young person, I had a "mechanical bypass" and simply do not grasp some of the technical and mechanical details that seem to come so naturally and easily to other people. On the other side of the scale, I am extremely comfortable selling educational programs or tangible products of almost any kind. When I can see the benefits for the prospect, I get extremely enthusiastic about whatever the product or service may be.

## THE TIME OF YOUR LIFE

The discipline we all need is attainable. Specifically, if you and I can look at the benefits for starting our day at the proper time—ON A REGULAR BASIS—we will be inclined to do what is best.

Sales giant Walter Hailey says research proves that 70 percent of all sales are made between 7:00 A.M. and 1:00 P.M., 20 percent between 1:00 P.M. and 4:00 P.M., and 10 percent after 4:00 P.M. When people are energetic and just getting their day started, they're obviously in a more optimistic and responsive frame of mind. In addition, these sales result from the fact that salespeople are also more excited and motivated about what they are doing.

Discipline and organization make a difference in sales. If you're going to make it big, the odds are good that you've got to make it early. The obvious exception to this would be in direct sales businesses where calls are made in the evenings, but in the 1990s even people in traditional sales positions (like insurance) are finding the daylight hours to be most productive.

### DON'T KID YOURSELF

Because salespeople have so much freedom and independence in the world of selling, they do not always exercise good judgment or sound integrity as they go about the business of selling. They don't really get to work or to the presentation on time; they don't really make all of the calls they claim to make; they don't really follow through as they should; they don't really work the number of hours they put down on their reports. In the process they can fool their managers or employers. It is an absolute impossibility for a manager to know every thought, every action, and every moment that the individual salesperson invests in the sales process. Yes, you can fool your manager and "get by" with some of that inactivity, but who are you really hurting? Who are you really kidding? What does it do to *your* bottom line?

**Discipline yourself to do the things you need to do when you need to do them, and the day will come when you will be able to do the things you want to do when you want to do them!**

According to Terrence Patton, a crisis sales training consultant from Roanoke, Virginia, 20 percent of sales calls reported never take place, and over 15 percent of a salesperson's calls involve absolutely no precall planning. Tragic. Foolish. And expensive—for the salesperson, the family, and the company.

## WHEN DO YOU DO WHAT?

Figures vary enormously as to where the typical salesperson spends time. Many have calculated that less than two hours of the working day are actually spent in the sales process. The rest of the time is spent going from prospect to prospect, waiting in offices, looking for parking spaces, taking care of administrative details, and handling service calls and a host of other things. Obviously, some of these are critical and must be done on a regular basis.

The question the sales professional must ask is this: Can I more effectively—or equally effectively—handle this assignment during nonselling hours? I particularly think of answering correspondence, filling out reports, coping with administrative details, obtaining credit reports, and taking care of personal business (seeing the dentist, buying clothing, visiting friends, paying bills, etc.).

When the car is in the shop, do you deliberately create a number of administrative tasks to do during that day so it won't be wasted, or do you rent a car and get on with the sales process, taking care of the administrative details during the nonselling hours? This comes under the heading of organization (which is frequently missing in "average" producers). Does it surprise you to learn that real sales professionals, with no more time than average performers, will spend twice as many hours in front of prospects as average producers do? They make sales not because of exceptional sales ability but because they have prioritized what's important in what they do on a daily basis.

## RECIPE FOR SALES SUCCESS

Generally speaking, the high-producing sales professional does work harder than the average producer. The reality is, simply outworking your competition will put you in the upper echelons of selling. I'm not talking about working 80- and 90-hour weeks. One extra hour per day in high-payoff activity will allow you to outdistance most of the field and surprise yourself in terms of people helped and dollars earned.

Next, add integrity, discipline, and organization to the recipe, and you catapult very quickly into the top 10 percent of all salespeople. Throw in a constant quest for knowledge and learning about how to become "even better" as a professional salesperson while becoming adept at the new procedures and latest industry trends and you will move into the upper 5 percent.

I'm really talking about using all of your resources—physical, mental, and spiritual—and taking care of all facets of your life.

## "TIME" TO BE SUCCESSFUL

Each one of us is unique. Every salesperson has qualities and characteristics as well as mannerisms, procedures, and habits that will vary from anyone else. However, outstanding salespeople have many things in common.

A common trait of the top producers is being "time-conscious." Professionals know that everyone has the same amount of time— twenty-four hours per day— and that one of the keys to success is the use of this allotment of time.

Through careful record keeping, top selling professionals account for time spent with prospects, time spent waiting, and time spent in travel. Not so coincidentally, those who are serious about success turn their travel time to productive time by listening to educational and motivational recordings or rehearsing the verbiage for the next presentation. While "cooling their heels in the outer office," real sales professionals have a plan of action to utilize this hopefully brief (but frequently too long) period of time. Often, the time is invested in reviewing the information or expanding the information they have on the prospect they're waiting to see.

Sales professionals don't count time; they make time count. Independent sales professionals who discipline themselves to keep detailed records are more productive, and companies that require detailed reports of a salespersons' activities have a more productive sales force.

## GET SOME HELP

Just because you see or remember something that needs to be done, or just because others call your attention to something they want you to do, does not necessarily mean you have to change your course of action. When your direction is clearly set and you're working toward a specific objective, you are far less likely to let friends, neighbors, or relatives with "time to kill" murder your time in the process.

Consider the "time-killing" activities that the nonprofessional salesperson permits to occur and the fact that most salespeople spend too much of their time doing nonproductive tasks, and it is easy to understand why authorities estimate that as much as 80 percent of the salesperson's time is involved in activities that do not directly generate business. The prime reason the high-producing sales professionals are careful in their record keeping is to make certain they devote the bulk of their time to face-to-face sales and service situations that directly and indirectly lead to increased sales.

## EFFICIENCY VS. EFFECTIVENESS

You have heard before that "efficiency" means doing things right; "effectiveness" is doing the right things.

One of the most effective and efficient men I know is Dave Liniger, the founder of Re/Max Realtors. He has established an atmosphere that encourages the people around him to get the most out of their time and themselves.

Dave discovered that 47 percent of the top one hundred Re/Max producers had personal assistants who handled some of the "nonsales" responsibilities. These "helpers" were involved in activities like putting up and taking down "For Sale" and "Sold" signs in yards, having cars serviced, making routine phone calls, picking up dry cleaning, dropping mail at the post office, and handling the 1,001 details that can consume time.

Delegating nonselling tasks frees the professional salesperson to spend more time prospecting for and talking with clients, which are far more likely to lead to more sales more often. Increased sales means a boost to the economy AND the income of the Re/Max associate. Interestingly enough, while these top producers work longer hours each week than the other sales associates, they are far more likely to take vacations—often taking as much as four weeks off per year.

The conclusion is clear: The better you utilize your time, the more income you will generate; and the more income you generate, the more free time you will have for your family and for taking those really nice trips. In short, higher income salespeople work smarter, not necessarily harder, and they utilize other people more efficiently and effectively so that everybody wins!

## BEWARE

Please be sensitive to your spouse when delegating nonselling tasks. Some families thrive on working closely in this area, and some terrible frustrations and even devastating breakups have been caused by unrealistic expectations. Too many times, the spouse who does not work outside the home is expected to do EVERYTHING! Working in the home, especially if there are children involved, IS a full-time job.

Most homes in the nineties have both the husband and the wife in the work force. Both spouses will have tasks that fall in the "nonproductive" category. Please DISCUSS the best way to keep the "balance" so that one person (or one person's career) is not always given priority.

If you have experienced any concerns or challenges in this area, I would recommend a book to you called *COURTSHIP AFTER MARRIAGE: Romance Can Last a Lifetime.* Humility prevents me from sharing the author's name, but his first and last names begin with the letter *Z*.

## AND EVEN MORE SUCCESSFUL SALES CHARACTERISTICS

In the nineties, more than ever before, there are some ever-present companion traits of highly successful sales professionals. One is the conviction that customers must be given superior service if they expect to build customer loyalty. Selling a product that is not serviced is corporate suicide. And with the high level of expectation of today's consumer, the option of not giving exceptional customer service no longer exists.

For example, the salesperson who sells a product that requires instruction or know-how to use will check back within two or three days to make certain the prospect understands how to use the product to get maximum benefit. We once bought a vacuum cleaner with 287 (and that's only a slight exaggeration!) attachments. It looked so easy when the salesman was demonstrating, but after he departed, The Redhead and I could remember and use only a fraction of those attachments. How neat and wise it would have been had he stopped by within the next few days and given us a refresher course when our excitement was at its peak. We would have benefitted greatly, and we would undoubtedly have supplied him with prospects.

This again ties in to the philosophy I espouse in every book I have written and will ever write: "You can have everything in life you want if you will just help enough other people get what they want!" We wanted maximum use of our vacuum cleaner; the salesman obviously wanted to make more sales. He didn't help us get what we wanted and never asked us for those prospects, so both parties lost as a result of his lack of concern, service, and follow-through.

Tied to customer service are the salesperson's love for people and for the profession of selling and a conviction that the product is a perfect "fit" for the prospect. This next "vignette" explains what I am talking about.

## HELPING OTHERS GET WHAT THEY WANT

One winter evening in 1990 The Redhead and I were casually walking through Prestonwood Mall in North Dallas. We strolled past Marvin D. Anthony's men's store, which had a beautiful window display featuring the most gorgeous black cashmere sports coat I've ever seen—and it was on sale at a terrific price. We paused, The Redhead commented on the coat, and Marvin himself "just happened" to be standing at the front, close to the door. He recognized my wife since she had bought a couple of items from him for my birthday. Needless to say, Marvin enthusiastically invited us to "come on in."

In short order I bought that coat. And what good is the most gorgeous coat "in the whole world," as Marvin modestly put it, without a perfectly matched pair of trousers—or even two pairs? I bought. The pièce de résistance, though, was the tie. Marvin is a real professional, working within the framework of his personality to use his skills to the best of his ability. He is slightly dramatic, tremendously enthusiastic, and very sincere. With a flourish and without any hesitation, he made a beeline for the tie that was the perfect complement for the coat, and it was absolutely magnificent—love at first sight! But the price was "out of sight." Though it cost twice as much as I had ever paid for a tie, I bought. Here's why: I liked it, I wanted it, and it completed the outfit. Plus (and this was the deciding factor), I'm convinced, and The Redhead is even more convinced, that Marvin sincerely wanted me (and nobody else) to have that tie. During the interchange and decision-making process, as Marvin was bringing other items out, The Redhead said, "You know, honey, it is a beautiful tie, and Marvin really wants you to have it. I think you should get it." I did.

Two bottom lines: I love that tie and have gotten more compliments on it than any I've ever owned. And Marvin's conviction that it was "my" tie and his sincerity in wanting me to have such a beautiful tie were the determining factors in my decision to buy. Message: Your sincere interest in doing what is best for your prospect and your conviction that what you are offering meets that criterion will be the determining factors in many, many "yes" decisions.

## THE "PICTURE" OF SUCCESS

Now wrap this portrait of the truly professional salesperson (a time-conscious, service-oriented, product-believing, profession-loving person) in INTEGRITY, add a GENUINE LOVE FOR PEOPLE, and you have a solid foundation for sales success.

When you have these characteristics, you will always find a considerable amount of product knowledge and sales know-how mixed in with the formula. Think about it. If you love the profession, have genuine concern for people, and believe in the product you're selling, then you're going to feel a moral responsibility to persuade people to buy for their own benefit. You can't help acquiring a missionary zeal and believing that if everybody knew what you know about your product, everybody would buy your product. That feeling is transferred to an ever-increasing number of prospects who rapidly become customers because "selling is a transference of feeling." It's true. If you can transfer that "feeling" to the prospect through the professional procedures we are covering, then your prospect will become your customer if ownership is within the boundaries of the possible.

## LOOKING AND LISTENING

The highly productive professional salesperson is also a professional looker and listener who pays attention to the details of the sales call, observes the mannerisms of the prospect, and tunes in to the prospect's rate of speech. If the prospect is a slow, deliberate, methodical speaker, the selling professional emulates the style of the prospect. If the prospect is inclined to speak and move at a more rapid pace, the top performing salesperson will do the same and be compatible with the mannerisms and speech patterns of the prospect.

In other words, a true professional makes every effort to get in harmony and establish rapport with the prospect.

What I'm really saying is that the sales career is built before, during, AND after the sale is made. As we say down home, "Even a blind pig is going to find a good acorn every once in a while." It's also true that even inept salespeople, by the sheer process of making calls, will end up with an occasional sale. But I can guarantee you they won't build a rewarding sales career on that type of hit-or-miss approach.

## SELF-ANALYSIS NOTEBOOK

One of the reasons this handbook on professional selling skills has created so much interest among the salespeople we've talked with is that many of them are ambitiously dissatisfied with their productivity. They have come to understand that many of the things they do and the procedures they follow are habitual and in many cases are no longer effective, perhaps unnecessary, and possibly even harmful. This is why "self-analysis" is so important.

"Self-analysis" is a magnificent procedure designed to keep a carefully documented running account of your activities and regularly ask yourself some questions: "Do I need to perform this activity, or do I need to do it in another way? Can I increase my overall productivity by increasing my effectiveness? Do I really need to work this hard?"

Don't misunderstand. I'm convinced that more salespeople fail because of not working hard enough than fail because of working too hard. However, when I think of hard workers, I think of my lifetime friend Randall Manning from Winston-Salem, North Carolina. Randy is retired, but for many years he was one of the top producers for Pitney-Bowes. He probably got more business per hour worked than any professional salesperson I've ever known. He excelled at *networking* before the word was coined. He had an engaging personality, and people instinctively liked and trusted him.

As important as being liked and trusted is—and these characteristics are the most important to START—his productivity came from careful planning. He never left home unless he knew precisely where he was going, when he was going to arrive, the people he needed to see, the circumstances of the call, the presentation he planned to make, the approach he was going to use, and the third-party influence he hoped to bring to bear. He also knew the prospect's major interest and always worked toward a long-term relationship.

### A BUILT-IN "CLIENT" SALES FORCE

For those reasons, clients were loyal to Randy, and they went out of their way to help him generate additional business. The reason is very simple. He took magnificent care of them because it was the right thing to do AND the smartest thing to do. Randy knew that his success in getting new prospects and new sales depended to a very large degree on his success in satisfying the customers he had. He made each one of them an assistant salesperson. Throughout his lengthy career there were few, if any, of his customers he could not go back to and sell and sell again.

Randy also understood what all successful salespeople must understand: It costs roughly five times as much to acquire a new customer as it does to keep the ones you have. So he worked at keeping the ones he had.

## COMPANY EXPECTATIONS

With the emphasis placed on productivity today, I get many questions about what to do when company demands exceed the realistic. This is a sensitive issue, and frankly, the companies and the representatives of those companies have turned it into an emotional issue. Let me encourage you to consider the following, whether you run a company that needs more productivity from its salespeople or whether you are that salesperson who needs less pressure from the company.

My recommendation is that you move the discussion from the

emotional side of the table to the logical through scientific validation. The key issues that must be evaluated for validation are activity, pipeline, and results. Activity is "how you use your time." Pipeline means "number of qualified buyers being worked." Results mean "number of sales generated."

## ACTIVITY

One of the most meaningful activities I have ever been involved with was doing a time analysis chart. I will admit that when I first heard about tracking my time, I felt like I had just been given a prison sentence. Most of us feel we are not being trusted when someone asks us to account for every minute of every day. So why not get a head start and do it before being asked?

Any company that is going to be successful in the long term is going to ask you to keep accurate records of your sales activity. However, the Winner's Time Log allows you to track every minute of your day. If you will keep this chart for just two weeks, it will dramatically affect your life. You will discover (as I did) that little more than two hours per day are spent in actual revenue-producing activity. Most of the time is spent "getting ready" to participate in revenue-producing activity. Your objective is not to be judgmental or critical of yourself; your objective is to become aware of the activities you might add or delete.

My charts showed that I was spending incredible amounts of time on the telephone. I was shocked to learn that on days I had set aside for writing, there were mornings that my writing time was literally cut in half by time spent on the telephone. Interruptions (sometimes telephone, sometimes other things) were disrupting and stealing two to three hours per day. Now please understand, when The Redhead comes by for a hug, that is an interruption I look forward to and want to have occur. (Besides, the hug always inspires me to be at my creative best.) I mention this simply to say that if the phone calls and interruptions you TRACK are O.K. by you, be about enjoying them. Don't get so caught up in what psychologists call "Type A" behavior that you don't build in time for the activities important to you. One of the great things you can discover and improve upon is time spent with family members.

Date: ______________________

# WINNER'S TIME LOG

Instructions: The TASK (what you are doing) and CONCERNING (what project/area the task is related to) columns are to be filled in *as* the activities occur. The PRIORITY column is to be filled in at the end of the day with a 1, 2, or 3. 1 = *high payoff,* winning activities; 2 = *fair payoff,* but I won't meet all my goals doing these all day; 3 = *poor payoff,* too many activities like this and I'll be unhappy and unemployed.

| | TASK | CONCERNING | PRIORITY |
|---|---|---|---|
| | | | |
| | | | |
| | | | |
| | | | |
| 7:00 | | | |
| 7:15 | | | |
| 7:30 | | | |
| 7:45 | | | |
| 8:00 | | | |
| 8:15 | | | |
| 8:30 | | | |
| 8:45 | | | |
| 9:00 | | | |
| 9:15 | | | |
| 9:30 | | | |
| 9:45 | | | |
| 10:00 | | | |
| 10:15 | | | |
| 10:30 | | | |
| 10:45 | | | |
| 11:00 | | | |
| 11:15 | | | |
| 11:30 | | | |
| 11:45 | | | |
| 12:00 | | | |
| 12:15 | | | |
| 12:30 | | | |
| 12:45 | | | |
| 1:00 | | | |
| 1:15 | | | |
| 1:30 | | | |
| 1:45 | | | |
| 2:00 | | | |
| 2:15 | | | |
| 2:30 | | | |
| 2:45 | | | |
| 3:00 | | | |
| 3:15 | | | |
| 3:30 | | | |
| 3:45 | | | |
| 4:00 | | | |
| 4:15 | | | |
| 4:30 | | | |
| 4:45 | | | |
| 5:00 | | | |
| 5:15 | | | |
| 5:30 | | | |
| 5:45 | | | |
| | | | |
| | | | |
| | | | |
| | | | |

Here is my major point: The Winner's Time Log is not a limiting factor but a freeing factor. How can you correct poor performance habits of which you are unaware? How can you become aware of the way in which you are using your most valuable commodity—your time? How can you be certain that you are maintaining the proper balance in your life? The Winner's Time Log is the answer.

Incidentally, top students sit down and *start* studying. Mediocre or poor students spend a lot of time *preparing* to study. Top salespeople do their planning and preparing during nonselling hours. When selling time comes, they pick up the phone, briefcase, or selling samples and start selling. In addition, the true "pros" in selling seize every opportunity—expected and unexpected—to sell, sell, sell! The following example will explain what I mean.

## Acres of Diamonds

Selling is a profession that enables us to take advantage of opportunities almost regardless of the circumstances. Leonard Allen of Eau Claire, Wisconsin, sells special welding electrodes for the maintenance industry. This includes farmers because of the considerable amount of machinery they have to repair themselves to keep their rolling stock in operation. Leonard was calling on a local farmers' co-op, and the prospect was interested but extremely busy. While trying to listen to Leonard, he was constantly interrupted by necessary phone calls. During the time the prospect was involved in a phone conversation, Leonard talked with an older farmer dressed in coveralls, and as Leonard explained it, "his boots indicated he was in farming." Leonard calls the following concept his "Barnyard Close."

He started the conversation with the farmer, opened his demo case, and showed the special welding rod—the one that welds through rust, dirt, and all the other things the farmer encounters. This particular gentleman was extremely well informed, quite articulate in his statements, and decisive in the questions he asked. The bottom line is that Leonard ended up with a considerable order because he was able to specifically answer the technical questions the farmer asked.

By the time Leonard closed the sale, the co-op manager had finished his call and communicated to Leonard that this particular farmer was one of the wealthiest and most respected in the area. He wanted to know what the man had purchased. When Leonard told the prospect what the farmer had purchased and why he bought it, the co-op manager declared that because of his respect for the farmer, he, too, would buy. Two sales before 9:00 A.M. started a magnificent day for Leonard Allen!

Lesson: As a child I sang an old church song entitled "Brighten the Corner Where You Are." Salespeople need to be selling in the corner wherever they are. They also need to utilize their time most effectively. It would have been easy and risk free for Leonard to have ignored the farmer or indulged in idle chatter. Instead, he seized the opportunity, rendered a service, and made two sales as a result of his efforts.

## PIPELINE

Building a pipeline is the key to consistent results for the selling professional. The danger in this area is that based on our definition, the pipeline has some subjective quality. The "number of *qualified* buyers being *worked*" calls for a definition of *qualified* and *worked*. You will need to work with your supervisor/manager to determine a definition of these terms upon which you both can agree.

For our purposes, a qualified buyer is one who has the authority and the resources (usually dollars) to make the decision. Working that prospect means that the decision can be reached in the next thirty days. You will be working many potential buyers outside the thirty-day range, but I like to think of these as contacts or suspects rather than prospects. Are they less important than clients who will close within thirty days? Absolutely not! Do they require a different time allotment and means of "working"? Absolutely!

Now please don't get caught up in the semantics. Your business may not close anyone in thirty days. The parameters of the definitions ARE YOURS, TO BE ASSIGNED BY YOU. Just be sure that BEFORE you start, you have agreement with your supervisor or manager on what constitutes "working qualified buyers."

## RESULTS

Great managers begin by managing results. When results aren't there, they manage and train on techniques and skills. When technique and skill training is not getting results, outstanding managers focus on activity. All that is to say, as you get results, be sure you know how and why you are being successful so that you can replicate success. Nothing is more devastating than the salesperson who is "on a roll" and selling everybody in sight. Then one day the person just "goes dry." Nobody is buying anything. What happened? How could this happen? What can I do to get back "on the roll"? The only way to answer these questions is to evaluate activity, pipeline, and results.

Why did your last customer buy from you? Where did he or she come from (source)? How long did it take you to complete the sale? Was this longer or shorter than usual? How many referrals did you get from this satisfied customer? What is your current closing ratio? How does this compare to last week? Last month? Last year?

Some of you are obviously thinking that if you spent the time necessary to be able to answer these questions, you would be spending all your time in record keeping and none in selling. Please forgive me if what I am about to say is too direct for some of you, but that is a lazy, stubborn, close-minded, loser's response. (Bet I got your attention!) Salespeople who "fly by the seat of the pants" are nonprofessionals who cause the professional's reputation to suffer. Now let me hasten to add that from time to time we all fall into that negative category. I will be the first to admit that keeping the proper records, paperwork, and details is not something most of us enjoy. However, to be the professionals we were meant to be, we must find a comfort level. With the proper evaluation of activity, I promise that you will find more than enough time to keep the records that allow you to answer the questions that heat the warm water of mediocrity and turn it into the boiling water that steams you to success.

## THE DISCIPLINARIAN

Everyone needs a method, technique, or system for accountability. In athletics, the scoreboard tells who won and who lost the game. In the business world, some say the check stub tells who won and who lost the game. In both cases I disagree. The best team does not always come out on top on the scoreboard, and the best paychecks don't always belong to the top performers. The scoreboard and the check stub are indicators of performance, but they are not the final word.

True professionals (in any and all activities) have the peace of mind that comes from knowing that they did the best they could with what they had at any given point in time. They have the peace of mind of knowing that they are being true to the value system in which they believe. This can be accomplished only with a system that allows the people seeking success to hold themselves accountable for tasks and objectives.

None of us can manage time. But each of us can account for our use of this precious commodity. We cannot control the thoughts and actions of other people, but we can make choices about how we are going to spend our time and what objectives we will seek.

The Performance Planner is our answer to the questions: "How will I know when I am successful?" and "Is there a way to hold myself more accountable while becoming more organized?" I developed the Performance Planner as a "Disciplinarian" that would allow us to track tasks and results while planning objectives.

### THE RIGHT SYSTEM

Yes, the Performance Planner is a product available from the Zig Ziglar Corporation, but let me hasten to add that you do not have to own a Performance Planner to be successful. I do believe, however, that you have to use some system for accountability. Daytimers, Inc., the Franklin Institute, Inc., and Time Systems, Inc. (addresses in the back of this book)—all provide calendars and concepts that allow you to make the best use of the time you have. A pencil and a piece of paper can be the beginnings of developing your personal performance tracking system. The most important thing is not which system you use—the most important thing is that you have a system!

## KEY COMPONENTS

Regardless of whether you purchase a system or develop your own, the primary components of a successful sales tracking system are a calendar (keep only one for all areas of life); a "to do" list (an "idea warehouse" where projects and future tasks can be recorded and tracked); and a section for setting and tracking goals. If each of these can be kept in a single book or notebook that is with you AT ALL TIMES, you will be pleased with the impact this system can have on your life.

**The most important thing is not which system you use—the most important thing is that you have a system!**

From a sales perspective, you will want to include an alphabetized section for prospects (keep the information sheet on each prospect alphabetized, and put the last name—or the company's—on the calendar date you have the appointment or follow-up call). This prevents you from fumbling for information should the prospect call you back before the appointment. Your alphabet tabs can double as a listing of important phone numbers that you need with you at all times.

I understand that some of you have too many prospects to carry with you at all times. Obviously, you will keep alphabetical files in a file drawer, but these can still be coordinated with your calendar and "to do" list.

Also include a section for notes or ideas. A "journal" section will allow you to record key concepts that will help you to be successful in the future (as we have previously discussed).

## THE MOST COMMON "MISPERCEPTION"

Too many people think that organization and discipline restrict spontaneity; the exact opposite is true. When sales professionals take the necessary steps to become even more organized and disciplined, they are taking steps toward maximum utilization of time and effort, which frees them in all areas of life! I will make you this promise and guarantee. If you will follow the guidelines recommended in this chapter for thirty days (exactly as they are presented), you will increase your levels of productivity and enjoyment by a minimum of ten times your cost of this entire book! Then I want to challenge you to write me at the end of thirty days and share your victories. As the old TV commercial used to say, "Try it. You'll like it!"

CHAPTER SIXTEEN

# GETTING THE PERSON RIGHT

## *Get the Person Right, Then Get the Salesperson Right*

Dr. William James, the father of American psychology, said, "The most important discovery of our time is the realization that we can alter our lives by altering our attitudes."

## THE BUSY EXECUTIVE

Some of you will be able to identify with the busy executive who came home with a briefcase full of work. His six-year-old son was demanding time, but due to special deadlines, the father reluctantly told the boy he had several hours of work that took priority that evening.

As the young boy dejectedly walked from his dad's work area, he met his mother in the hallway. "What's the matter?" she lovingly inquired. "Aw, Dad has a briefcase full of work and can't play with me!" the little boy complained. "Why does he always bring all that work home?" With motherly wisdom and patience, she replied, "Well, your dad is an important part of his company, and he just can't get everything done during the day at work."

The young boy showed insight beyond his years when he asked, "Well, then, why don't they put him in a slower group?"

## PERSISTENCE

The lad was a persistent tyke and eventually found his way back to his dad's work area. The recurring question, "Can't you play now, Dad?" was not only painful but annoying.

Finally the young salesman had a brilliant idea. In front of him was a newspaper containing a map of the world. He proceeded to tear the paper into many pieces and gave it to the little boy to put back together, telling him that when the "puzzle" was finished, there would be time for playing together. The salesman figured he would have at least thirty minutes of uninterrupted time, but in a matter of minutes the youngster was calling his dad to look at the map. Dad stepped into the next room, and sure enough, the youngster had put the map of the world together perfectly. Dad asked how he had managed to do it so quickly. The youngster explained that on the other side of the map of the world was a picture of a man and that when he got the man right, the world was right.

## GET THE PERSON RIGHT

In the world of selling, when we get the "person" right, it's much easier to get the "salesperson" right. Realistically, until YOU get right, your SALES WORLD won't be right. The "secret" to getting YOU right is getting your "attitude" right. My intention throughout this book has been to allow you to get the information necessary to make the proper choices in all areas of life so that the choices you make will yield the attitude that leads you to success!

No one can separate personal, family, and business life. What happens at home (a sick baby, a child strung out on drugs, problems with a spouse) has a definite impact on job performance. An article in the January 8, 1990, *USA Today* stated that in companies of one hundred people or less, marital difficulty was the number one cause of productivity decline on the job; alcohol was in second place, and drugs were third. Likewise, what happens on the job (getting fired or promoted) definitely has an impact on relationships at home.

## A DEMANDING PROFESSION

Of all the occupations on earth, with the possible exceptions of psychiatry, counseling, and the ministry, surely the sales profession is the most demanding as far as the maintenance of the right mental attitude is concerned. In many ways your attitude in selling is even more important and at greater risk than the other professions mentioned because in those cases the "prospects" generally come looking for help. In the sales profession, we seek our prospects, and many times our calls come at inopportune times and are often made on people who are not always excited about seeing us.

Now add the fact that many do not feel a need or have an interest in what we are selling, and the stage is set for a fairly high "turndown" rate for discussing our goods and services—much less for doing a full presentation. When this process is repeated a number of times each day, the salesperson runs the risk of having the ego seriously damaged to the degree that a poor or negative attitude becomes a major problem.

## AN ATTITUDE "VACCINATION"?

How can you inoculate yourself and protect against the wrong attitude? Truthfully, there is no way you can completely build an armored shell to totally protect against feelings of frustration, disappointment, and fear. If you could, you would NOT be a very successful salesperson. The reason is simple: You and I are "emotional" people and "feel" a full range of emotions. If we didn't feel disappointment when a prospect refuses to take action on the "greatest product on the face of the earth," we couldn't feel enthusiastic about what we are selling. The same "feelings" that lead to excitement lead to disappointment. To be successful in selling, we must have the capacity to feel both "up" and "down."

Since we are not immune to those "down" feelings, the question is, What can we do to limit their frequency, length, and severity? Taking control is important because our attitude determines how many calls we make, when we start, how we finish, and the results we obtain each day.

## MENTAL HEALTH

With emotional health secure you need to look next at keeping your mental health in the proper focus.

Question: Have you ever gone to a movie and laughed? Question: Have you ever gone to a movie and cried? The odds are at least four thousand to one that you answered yes to both. Next question: Do you really believe you felt those emotions because of something they put in the seats? Or was it because of something put on the screen that went into your mind and in turn affected your thinking and your emotions? What you put into your mind does have an impact on you. Fortunately, you can choose what you put into your mind.

Your attitude is important, so we need to carefully look at what we can do to avoid "stinkin' thinkin'," which ultimately leads to "hardening of the attitudes."

At this point you should be thinking to yourself, "O.K., Ziglar, what can I do within my own limited time frame to maintain that positive mental attitude so that I can treat my belligerent prospects as graciously as I do the friendly prospects? How can I be pleasant to my mate and children as well as my neighbors and casual acquaintances when I've had a tough day out in the field?"

The answer is simple but not easy: YOU CANNOT CONTROL THE CIRCUMSTANCES IN YOUR LIFE, BUT THERE ARE MANY THINGS YOU CAN DO TO CONTROL YOUR MENTAL ATTITUDE AS YOU DEAL WITH THOSE CIRCUMSTANCES!

You begin by understanding this: You are what you are and where you are because of what has gone into your mind, and you can change what you are and where you are by changing what goes into your mind. In short, you choose what you READ, LISTEN TO, and VIEW. The following will provide more details.

## PRESSURE, STRESS, AND DISTRESS

Certainly one of the most significant aspects of a career in selling is a salesperson's health. The pressure in our great profession can often be overpowering. Think about just a few "stressors": the need to meet quota; the introduction of new products; the increasing competitiveness for the consumer dollar; the high-tech aspects of many phases of the business; an ever-increasing emphasis on customer service and quality products; the prevalence of alcohol and other drugs in the work force, accompanied by the social pressures to drink and do drugs; the heavily congested traffic situation—necessitating more time spent traveling from home to the office to prospects; the two-career family, which when children are involved includes baby-sitters, day care, schools, and many other complicating factors. These and a host of other "distress items" place mounting pressure—physical, mental, and spiritual—on the salesperson.

How can you, the professional salesperson, take care of yourself in this climate? As I have said before and will say again, mankind is tridimensional: physical, mental, and emotional (spiritual). The answer to your question lies in evaluating yourself in these three areas.

## SIMPLE, BUT NOT EASY

The advice I would like to share with you is relatively simple, but following it could well get complicated. Let's begin with some advice from a real superstar of selling, a man we have already discussed, Walter Hailey. Walter made a fortune in the life insurance business and then sold his company to K-Mart for somewhere in the neighborhood of $78 million (which is a *mighty* nice neighborhood). So he has made a lot of small sales, and at least one colossal sale, too. He's a man with enormous energy, unlimited enthusiasm, and a zest for life that makes you feel he's twenty years younger than his sixty-plus years.

Walter says that an incredibly high percentage of people spend most of their time "looking back in anger and forward in fear." And with the double burden of anger and fear, you are literally, as Walter puts it, "mortgaging your future." The anger of what has happened in the past creates fear of what is going to happen in the future. And even potentially successful people become paralyzed in the present.

## EMOTIONAL HEALTH

So, what's the solution? *Step number one:* Go ahead and blame the people who did whatever they did to you for all of the misery and problems you've suffered in your lifetime. My psychiatrist friends tell me it's O.K. to blame somebody else for your problem. So get started right now blaming Mom, Dad, Uncle Charlie, a former boss, a former mate, a former associate—and anyone else who comes to mind—for *every one* of your problems.

*Step number two*: Now that you've blamed others for your problems, forgive them for whatever they have done. In some cases that might be extremely difficult and could even require counseling. I think of physical, emotional, or sexual abuse as an example. If you need help in forgiving, I encourage you to do whatever is necessary to get the help you need. I feel so strongly about the importance of forgiveness because until you forgive those people for the roles they played, they are going to play a major part in your future. And your future is not going to be everything that it might be. As a matter of fact, it can be dismal—until you learn to forgive.

Forgiving is not necessarily forgetting. Archibald Hart, a Christian psychologist, defines *forgiveness* as "giving up your right to hurt someone back." When you forgive someone you agree to forfeit any revenge that you previously felt needed to be exacted. You may remember the deed, but you release its power to control you, and you release your desire to hurt the doer of the deed. This is not a "quick fix." Forgiving, as Dr. Hart defines the concept, is a process that works over a period of time.

*Step number three:* Now that you have blamed others for your past and forgiven them, you must ACCEPT RESPONSIBILITY FOR YOUR FUTURE. Until you accept responsibility for your future, you're going to relive your past and repeat the mistakes. One of the most meaningful statements I have been making over the past five years is this: FAILURE IS AN EVENT, NOT A PERSON. Yes, you may have failed, but you are not a failure.

When you follow that statement by *understanding* logically and emotionally that "yesterday ended last night and today is the first day of the rest of your life," you begin to truly accept responsibility for your emotional health. I want to encourage you with every fiber of my being to look forward with hope to the future! As my friend John Maxwell says, "If there's HOPE in the future, there's POWER in the present."

For me, my emotional health is in the hands of God. In no way am I trying to impose values on you, but in well over sixty years of living, I have learned that true emotional health comes from a personal relationship with our Creator. Every person has a choice. Mine is to serve God through Jesus Christ with the power of the Holy Spirit.

Let me encourage you to gather all the information you can on the spiritual aspects of life and make your own choice. When you know and understand this aspect of your health, all other areas of life are handled more effectively.

## FINDING AND KEEPING THE RIGHT MENTAL ATTITUDE

Here are some specific action steps for you to take in developing the right attitude:

*Number One*: Accept the fact that you CAN control your attitude.

*Number Two*: Make the commitment to do whatever is necessary to take control of YOUR attitude.

*Number Three*: Evaluate each book, television program, movie, and video before you actually start reading or viewing it with a question: "Is this going to help me in my personal, family, or business life, or is there a better use I could make of this time to advance my personal, family, and business life?"

*Number Four*: Learn one new word each day. In less than five minutes per day you can get amazing results. The average American learns only twenty-five new words each year and actually has a speaking vocabulary of five hundred words. One new word per day will mean that in one year you will have a "distinct advantage" over most people with whom you're dealing; within five years you will have a COLOSSAL advantage—not because you know the words but because those words give you a breadth and depth of understanding that will enrich your life in every way. Plus there is more good news: Every word has several "buddies"; when you learn one new word, you've just expanded your vocabulary by several more.

The International Paper Company has conclusively proven that your income and your vocabulary have a direct correlation. At age thirty-seven Vince Robert (a fifth-grade dropout) of Ottawa, Canada, was a taxi driver. He spent many hours each day waiting for fares at hotels and airports. One day he was overtaken with inspiration and bought a "twenty-pound dictionary." Vince put in on the seat beside him in his taxi and started learning those words. His knowledge increased so much, along with his confidence, that he started investing in the stock market. Bottom line—he bought the Eighteen Cab Car Company. Today he lectures to people on how to become successful. One word a day will make a difference, a dramatic difference in your personal, family, and sales life.

*Number Five*: Read something of value to you personally and professionally for at least twenty minutes every day—something that is informative, inspiring, and educational. If you're an average reader (reading 220 words a minute), in one year you will have read twenty 200-page books. The average American reads only two new books each year, so competitively speaking you will have another colossal advantage. You will be in a tremendous position to knowledgeably advise your prospects about the proper course of action to take for their own benefit.

Think of the enormous competitive advantage you will have. Your reading might relate to our profession, personal growth and development, psychology and human nature, or just about any subject you determine is beneficial to you. Every book I write includes a bibliography, which I encourage you to review. Look for titles that "jump out" at you, and read these books and magazines—information that will help you become even more professional.

*Number Six*: Turn your car into the University of Automobile—or Auto U. Sales trainer Don Hutson says that the typical professional salesperson spends over five hundred hours each year in an automobile. That's roughly ten hours each week. In ten hours a week you can become the consummate sales professional while you're in your car. You can master the arts of handling objections, prospecting, being persuasive, building presentations, and working with every conceivable sales close known to mankind. You can build an extensive vocabulary, learn a foreign language, acquire communication skills, or even become an expert on the Bible.

Innumerable sources for acquiring this material range from the public libraries and universities to scores of companies that specialize in providing up-to-date, highly informative, and motivational cassette recordings. This obviously includes our own company. As a visiting scholar for two years at the University of Southern California, I learned of a study revealing that if you live in a metropolitan area and drive 12,000 miles each year, in three years' time you can acquire the equivalent of two years of college education while you're in your automobile. If you can read even at the fifth-grade level, there is literally no excuse for not acquiring a marvelous education.

By far the most important benefit of listening while you're in your car is the pure motivational impact you will receive. For years salespeople have told me that between calls they would pop in one of my tapes and immediately receive quite a "lift." Frankly, I always thought they were talking about a psychological lift, but in addition to the psychological lift, they receive a physiological lift.

To achieve the best results from what I'm talking about, start every day by listening to an exciting motivational recording. Psychologists say that the first significant encounter each day has more influence on attitude than the next five people encountered. If you've spent anywhere from five to thirty minutes listening to something that turns you on, you're ready to make that call. The next best time to listen, from a sheer energy point of view, is after lunch. This makes certain those endorphins are hoppin' again, and your energy level and creativity are high.

Reinforce this each evening just before you turn those lights out by reading something encouraging and educational. The last thing that goes into your subconscious mind each night is some data and information that your subconscious can mull over during the course of the night. The proper information really can make a difference in your career.

*Number Seven*: Choose your associates carefully. Several years ago the *Los Angeles Times* did a study on some phenomenally successful people and discovered one of the things they had in common: At some point in their careers they consciously made a decision to upgrade the people with whom they were working, spending time socially, and hobnobbing in general. They all said this was an essential factor in their success. For that reason, I encourage you to think carefully on this subject.

# PHYSICAL HEALTH

The third aspect in the quest for the right attitude is physical health. Incidentally, it is impossible to separate the physical, mental, and emotional (spiritual) aspects of attitude. I'll spend more time on the physical because most salespeople neglect this area. A number of superb books give you a considerable amount of information on the subject.

As a physical fitness devotee since the early 1970s, I can tell you that taking care of your health will pay you enormous dividends in increased energy and fewer days spent in sickness. Your extra energy will produce increased revenue for your family. We will never be able to accurately calculate the billions of dollars in lost income American salespeople suffer every year. Think about what happens because the salesperson is simply too tired to get an early start in the morning, ran out of gas before the day was over, or had that "inevitable energy drop" after eating a heavy noon meal. For these salespeople the idea of making "one more presentation" before they call it a day becomes a physical impossibility. Their energy bucket is drained.

## THE PHYSICAL "HOW TO'S"

So what are some keys to taking care of physical health? Let's begin with DISCIPLINE, which is critical but often neglected. One hundred and seventy-five CEO's of the Fortune 500 companies are former United States Marines. Six of our last seven presidents served in the navy, and twenty-six of our presidents served in the military. Obviously, our armed services teach discipline, loyalty, commitment, and personal responsibility, along with a host of other positive qualities. As I said before, "When you discipline yourself to do the things you need to do when you need to do them, the day will come when you can do the things you want to do when you want to do them."

## START YOUR DAY THE PROFESSIONAL WAY

The discipline starts with an early morning wake-up call. For you and your mate to arise together would be ideal. A few minutes spent together planning the day's activities, just being with each other and relaxing will do wonders for the relationship, and this procedure will also do wonders for starting the day in the proper frame of mind. If there are no children, husband and wife could take a walk, jog, or enjoy a cup of coffee together. This will vary with individuals because some are morning people while others are night people. In my book *Courtship After Marriage: Romance Can Last a Lifetime*, I share some specific ideas on the importance of this time together and how it can best be spent, but the key is this: If you start your day in the proper manner, it sets the "tone" for the entire day. You are accepting responsibility for your health—mentally, physically, and spiritually.

## A HEARTBEAT AWAY FROM SALES SUCCESS

Establishing the tone for your day will make it much easier to follow through on the most important aspect of your physical health program. The key to a healthy heart (which is where the healthy body is centered) is this: Several times each week you need to choose an activity that causes your heartbeat to be accelerated into the "target range" recommended by your physician and keep your heart working for a certain number of minutes. Now I know that sounds somewhat vague, but please read on—your life (and your success) depends upon your attentiveness!

Let me urge you NOT to accept the tables in any of the books on the subject that show heart "target ranges" based on age, body frame, and level of fitness. We are not good personal diagnosticians, so ask your doctor to tell you what your "target range" for exercise should be. Your physician can also help you choose an activity that will fit your personality and your life-style—an activity that accelerates your heart in a healthy manner.

Once this is determined, you will *work toward* keeping your heart rate within that certain range for the period of time your physician recommends. The few dollars and few minutes you INVEST in discussing this with a physician will benefit you in many ways. Dr. Ken Cooper is the expert I believe in strongly, and he says that to maintain our fitness level, we need to work out three times per week; for minimal changes over time, we need to work out four times per week; for maximum changes in fitness, we need to work toward (not begin with) working out five times per week.

Dr. Cooper has me keeping my heart rate up for twenty minutes, and my activity of choice is jogging. I jog for thirty to forty minutes (never for distance, always for time) using the first four to eight minutes to accelerate my heartbeat into the target range, the next twenty minutes to maintain, and the last four to eight minutes as a "warm-down" (a time for my heart to gradually return to the normal rate). I do my best to arrange my schedule to jog three consecutive days, take a day off, then jog for two consecutive days, and take another day off. At my age and with my habits (including a special fondness for sweets, which I limit to one major dessert once each week with a few little nibbles in between), working out five days is best for me.

This schedule does remarkable things for controlling weight, reducing stress, and lowering cholesterol and blood pressure, not to mention what it does for maintaining my energy level. The late afternoon or early evening run works best for me.

Even as I write these words, I am feeling extremely good because—roughly one hour ago—I finished a very invigorating run here in Chattanooga, Tennessee. The weather was absolutely magnificent with the temperature hovering around seventy. Had it been too cold or rainy to run outside, I would have run inside the ballroom of the hotel, run up and down the corridors of the hotel, jumped rope in my room, or gone to the exercise room and worked out on the rowing machine, stair steps, or whatever was available. In short, once you've made the commitment and started disciplining yourself to do these things, it gets to be a habit, and what a wonderful habit exercising becomes.

Many sales executives choose the first part of their lunch hour for a brisk walk or jog and feel dramatically energized for the rest of the afternoon as a result. In my case, the energy surge after exercise extends from two to four hours, and my creativity goes up. My energy level is higher, and my endurance is greater. Exercise is not something you spend time doing; it's something you INVEST time in—with enormous immediate and long-range rewards!

## WHAT ABOUT YOUR DAY?

Instead of setting the proper tone for the day and scheduling exercise, how do many people react each morning? Too many people are like your neighbors (I know YOU wouldn't handle your morning this way) who awaken at the last possible moment—they're in a dead run awakening the kids, getting them dressed, plopping them down in front of the TV set with a bowl of sugar-laden cereal so that their minds and bodies can be ruined at the same time.

Husband and wife are madly dashing around with much shouting and often weeping, wailing, and gnashing of teeth, getting their cup of coffee, doughnut, or cinnamon roll, while dressing, shaving, or applying makeup at the same time. At about the time they should be arriving at work, our couple make a mad dash to get the kids into the car so they can speed out into the traffic. Woe be unto the unwary driver who impedes their progress in any way as the parents frantically rush to drop the kids off at the day-care center—sometimes even slowing down before opening the door and letting the kids out.

All this so they can rush helter-skelter to a hectic eight- to twelve-hour workday, aided by the three to eight cups of coffee consumed during the day to "keep their energy level up." Because of the time crunch and pressures of the fast-paced day, the only option for lunch is to pick up a quick bite at the fast-food place, wolf it down, and take off in nine different directions to make their calls for the afternoon.

At the end of the day, they reverse the process. Pick the kids up, hurry home, perhaps picking up some more fast food along the way, unless they can look forward to the luxury of a frozen (now microwavable) TV dinner. Since the meal is "lite," "lean," or "heart healthy," it is certainly justified—at least in their minds, if not their bodies. The meal is "enjoyed" while watching the evening news.

Around bedtime, our couple will have a little snack, something high in calories, cholesterol, and fat. Then an hour and a half after they should be asleep, they go to bed exhausted. Not the best way to spend a day.

## BUT SERIOUSLY...

If you have fallen into this trap, I encourage you to stop right now and THINK! Project in your mind where this will take you, even a year from now, much less five or ten years from now. Something will have to give. It might be the marriage, the kids, or your health, but something will give. "If you keep on doin' what you been doin', you're gonna keep on gettin' what you been gettin'." Grammatically, the statement may be lacking, but from a practical perspective, it is right on target.

Some people, in an effort to relieve the stress and pressure built up by developing poor habits, start having a cold beer or a cocktail to relax, then another and another. Since we now know that one person in nine who takes an occasional drink will end up with a drinking problem, there is an inherent danger is this life-style. I'm not "meddling," just asking you to examine what you want in this area of your life.

In the first place, does drinking provide the benefits you seek? Would you recommend it to a family member or close friend who was under stress and duress? If you were developing a sales presentation, how would you sell your spouse or someone else on the importance of the social or occasional drink? What are the three things you like best about drinking? The money spent on the product? Your return investment? The influence you can have on your children?

No, I'm not "preaching" or even "playing parent." I am encouraging you to think, long term, about what is best for your personal, family, and business life. I challenge you to find one person, just one, who took the first drink with the announced intentions of becoming an alcoholic. I also challenge you to put alcohol to the "Ben Franklin" test. On one side of the page, list "potential benefits," and on the other side, list "possible costs." P.S. Don't forget to include the fact that in 90 percent of all divorces, 70 percent of all wife and child abuse, 69 percent of all drowning deaths, and 50 percent of all highway deaths, alcohol is a contributing factor.

## THE RUSH-RUSH LIFE-STYLE

When you evaluate your daily routine, are you guilty of using this "hurry-hurry" style? How have you spent the last three months, six months, or even longer of your life? Doesn't it make sense to stop right now and evaluate where you are and where you want to go?

At this point you might be saying, "Zig, I *am* on a hectic schedule, but things are tough. I have kids to feed, a mortgage to meet, heavy insurance payments, an uncertain economy, and things you just don't understand. If I don't 'hustle,' then I might not be able to meet my commitments, which are so important."

Good point. I never said that becoming the healthy and successful sales professional you wanted to be when you started reading this book was going to be easy. But I can tell you that while you might be temporarily productive on that pressure-packed, undisciplined schedule, at the end of the year you will not have made as many sales, have earned as much money, have had as much fun, have been as good a provider/family person as you will be on a more sensible schedule.

## THE WRONG BENEFITS

The kind of schedule I described earlier will cause you to become impatient to get everything done right now, including getting that order from the prospect. You will have a tendency not to see all of the small signals given by the prospect or listen properly to what the customer has to say. A number of things will make a big difference in establishing permanent personal and professional relationships.

Prospects have more confidence in doing business with the salesperson who is calm, who is confident, who will spend that extra five minutes with them reassuring them that they made the right move (or that they should make the right move). The same patience that leads you to get involved on a regular basis with the proper physical exercise program leads you to handle prospects and customers with expertise.

## WHAT YOU ARE IS WHAT YOU EAT

Doctors Furman and Cooper can give you considerable advice on the foods you should eat. But I would encourage you to follow the basic rule that's been around for many years. Eat breakfast like a king, lunch like the company is cutting back the payroll and you don't know if you may be next, and dinner as if you had just lost your job. I especially encourage you not to fall into the "quick meal" trap.

Instead of dashing helter-skelter into the fast-food place for a fat-filled unbalanced meal, pick up chicken, tuna salad, or turkey on whole grain bread, complete with a piece of fruit for dessert. Many fast-food chains are now offering lowered fat and cholesterol foods from which you may choose. The key is making the proper *selection*.

Close the door in your office or get off in a deserted area. Sit there and slowly eat and enjoy that simple meal. If humanly possible, take a short walk after the meal. Even a brief five-minute walk will do wonders for reducing stress, giving you a chance to assimilate your thoughts and get ready for the afternoon in front of you.

## ELIMINATING THE POISONS

In addition to eating properly and exercising regularly, your physical health is determined to a large degree by eliminating (or avoiding) the poisons. I'm thinking primarily of tobacco and alcohol. I hope you won't be like the person who had read so much about the dangers of tobacco and alcohol that he quit . . . reading.

In all seriousness, did you realize that every time you light up a cigarette, you have decided to die fourteen minutes earlier than you otherwise would have died? In 1989, 432,000 Americans died premature deaths because they smoked. According to *U.S. News and World Report*, an additional 40,000 to 50,000 Americans also died premature deaths because they were with and around people who smoked. Those are serious numbers.

Now, I'll confess to a degree of prejudice here. Among my eleven brothers and sisters, the difference in life span of those who smoked versus those who did not smoke is thirteen years—thus far. With every passing year that the remaining four of us live, that spread gets even larger. Tobacco is a killer.

In today's competitive world, the salesperson who lights up is courting the loss of a sale for sure. Again to quote my friend Walter

Hailey, he says that with all the evidence we now have about what tobacco does, he would never get in business with people who smoke because it's a clear indication that they really aren't very bright. I know that will offend some of you, but since I have your attention, let me emphasize that *smoking kills people*. Even as I write, I'm deeply concerned that other members of my family still smoke. And late in 1990, I buried my younger brother as a direct result of his smoking cigarettes.

If you are a smoker, I strongly encourage you to quit. Chances are good you've already tried and didn't quite make it. Every study that I've ever read indicates that those who successfully quit usually do so on or after their third attempt to quite. I remind you again: "Failure is an event, not a person."

When you quit (or choose not to start), you will breathe easier, you will smell better, and you won't offend anybody on earth by not smoking (except the tobacco companies, and after all, you've already financed them long enough, haven't you?). The additional sales you make will contribute to our economy. If you're married, your mate and children will applaud the effort. You'll be able to trade your car in for more money. You'll spend less on repainting the interior of your home. The money you save will be significant, and the life you save will be your own.

**Failure is an event, not a person.**

In addition, I cannot think of one benefit that smoking brings to your career. I have never seen a sale made due to smoking, but I have seen several lost. Smoking is an insidious habit that grabs us when we are young (for the most part) and hangs on for as long as we allow it to control our lives. For your life, for your family, for your career—FIND A WAY to stop smoking. And if you don't smoke, please don't start.

## THE DEATHS MOUNT

The second poison to avoid is alcohol. More than 110 *million* Americans drink, and over 18 million people have a serious drinking problem. A study reported in the *Atlanta Journal and Constitution* revealed that of the 104,000 who died in 1987 (from illnesses and accidents brought on by alcohol) the average length of life span lost by Americans was twenty-two years. That's an incredibly steep price to pay.

Believe me when I say that I understand the social pressures to drink are incredible. But one thing I have observed without fail is that people who have the courage and character to refuse to be "stampeded" into having a beer or a cocktail gain universal respect from those who also wish they had the discipline, the will, and the courage to say no.

I would like to emphasize that from my perspective this really is not a moral issue, though I believe I could make a pretty good case along those lines. When you look at the economic damage wrought by alcohol and tobacco use, the number of careers that have been curtailed or destroyed, and the number of lives that have been disrupted, you can see how horrible the poisons really can be. But if you will consider for the moment what these poisons do to your career and your future, you can see it really is a practical issue.

## WE DON'T MISS IT UNTIL IT'S GONE

Health seems to be one of those things we become enormously concerned about when there's a possibility we're going to lose it—and yet we take it for granted while we have it. I encourage you to think about your health before you have placed yourself in jeopardy!

## ILLEGAL DRUGS

I've purposely not discussed illegal drugs because they are in violation of the law and really should not be a factor. Comparatively speaking, illegal drugs are not nearly the problem that legal drugs are. In 1989, for example, we lost "only" 20,000 to 25,000 lives to illegal drugs while losing 432,000 lives to tobacco and considerably more than 100,000 lives to alcohol.

Now combine that information with this: According to the September 11, 1989, issue of *U.S. News and World Report*, there's seldom a case of a person using illegal drugs who did not use tobacco and/or alcohol as the "entrance" drug.

## ANOTHER REMARKABLE STUDY

Forest Tennant, M.D., Ph.D., is perhaps the number one drug authority in the world. When Howard Hughes and Elvis Presley died, results of their autopsies were sent to Dr. Tennant for him to evaluate. For several years he was a drug consultant for the NFL, the Justice Department, NASCAR, the Los Angeles Dodgers, Abbott Laboratories, Texaco, and many others.

Dr. Tennant was in attendance at a seminar I conducted in Anaheim, California. Before I started speaking he took blood samples from five of the people (actually, they gave him the blood). When the seminar ended four hours later, he again took blood samples from those same five people. The endorphin and cortisol levels were up to 300 percent higher. Since then Dr. Tennant has conducted additional experiments and has made some fascinating discoveries.

Dr. Tennant reported some of his findings in the May 1989 issue of *Meetings & Conventions* magazine. Here are the scientifically validated findings:

> There is a biochemical basis for why people feel good after these talks. Something about hearing about success gives us an emotional charge that releases those chemicals into the bloodstream and that makes the body function better. And while these effects last for no more than a few hours, regular doses of motivation will lead to better health, happiness, and achievement.

Dr. Tennant and I have been friends for a number of years, and in private conversations he has said to me that his discoveries prove that we can store creativity, energy, and endurance. When you're between calls, insert the tape of a speaker you really trust and believe in; make certain the recording itself is done in front of a live audience.

Now let me emphasize something. You can get education and information from studio recordings, but if you're going to get the full benefit of the inspiration and sheer enthusiasm and motivation, the recording must be done in front of a live audience. To repeat what Dr. Tennant said, "The combination of hearing about success delivered in an enthusiastic manner activates the pituitary gland which, in turn, floods the system with those endorphins, dopamine, norepinephrine, and some of the other neuro-transmitters." When this happens, you literally are storing energy, creativity and endurance.

I'm absolutely convinced that the closing statistics I shared earlier (70 percent of all sales are made between 7:00 A.M. and 1:00 P.M., and only 10 percent of sales are made after 4:00 P.M.) are accurate because the saleperson's motivation has run down and the energy level is lower.

When you are physiologically energized and psychologically confident, you've just added two powerful ingredients to your way of life and approach to selling. And in the process you will be able to handle the one thing that probably costs salespeople more money and breaks more sales careers than any other single thing: lack of action. Being healthy physiologically and psychologically will enable you to focus on the things going right instead of the things going wrong. Instead of suffering from "paralysis of analysis" as my friend Cavett Robert says, you will get into action and make those calls. When you do miss a sale, your optimistic nature—fueled by that proper input—will force you to realize that the missed sale simply leads you closer to the one you are going to make.

Psychological and physiological health also helps you in another critical area. When your energy and confidence are high, the natural tendency not to call on people of wealth and prestige will gradually diminish until it disappears altogether. You will also be far more inclined to wear the badge of your profession with considerably more confidence. You'll even catch yourself saying, as my friend and fellow platform professional Rita Davenport says, "When people ask me what I do, I say, 'Please forgive me for bragging, but I'm in the world of sales.' "

The benefits to getting the person right and *then* getting the salesperson right are astronomical. Go out and establish the habits that will allow you to maintain the proper attitude for the healthy and successful life you deserve to live!

## HOW DO YOU MAINTAIN THE RIGHT ATTITUDE?

In our hurry-hurry, competitive world, if we constantly are striving to beat everybody else and be number one, over a period of time the toll can be horrendous. This is especially true if, try as hard as we might, we never quite seem to reach the pinnacle we have set for ourselves. Despite the fact that we get up early and stay up late; despite the fact that we're avid students and are constantly researching, learning, and practicing new techniques; despite the fact that we do all of the things this book and other success books teach, we still consistently end up on the short end of the stick and never achieve our goal of being number one. What's the answer?

I believe the problem lies in the definition of *success* in our profession. I sincerely believe each of us can be number one. No, that doesn't mean I believe that everybody can be the biggest, fastest, strongest, smartest, most persuasive, most productive, and most capable; but I do believe YOU ARE NUMBER ONE when you can honestly look in the mirror at the end of the day and say, "I used my ability today. I gave it my best shot." In short, you realize that true success is not necessarily beating someone else; real success, enjoyment, and happiness come from using your own ability. Success is not determined by beating the other fellow; real success is measured when you use the ability you have.

## MAKING SURE YOU HAVE THE PERSON RIGHT

If you take the steps I have outlined, you will be extremely pleased with your results. However, even if you have the right attitude, there are going to be times when prospects are not going to buy from you. I hate to break that hard news to you, but in all truth, some folks are going to say no!

People do not buy because of what we tell them or show them. They buy because of what we tell them and show them that they believe. Fact: Prospects believe those people they TRUST! Without TRUST people won't listen, and without TRUST people won't buy.

Since everything is selling and all of us are salespeople, we must ALL be trusted to be effective. The teacher whom the students trust is infinitely more effective. The athlete must trust the coach before he will fully accept instructions and give his wholehearted effort.

What you know is important. Who you know is also important, but WHAT YOU ARE is most important, especially in the world of selling.

## SUCCESSFULLY SELLING TRUST

In March 1991 I had lunch with Bob Forrest, who is the mayor of Carlsbad, New Mexico. He has several tire dealerships in that section of New Mexico and is a third-generation owner. Bob says, "We don't attempt to compete price-wise, but we can more than compete service-wise." His family's reputation has been established for three generations, and the service is solid. People instinctively know, based on years of experience, that Bob is going to deliver what he sells. I believe this factor is going to be even more vital in the years ahead. We (consumers) are going to look to people we can trust.

Think about it for a moment. All of us like to do business with people we can trust. Can you imagine going to a doctor and not having any confidence that the treatment is any good? Can you imagine doing business with a financial institution whose trustworthiness was suspect? Could you be happy with a mate you do not trust? No way.

The same rule applies in selling. If people really trust you, if everything else is even close to being equal, they will do business with you.

## BUT WHY DO PROSPECTS SAY NO?

As I have said for almost all of my sales career, there are five reasons people will not buy from you:

No Need
No Money
No Hurry
No Desire
No Trust

The last of the five—No Trust—is the most difficult to understand and the most fundamental to possess. The only way to separate personal rejection from business refusal—when the prospect says no—is to understand the importance of TRUST in the sales relationship. People MUST trust you before they buy from you, and if you are not the right kind of person, people will not buy your goods or services.

If a prospect does not buy from you because of a lack of trust, then aren't you justified in feeling personally rejected? Absolutely not! When you are told, "NO!" you are justified only in examining the reasons for the prospect's response. Has anyone ever trusted you with anything? Do you perceive yourself to be completely untrustworthy? Are you dealing with a reputable product or service in which you sincerely believe? What "silent signals" might you be sending to the prospect with body language or facial expressions? Without even knowing many of you personally, I am going out on a limb and saying that my guess is you are a trustworthy person. You may not be communicating that trustworthiness to the prospect, and that lack of communication is the real key.

The "kind of person you are" is the determining factor in the kind of sales career you will have, and since trust is the most important factor in the prospect's decision to say yes or no, let's look more carefully at the trust factor in the sales process. Somebody once said, "A lie might get you ahead, but it won't bring you back." To express it another way, "You can shear a sheep once a year, but you can skin him only once."

## WHY WILL YOU MAKE SALES IN THE FUTURE?

For you to make the sale and for your prospect to move from the "no" side of the ledger to the "yes" side (to move from a mind that's absolutely closed—"I have no need or desire to do business with you since what you are asking in dollars is worth more than the benefits I will receive"—to a smiling face, a mind that's open, and a pen in hand to sign the order—"I'll take it!"), you must take a series of steps (represented in the diagram by a series of dots).

"NO!"......................................................"YES!"

The series of small steps you must take to make the move and close the sale include getting the prospect to like and trust you. The prospect must like you before trusting you, and the prospect must trust you before buying from you.

## DEVELOPING TRUST

Since TRUST is such an integral element in the sales process, let's look at a series of steps that will allow you to develop trust in the proper manner so that you can close more sales more often. Trust begins with a favorable first impression. Creating a favorable first impression, as stated earlier, begins with your appearance. Being dressed appropriately (whether making calls in person or on the phone) has a great bearing on your feelings as well as the prospect's perceptions. All studies show that being dressed to the level of the prospect—again, whether in person or on the phone—significantly increases the closing ratio when other factors are equal.

## A SECOND CHANCE

Often, salespeople with lesser skills but a greater "positive appearance quotient" will sell more effectively than those with more skills who don't pass the appearance test. Remember, appropriateness is the key. How do the people upon whom you are calling dress? And though the statement has become something of a cliché, it is still vividly true: "You never get a second chance to make a first impression."

## TRUST AND CONFIDENCE

If you have passed "inspection," the next judgment the prospect makes happens when you open your mouth. Here is where you begin to reveal your level of CONFIDENCE, and confidence is the second factor in gaining trust.

Appearance gives clues, and your words and tone of voice are the "icing on the cake." In his book *Silent Messages*, Dr. Albert Mehrabian explains that 55 percent of our attitudes and feelings are expressed through *nonverbal* skills including our appearance, posture, and gestures; 38 percent of our attitudes and feelings are expressed through *tone* of voice; and 7 percent of our attitudes and feelings are expressed by the *words* we choose. Which carries the most impact: What you say (7 percent) or how you say it (93 percent)?

At the risk of offending you with oversimplifying the process, you will make more sales when you do what your mother told you: "Stand up straight, look people in the eye, and speak up!" The BEST selling professionals return to basics; the little things make the big difference; YOUR SUCCESS is dependent on returning to basics and paying attention to the little things.

## TRUST AND YOUR COMPANY

I receive many letters from people who are struggling in their careers in the sales profession, and one common factor is their choice of organization. If your company is not credible and trustworthy, it is very difficult for you to be credible and trustworthy. If your company is credible and trustworthy and you do not BELIEVE this to be true, you (and your prospect) have a problem. Be sure that the seeds of doubt that are growing weeds in your attitude are accurate. Ask questions from those with responsibility in the areas of disenchantment; offer ideas to departments with apparent shortcomings; do not accept the "grapevine" as gospel truth.

The key is to choose a company you can believe in. During the interviewing process, you are interviewing the company as much as you are being interviewed. This applies even to organizations with a good, solid reputation. Having worked with many different organizations in many different fields, I can tell you from experience that what a company looks like from outside and what a company looks like from inside are often completely different.

Don't be afraid to ask the tough questions (with the right attitude) during the interview process—regardless of how badly you need a job! You might get the position, but in the great profession of selling, credibility and belief go hand in hand. If you have doubts, your career (and especially your compensation) will be affected. Be strong-willed in seeking the right organization for you—an organization that complements your basic beliefs and values.

If you are already with a company that you have doubts about, take it upon yourself to be the example for change by doing your part extremely well. Working from within an organization to make it better is one of the greatest thrills you can have in your professional life. At the point you see that you cannot work from within to improve your organization and yourself, your decision is made; you have no choice but to seek other employment.

## TRUST AND REFERRALS

When you approach a new friend (*stranger* seems like such a harsh word) with the name of the person's old friend who recommended you call, you are developing trust. From the perspective of trust, referrals pay off hugely for the sales professional who asks for them. Put yourself in the prospect's place. Think of the name of your oldest and dearest friend. If he or she asked you to talk to a person—even one selling time shares in Iraq—you would probably be willing to listen. "Well, the idea sounds crazy to me, but ______ (insert your friends's name) is my oldest and dearest friend (or has sound business judgment, etc.) so I guess I should listen." Referrals are of great benefit to you, your organization, and your clients.

## TRUST AND THE "LITTLE THINGS"

Many seemingly minor elements can affect your prospect's feelings of trust toward you. In my case, if someone tries to sell me something when I am physically tired, his chances are substantially diminished, especially if it's a major investment. Many years ago I recognized that I am not at my mental best when I am extremely tired, so regardless of how attractive the offer is, I will almost always say no until I am rested and can clearly think it through. Your prospect might be one of these people and you might do everything else right, but the timing might be wrong.

Sensitivity is a key part of the sales process. If you sense that there are some factors over which you have no control, you might want to reevaluate your timing for the presentation. However, I caution you about playing "psychologist" on every call, else you find yourself developing the habit of talking yourself out of making every presentation, and you know the obvious result of doing that. The secret to getting the sale is getting the mind of the prospect open.

## TRUST AND REPUTATION

Several years ago while I was serving on the board of a small college in a rural area of Texas, a decision was made concerning a heating and air conditioning unit for one of the buildings. The budget was extremely tight; funds were limited. We had no choice, however. We had to correct an intolerable situation. Unfortunately we were able to get only two bids on the job. There was a dramatic difference in price to do what ostensibly was exactly the same job with all the equipment meeting the specifications the board had set forth. Nevertheless, without hesitation or delay the board unanimously voted to accept the more expensive bid. Reason: The other company had a reputation that indicated very strongly that the work was shoddy and the follow-up, as far as service was concerned, was nonexistent.

The point I'm making, whether you're new in selling or old in selling, is that if your product is approximately the same as someone else's, you—the salesperson—can make the difference. Give your prospects every reason to trust you, namely, by being trustworthy, and they will come up with an excuse to buy from you.

## REAL MOTIVATION

On a recent trip, I was seated next to a gentleman who was busily working on some papers, and since I was engrossed in a book, conversation was nonexistent. When the flight attendant brought our meals, we each put our work down in order to eat. He commented, "What is the book you're reading? Is it a good one?" With considerable enthusiasm I responded that it was. Then I elaborated that just the evening before I had finished the book, and I was now going through reviewing the parts I had underlined or highlighted. In the process I noticed the large number of notes I had made on the pages, so I turned all the pages and counted in excess of 125 notations. I explained that in my opinion a book of value will always do two things. First, it will give you some information that is inspirational, interesting, applicable, and usable. Second, it will provoke thoughts and ideas in the reader. This particular book had inspired 125 ideas or thoughts.

As you know by now, *to motivate* means "to draw out" or bring out what is inside. *Ziglar on Selling* was written to "motivate" you as a professional persuader: (1) to see what you already know; (2) to give you new information; and (3) to inspire you to combine the two so you will have new and even more creative ideas to enrich your life.

Your purpose should not be to "get out" of the book as quickly as possible, but to "get out" of the book what is there and, far more important, let the book GET OUT OF YOU WHAT IS THERE!

Please don't misunderstand. Not by any stretch of the imagination am I implying that with the right attitude and proper motivation you're going to be "high" 100 percent of the time. The only people who accomplish that objective are those who are "high" ON something, and that "something" will end up shortening their lives and their careers. What I'm speaking of is a balanced attitude, with a heavy leaning toward the optimistic and positive. I don't believe positive thinking will let you do "anything," but I know that positive thinking will let you do everything better than negative thinking will. Positive thinking will let you use the ability you have while negative thinking prevents you from fully using your ability. Use the ability YOU possess to apply the principles YOU have been learning, and sales success and professionalism are sure to be YOURS!

# APPENDIX

## *Successful Selling Skills Summary*

**Part I. Personal Inventory**
Please complete the following statement to the best of your ability at this point in your sales career.

1. I choose a career in sales because ______________________________.
2. I choose my present company because______________________________.
3. The thing I like best about selling is ______________________________.
4. The thing I like least about selling is ______________________________.
5. My family thinks selling is ______________________________.
6. My closing percentage is ______ percent (number of sales divided by number of presentations).
7. The number of attempts I must make to get the opportunity to make my presentation is ______.
8. The number of presentations I must make to make one sale is ______.
9. To reach my financial goals, ON A DAILY BASIS I must have ______ prospects and make ______ attempts; which will yield ______ presentations.

10. The number of presentations listed in question 14 will average out in 30 days to yield ______ sales, which will yield $______.
11. The high-tech equipment I deal with in selling is ____________________________________________.
12. The best method I have discovered for prospecting is ____________________________________________.
13. I deal with call reluctance (fear of making the call) and sales rejection (being told no) by ____________________________________________.
14. In my world of sales, travel means ____________________________________________.
15. My sales support staff is ____________________________________________.
16. Regarding the selling profession, in one year I will be earning ____________________________________________.
17. Regarding the selling profession, in five years I will be earning ____________________________________________.
18. Regarding my career in sales, in one year my position will be ____________________________________________.
19. Regarding my career in sales, in five years my position will be ____________________________________________.
20. My ultimate goal as it relates to my career is ____________________________________________.

**Part II. Selling Skills Rating.**

Rate yourself in each of the following strategic areas on a scale of 1 to 5. Then add the numbers to see which successful Selling Skills Level you have achieved.

1 = No skills evident
2 = Skills just beginning to develop
3 = Skills inconsistent and needing work
4 = Solid skills
5 = Excellent Skills

____ 1. ENTHUSIASM. Selling excitement comes from deep within. I am proud to be a salesperson, and I delight in letting others know what I do and what I sell.

____ 2. CONFIDENCE. Beyond believing in what I sell, I strongly believe in myself and my ability to sell.

____ 3. CHARACTER. I carry out my plan even after the emotion of the moment in which I made the commitment has passed. I do what I say I will do. I persevere.

____ 4. INTEGRITY. I sell my products and services only to those I sincerely believe can truly benefit from them. I sell for the benefit of others as well as for my own well-being, using money as a scoreboard and not the sole sales objective.

____ 5. SINCERITY. I say what I mean (tactfully) and mean what I say. I am honest with myself and with my prospects. I carefully consider comments for validity. I under-promise and over-deliver.

____ 6. MOTIVATION. I know why I am doing what I am doing. I have carefully considered my motives, reasons, and purposes for all action steps.

____ 7. POSITIVE EXPECTANCY. I look for the best in all people and all situations. I expect to be treated fairly and with respect. I expect to treat others the same way.

____ 8. INITIATIVE. I make things happen instead of waiting for things to happen. I take personal responsibility for my attitude and actions. I am proactive instead of reactive.

____ 9. ATTITUDE. I am bright and cheerful and optimistic. I understand that positive thinking is important and positive believing is even more important. I rarely criticize or complain.

____ 10. SMILE. I understand that I am never completely dressed without a smile. I smile and "smile big" to show people I am happy to meet them and happy to greet them. I give a smile to those who don't have a smile of their own.

____ 11. APPEARANCE. I dress appropriately, taking my prospects' and clients' level of dress into consideration. I preplan my wardrobe and am always neat and clean.

____ 12. SELF-ANALYSIS. I keep excellent written records and know where my sales are coming from and why people buy from me. I know how I did last year, how I am doing this year, and how I am planning to do next year.

____ 13. ORGANIZATION. I know how I use my time. I know which tasks and activities have the highest payoff based on my goals. I know, understand and take action on the ten most important tasks I must complete to be successful each day.

____ 14. SUPPORT SYSTEM. I deal with my family and coworkers tactfully and diplomatically, involving them at every opportunity. I understand that family and coworkers are my *internal* customers and are just as important as my *external* customers.

____ 15. TRAVEL. I understand the dangers and the advantages of the road and am prepared to deal efficiently and effectively with both.

____ 16. CUSTOMER SATISFACTION. I understand that almost everyone is capable of customer service and that to be successful in the world of selling, I must go beyond customer service to customer satisfaction. I have a specific plan of action to accomplish customer satisfaction.

____ 17. TELEPHONE SELLING. I enjoy the advantages the telephone offers me in the world of selling. I feel no "telephone terror," and I look forward to using this tool to return calls quickly, initiate calls to save money and time, and answer calls promptly and courteously.

____ 18. HANDLING OBJECTIONS. I understand which objections I will be getting on a regular basis, and I have preplanned methods for handling these objections. I also have a methodology for handling the "surprise" objections.

____ 19. HANDLING REJECTION. I know the difference between a personal rejection and a business refusal. I de-personalize turn downs and often use the prospect's reason for not buying as the reason for buying.

____ 20. PICTURE PAINTING. I understand that I am a word-merchant and picture-painter and that to be successful I must carefully select words that paint the most vivid emotional pictures for the prospect.

____ 21. CLOSING. I know how to close sales, when to close sales, and which sales closing techniques are most effective for me and my product or service. I always ask for the order.

____ 22. GOALS. I understand that a goal is a dream I am willing to take action on. I break down my goals into bite-size pieces and work toward achievement on a daily basis.

____ 23. LISTENING. I know and demonstrate by my actions that "telling is sharing, but listening is caring." I listen with my eyes and heart as well as my ears.

____ 24. EDUCATION. I regularly read and listen to upbeat, inspirational, informational, and insightful information that helps me to become even more professional. I know that education is an ongoing and continual process that I will enjoy all my career.

____ 25. COMMONSENSE. I understand that commonsense is not a common practice. I work to run all information through the commonsense filter. I plan to win, prepare to win, and therefore I have every right to expect to win in the world of selling!

____ TOTAL SCORE

**SUCCESSFUL SELLING SKILLS RATING LEVELS.**

0 - 50 = You are at the right place at the right time! The good news is that your best selling years are in front of you. The other good news is that you have all the information necessary to become successful in your hands!

51 - 75 = *Ziglar on Selling* is for YOU! You have a strong foundation upon which to build your selling career, and with the information available, you will be able to go over the top! Read and review this information daily (in your nonselling time).

76 - 99 = You are knocking down the door to success! With just a little extra oomph you will be accomplishing what you want to accomplish in your professional career. This book is the icing on the cake for you and will help you as you continue on your winning ways by becoming an even bigger winner!

100 - 125 = You should have written the book! Now don't get overconfident and forget to review the fundamentals. Part of the reason you are as successful as you are is because you have recognized the importance of ongoing education. Congratulations!

# EPILOGUE

## *Something Personal for You*

I heard a wise person say once, "It's not where you start; it's where you finish that counts." Since I began this book with a story of my less-than-spectacular start, perhaps I should finish with "the rest of the story"—at least up to this point! (I do believe the best is yet to come.)

I include this personal information because with three exceptions, chances are excellent that in my life and career I have walked in every pair of shoes represented by the readers of this book.

The first pair of shoes in which I have not walked belongs to a person who has suffered through any kind of serious physical or mental illness. I've always been blessed with incredibly good health in both departments, so I can't honestly say I know how you feel.

The second pair of shoes in which I've never walked is represented by those who have lost a mate or a child through either death or divorce. I've been most fortunate in those areas and have four strong, healthy children and a beautiful, loving wife of over forty-five years.

The third pair of shoes in which I've never had to walk is that pair worn by those who have never really been loved. I've been more than blessed with love all my life. First, by a mother who loved me and expressed that love repeatedly. Second, by my brothers and sisters who have always loved me and have been extremely supportive of me. My older brothers and sisters supplied many of my physical and financial needs after the death of my dad when I was only five years old. And there's the love of The Redhead, which has been steady, dependable, and boundless throughout our marriage. Additionally, I've had the love of my children and grandchildren who have all expressed that love and demonstrated it as well. Last, I've enjoyed the love of the people whose lives I've been permitted to touch over the years.

For those three kinds of persons, I can say to you that I "know how you feel," but in reality there is no way I really can.

## THE SIMILARITIES MAY SURPRISE YOU

However, there are many shoes in which I have walked. I know how it feels to be spiritually adrift in my relationship with God and wondering what really would happen when I closed my eyes that last time. I know how it feels to be broke. I've walked in those shoes many times over the years. I know how it is to feel despondent and "down in the dumps." I know how it is to feel you have no purpose and no future.

I believe I have been as deeply in debt, as broke, and as concerned about my financial wherewithal as 99.9 percent of the people who will ever read this book. Yes, for many of you I have walked in your shoes.

I share this information because chances are excellent that those of you who have read my books, or heard me speak, or listened to my tapes have gotten the idea that somehow I just picked up a pen and wrote books, grabbed a microphone and made speeches, and turned on the recorder and made recordings. Such is not the case. If I have skills in those areas, it is because I have taken whatever gifts God gave me in those areas and invested a tremendous amount of time, effort, and research to develop those talents.

I have spoken for no fee to every size and conceivable kind of organization—the Lion's Club, Rotary Club, and Jaycees, not to mention the schools, churches, prisons, drug rehab centers, and a host of other nonprofit organizations including the Salvation Army and branches of the military. I've spoken to sales meetings at automobile dealerships, cookware franchises, vacuum cleaner organizations, real estate companies, and countless other groups. I've driven fifty miles, a hundred miles, and on three different occasions two hundred miles at my expense to speak to a group of a dozen people and then of necessity driven home that night because I did not have enough money to pay a motel bill.

I mention these things because I want you to know as you commit yourself to your career that it might not necessarily be easy, but I believe that with persistent physical, mental, and spiritual effort you can learn the skills you need to develop to reach your objectives.

Obviously, some of you have more talent than others, but undeveloped or sparingly applied talent simply will not get the job done in the world of selling or in life in today's marketplace.

## WHEN THE PUPIL IS READY, THE TEACHER WILL APPEAR

In your life, there will be many instances when the right person will come your way and make a difference. I believe this book can make a difference, but only if the lessons are learned and put into practice. I vividly remember one of those occasions when that teacher came into my life. After two and one-half years of selling, my credit had run out, my patience was exhausted, my frustration was at an all-time high, my creditors were not overly happy with me, and even The Redhead was beginning to wonder if perhaps I had chosen the wrong profession. She never voiced it, but somehow I've got to believe there was concern on her part.

Then one day I went to a meeting, spent the day in Charlotte, North Carolina, at a training school, and did not learn a thing. I drove back to Lancaster, South Carolina, late that afternoon and conducted a demonstration that evening. I finally got back to our little apartment about 11:30 P.M., and the baby kept us up most of the night. The next morning at 5:30 the "alarm clock" (that was before I learned that it is actually an "opportunity clock") sounded off to alert me that it was time to drive back to Charlotte for day two of the training meeting.

Force of habit rolled me out of bed, but when I looked at the snow that had fallen overnight and my little Crosley automobile without a heater, I decided to do what most intelligent human beings would do—I got back in bed. But even as I lay down, the words of my mother came back to me: "Son, if you're in something, get in it. If you're not in it, get out. If you're not giving your best effort, you're not being fair to the man you're working for, and you're not being fair to yourself."

I remember that it had taken me over two months to persuade the managers of the company to give me the job. They did not believe that I could sell, and for the next two and one-half years all I had done was prove they had been right in the first place. However, I had promised them that I would attend all sales meetings and all training sessions, and in two and a half years I had not missed a meeting, and I had never even been late for one. I rolled out of bed and drove to the meeting, and that's the day my world turned around.

Mr. P. C. Merrell, my hero, the man who had set all the records and written the training program, was in charge of this most important day. When the training session was over, he literally got me into a corner and said, "Zig, I've watched you for over two and a half years, and I've never seen such a waste." Naturally, he got my attention very quickly, and I asked him what he meant. He responded that in his judgment I had real ability, that I could be a national champion, that I could go to the top and someday become an executive in the company if I went to work on a regular schedule and believed in myself.

From the very beginning I had been told to go to work on a regular schedule, but when you're a "little guy from a little town who's never really going to do anything," you rationalize, "Why should I beat my head against the wall when nothing good is ever going to happen to me anyhow?" Now, however, a man in whom I had complete TRUST and FAITH, a man whose INTEGRITY and CHARACTER were beyond question, was telling me that I could be a national champion. I believed him.

## WHAT A DIFFERENCE A DAY MAKES!

On the way home that little Crosley scarcely touched the ground! I had a demonstration that evening with three prospects, and little did they realize what was about to happen to them. They never had a chance! They were not dealing with a little guy from a little town who would struggle all of his life. They were dealing with a national champion, a man who was destined to go to the top, who could even be an executive in the company if he really put his mind to it.

Not only did I sell all three prospects that evening, but I completed the year second in the nation out of over seven thousand people and received the best promotion the company had to offer. I swapped the Crosley for a really nice car, and the next year I was the highest-paid person in the United States with that company. Three years later I became the youngest divisional supervisor in the sixty-six-year history of the company and set some records that stand to this day.

I hasten to add one other important point. At the time I had the encounter with Mr. Merrell, I was a "trained" salesman. I knew how to get prospects, make appointments, conduct demonstrations, handle objections, and close the sale. The salesman was ready—Mr. Merrell got the man ready. That's really what I'm saying to you. I could teach a twelve-year-old all the procedures and techniques necessary for any salesperson to be successful. I could take the biggest crook in town and the number one con artist in operation today and teach them the procedures, but neither the twelve-year-old nor the con artist would build a successful sales career. The twelve-year-old would lack the credibility that comes only with having a few more birthdays. The con artist would self-destruct in a short period of time, perhaps selling well in the initial stages but ultimately reverting to form and destroying the trust and confidence of those with whom he deals. No, the kind of person you are is the most essential facet in building a professional sales career.

I might also point out that upon Mr. Merrell's suggestion, I did start making an appointment with myself to be talking to a prospect at exactly the same time each day. That one concept made a tremendous difference in my effectiveness. Despite the fact that I finished second in the nation, out of the seven thousand salespeople, I never placed in the top twenty for a single week or for a single month, but neither did I come up with a complete blank in any week. That consistency of effort for the entire year was the reason I finished second in the nation.

## MR. MERRELL'S MESSAGE FROM ME TO YOU

Before I speak to an audience, I ask God to make me a P. C. Merrell in the life of each person there. I do this whether it's for the 23,000-plus beautiful young men and women with the Future Farmers of America or whether it's for a dozen retired Baptist preachers.

One of the few things I do not like about my chosen profession is that I never really have a chance to get to know many people on a personal basis. As a rule, I fly into a town one day and out of that town the next day. It's a rare occasion when I spend two nights in the same place, except when The Redhead is traveling with me and we have occasion to spend three or more days together. Needless to say, when that happens, any free time I have is spent with her. Even during the three-day Born To Win Seminars we hold every other month here in Dallas, I really don't get much of an opportunity to form close relationships with the two hundred or more people who attend. I simply cannot spend much time with any one person, though I definitely make it a point to at least shake hands, share time together at a meal, or chat in the hallways during breaks in those sessions so that I have a speaking acquaintance with every person there. But I think you'll agree that's not really building a relationship.

I've often wondered what it would be like to be able to spend time with every person who has ever attended one of my seminars, read one of my books, or listened to one of my recordings. Realistically, I know that is the "impossible dream." However, I'm going to ask you to use your creative imagination and right now visualize me standing directly in front of you, calling you by name, and saying some of the things Mr. Merrell said to me and adding some of my own thoughts with the hope that they will have an impact in your life as Mr. Merrell's words and thoughts did in my life.

## A MESSAGE FROM MY HEART

Here's what I would love to say: "You, ______, are rare; you're special, unique, and important. You can make a difference in the lives of other people. Over ten billion people have walked the earth, but there is not now, there never has been, and there never will be another one quite like you. Your voice pattern is different from any other voice on earth; your fingerprints are different; your very genes leave their trail of identifying marks completely different from any human being who has ever lived. You're a special individual. Develop your uniqueness; apply it by utilizing the principles we've been discussing, and make a real effort to be a difference maker in other lives."

I would conclude my thoughts to you by saying, "I hope you're active in our electoral process in America. I hope you vote in the national, state, local, city, and county elections. Whether for the local justice of the peace or president of the United States, your vote is important and can make a difference.

"But now, ______, I'm going to give you an opportunity to cast a vote that is infinitely more important than any vote you've ever cast in any election anywhere at any time for anybody. This vote is going to be cast in the privacy of your own mind, and while its impact might be substantial on other lives, the biggest impact will be on your own.

"Since this vote is so important, I'm going to ask you to take the following steps AS SOON AS YOU FINISH READING THIS. Close your eyes and in your imagination reach up and close the draperies to the polling booth because this vote is extremely important and very, very personal and private. Now, look carefully and you'll see a number of levers indicating a number of different names for whom you could vote. However, one name sticks out more clearly than any other name. That name is your own, and it is emblazoned in pure gold on the voting lever. Reach for that lever. Pull it down with force, vigor, conviction, and enthusiasm. Vote for you, and when you do, you will discover that long ago God had already voted for you.

"With those two votes, my friend, you can win any election or any contest you ever enter. That eternal arithmetic is so powerful and so true! It clearly says that you—plus God—equals enough."

Accept that as a basic fact and I really will see you—and yes, I do mean YOU—AT THE TOP!

# BIBLIOGRAPHY

This Bibliography contains the majority of the body of research I used in writing this book, plus some information recommended by friends and associates. I have not personally read each book but trust those who have.

**Sales Training and Sales Motivation**

Allesandra, Anthony J. *Non-Manipulative Selling*. Reston, Virginia: Reston Press, 1981.

Bettger, Frank. *How I Multiplied My Income and Increased My Happiness in Selling*. Englewood Cliffs, N.J.: Prentice-Hall, 1982.

Bettger, Frank. *How I Raised Myself from Failure to Success in Selling*. Englewood Cliffs, N.J.: Prentice-Hall, 1975.

Evered, James F. *A Motivational Approach to Selling*. American Management, 1982.

Herman, Fred. *Selling Is Simple—Not Easy, But Simple*. New York: Vantage Press, 1970.

Hopkins, Tom. *How to Master the Art of Selling*. New York: Warner Books, 1982.

Kinder, Jack and Garry. *The Selling Heart*. Indianapolis: R & R Newkirk, 1974.

Linkletter, Art. *How to Be a Supersalesman*. Englewood Cliffs, N.J.: Prentice-Hall, 1974.

Mandino, Og. *The Greatest Salesman in the World*. New York: Bantam, 1974.

Qubein, Nido. *Nido Qubein's Professional Selling Techniques*. Rockville Center, N.Y.: Farnsworth, 1983.

Roth, Charles B., and Roy Alexander. *Secrets of Closing Sales*. Englewood Cliffs, N.J.: Prentice-Hall, 1982.

Walters, Dottie. *The Selling Power of a Woman*. Englewood Cliffs, N.J.: Prentice-Hall, 1962.

Wilson, John M. *Open the Mind and Close the Sale*. New York: McGraw-Hill, 1953.

Ziglar, Judge. *Timid Salesmen Have Skinny Kids*. Martinez, Ga.: Action Now, 1978.

### Management and Motivation

Blanchard, Kenneth, and Spencer Johnson. *The One Minute Manager*. New York: William Morrow and Company, Inc., 1982.

Blanchard, Kenneth, and Robert Lorber. *Putting the One Minute Manager to Work*. New York: William Morrow and Company, Inc., 1984.

Brown, W. Steven. *13 Fatal Errors Managers Make*. Old Tappan, N.J.: Fleming H. Revell Company, 1985.

Gschwandtner, Gerhard. *Superachievers*. Englewood Cliffs, N.J.: Prentice-Hall, 1984.

Hunsaker, Phillip L., and Anthony J. Allesandra. *The Art of Managing People*. Englewood Cliffs, N.J.: Prentice-Hall, 1980.

Smith, Fred. *Learning to Lead*. Waco, Tex.: Word Books, 1986.

### Inspiration and Self-Help

Billigmeier, Shirley. *Inner Eating: How to Free Yourself Forever from the Tyranny of Food*. Nashville: Oliver Nelson, 1991.

Carnegie, Dale. *How to Win Friends and Influence People*. New York: Pocket Books, 1982.

Conwell, Russell. *Acres of Diamonds*. Old Tappan, N.J.: Fleming H. Revell Company, 1975.

Cooper, Kenneth, M.D. *The Aerobics Program for Total Well-Being*. New York: M. Evans, 1982.

Dobson, James. *What Wives Wish Their Husbands Knew About Women*. Wheaton, Ill.: Tyndale House, 1975.

Furman, Richard. *Save Your Life Cholesterol Plan*. Nashville: Oliver-Nelson, 1990.

Glass, Kinder, and Ward. *Positive Power for Successful Salesmen*. Dallas: Crescendo, 1972.

Maltz, Maxwell. *Psycho-cybernetics*. New York: Pocket Books, 1970.

Mandino, Og. *The Greatest Miracle in the World*. New York: Bantam Books, 1977.

Peale, Norman Vincent. *The Power of Positive Thinking*. New York: Fawcett, 1978.

Schwartz, David J. *The Magic of Thinking Big*. St. Louis: Cornerstone, 1962.

Smith, Fred. *You and Your Network*. Waco, Tex.: Word Books, 1984.

### Family Books

Blue, Ron and Judy. *Money Matters for Parents and Their Kids*. Nashville: Oliver-Nelson, 1988.

Chapin, Alice. *Building Your Child's Faith*. Nashville: Thomas Nelson, 1990.

Ketterman, Grace. *Depression Hits Every Family*. Nashville: Oliver-Nelson, 1988.

Mowday, Lois. *Daughters Without Dads*. Nashville: Oliver-Nelson, 1990.

Scott, Buddy. *Relief for Hurting Parents*. Nashville: Oliver-Nelson, 1989.

Stanley, Charles. *How to Keep Your Kids on Your Team*. Nashville: Oliver-Nelson, 1986.

Strack, Jay. *Dad, Do You Love Mom?* Nashville: Thomas Nelson, 1989.

Swindoll, Charles R. *You and Your Child, Expanded Edition*. Nashville: Thomas Nelson, 1990.

### Other Books by Zig Ziglar

*Confessions of a Happy Christian*. Gretna, La.: Pelican, 1978.

*Courtship After Marriage: Romance Can Last a Lifetime*. Nashville: Oliver-Nelson, 1990.

*Dear Family*. Gretna, La.: Pelican, 1984.

*Raising Positive Kids in a Negative World*. Nashville: Oliver-Nelson, 1985.

*See You at the Top*. Gretna, La: Pelican, 1974.

*Steps to the Top*. Gretna, La: Pelican, 1985.

*Top Performance*. Old Tappan, N.J.: Fleming H. Revell Company, 1986.

*Zig Ziglar's Secrets of Closing the Sale*. Old Tappan, N.J.: Fleming H. Revell Company, 1984.

### For Your Continuing Education

*Guideposts*. Published monthly by Norman Vincent Peale and Ruth Stafford Peale, Carmel, New York 10512.

*Harvard Business Review*. Published bimonthly by the Graduate School of Business Administration, Boston, Massachusetts 02163.

*Personal Selling Power*. Published monthly by Gerhard Gschwandtner and Associates, P.O. Box 5467, Fredericksburg, Virginia 22403.

*Reader's Digest*. Published monthly by the Reader's Digest Association, Inc, Pleasantville, New York 10570.

*Success*. Published monthly by Success Unlimited, Inc., P.O. Box 2240, Boulder, Colorado 80322.

**Addresses Referenced in *Ziglar on Selling***

Carlson Learning Systems, Inc. Personal Profile Systems, 3140 Harbor Lane North, Suite 200, Minneapolis, Minnesota 55441. 612-540-5110.

Day-Timers, Inc., One Day-Timer Plaza, Allentown, Pa. 18195. (215) 395-5884.

Debtors Anonymous. General Service Board, P.O. Box 20322, New York, NY 10025, (212) 642-8220.

Franklin International Institute, Inc. 2640 Decker Lake Boulevard, Salt Lake City, Utah, 84119. (800) 767-1776.

The National Foundation for Consumer Credit. 8701 Georgia Ave., Silver Spring, MD. 20910.

National Speakers Association, 4323 N. 12th Street, Suite 103, Phoenix, Arizona 85014. 602-265-1000.

Ronald Blue & Company, 1100 Johnson Ferry Road NE, #600, Atlanta, Ga. 30342.

Time Systems, Inc., 5353 North 16th St., Suite 400, Phoenix, Arizona 85016. (602) 265-3220.

Walter V. Clark Associates, Inc., 2 Jackson Walkway, Providence, Rhode Island 02903. 401-421-2008.

# WOULD YOU LIKE TO BE A "CONTRIBUTING EXPERT" ON A FUTURE ZIG ZIGLAR BOOK?

If you would like to share your experiences with other people who are on the "firing line" and using the principles we teach at The Zig Ziglar Corporation, I would like to involve you in future books.

One of the ways we learn best is through real life experiences. When you use one of the concepts or principles talked about in this book or any of my other books, please write to me and tell me how it worked (or failed to work), and I will make every effort to use your experiences in teaching others. Any and all kinds of experiences are appreciated.

If we are able to use your story, anecdote, or teaching lesson, you will be listed as a Contributing Expert as those are listed in the front of this book, and you will receive (at no charge) an autographed copy of the book you help write (but only if you will autograph one for me).

Write to me at the address below, and help me to help others to, "See You (and them) At The Top!"

**THE ZIG ZIGLAR CORPORATION**
3330 EARHART DRIVE
CARROLLTON, TEXAS 75006